A Publication Distributed by Heron Books

THE MASTERPIECES OF

Guy de Maupassant

I

GUY DE MAUPASSANT
1850–1893

Guy de Maupassant

PIERRE ET JEAN

AND

OTHER STORIES

DISTRIBUTED BY HERON BOOKS

CONTENTS

GUY DE MAUPASSANT
(1850–1893)

Guy de Maupassant's birthplace was Normandy and it was close observation of his fellow Normans (farmers, bourgeois and officials) which was to produce the greater part of his incomparable short stories.

His mentor and master, Gustav Flaubert, also came from Normandy and under his stern tutelage De Maupassant became the most brilliant and versatile of those writers who enriched French literature in the nineteenth century. He developed slowly, spending many years perfecting his work and it was not until the age of thirty that he published his first volume—a book of poems. His first and most successful short story was *Boule de Suif* (Ball of Fat). It was published in 1880, in a book of short stories by various authors entitled *Les Soirées de Médan*.

From 1880, for the next ten years, he wrote unceasingly and this decade was productive of no less than three hundred short stories, six novels and several plays and travel books.

De Maupassant reached the height of that school of Romantic realism which had as its founders Mérimée and Balzac and he surpassed Flaubert in the scope and vividness of his writing. His was the conviction that in life there could be "no aspect so noble or so mean, so lofty or so low, so honourable or so contemptible" that it did not merit analysis in its minutest detail.

Apart from his novels De Maupassant's stories may be divided into three groups: those which are concerned with Norman peasant life; those that deal with government officials (he was one himself for a long time), the Paris middle classes and the fashionable world and those later fantastic tales of his tragic phase. Of his novels the best known are *Pierre et Jean* (1885), the dramatic tale of a mother's past uncovered by her son. This is the book in which he defines his aesthetic ideas. *Bel Ami* (1885), a portrait of unscrupulousness in the world of politics and the press. *Une Vie* (1883), the tragic story of a suffering wife and mother, victim of her own weakness, and *Fort Comme la Mort*. Of his short stories, *Madam Tellier's Excursion, Moonlight, The Rondoli Sisters, The Horla, Useless Beauty, The Story of a Farm Girl, An Enthusiast* and *Miss Harriet* are among the most renowned.

In 1891 began the tragic phase of De Maupassant's life. The fears and morbidity which had begun to possess him, the everlasting struggle between his noble vision of life and its reality, were breaking him. Towards the end of his life this led to his complete mental collapse and finally to his death at the early age of forty-three.

PIERRE ET JEAN

CHAPTER I

THE SOWING OF THE SEED

OLD Roland had sat motionless for a quarter of an hour, gazing intently into the water, every now and then pulling gently on his line, which trailed idly in the sea.

"Zut!" he at last suddenly exclaimed.

Madame Roland, who had been dozing in the stern of the boat beside Madame Rosémilly,—the latter the guest of the fishing party,—woke up, and turning to her husband, said: "What's the matter, Gérome?"

"Not a single bite," replied the old man in a rage. "I have caught nothing since midday. Men should always go fishing by themselves. Women are never ready to start till it is too late."

His two sons, Pierre and Jean, one on the port, the other on the starboard side, each with a fishing line twisted round his forefinger, began to laugh. "You are not very polite to our guest, father," said

1

Jean. Mr. Roland was abashed and hastened to apologize.

"Pardon me, Madame Rosémilly; that is just like me. I invite ladies because I like their company, and then, whenever I get afloat, I think of nothing but the fish."

Madame Roland was now wide awake. She gazed with a quiet look round upon the wide expanse of cliff and sea, and murmured: "You have had good sport, nevertheless."

Her husband shook his head, but, notwithstanding, he looked complacently at the basket where the fish caught by the three anglers still lay gasping, with a faint rustle of clammy scales and quivering fins, and feeble, ineffectual struggles, dying in the fatal air. Old Roland took the basket between his knees and tilted it up. The silvery heap of fish slid to the edge, displaying those lying at the bottom, and their death-struggles became more convulsive, while the smell of the briny sea ascended from the depths of the creel. The old fisherman sniffed it as we smell roses, and exclaimed:

"Well! they are fresh enough!" and after a pause, "How many did you catch, doctor?"

The elder son, Pierre, a man of thirty, with black whiskers trimmed like a lawyer's, and mustache and beard clean shaved, replied: "Oh, not many; three or four."

The father turned to the younger son. "And you, Jean?" he asked.

Jean, a tall fellow, much younger than his brother, fair and bearded, smiled and muttered: "About as many as Pierre—four or five."

2

This was the little fib they always told and it delighted their father. He had fastened his own line round a rowlock, and folding his arms, he said:

"I will never again fish in the afternoon. After ten o'clock in the morning it is useless. The fish are too lazy to nibble; they are taking their *siesta* in the sun." And he swept the horizon with the satisfied eye of a proprietor.

Old Roland was a retired jeweler, whose passion for the sea and sea fishing had led him to give up his business as soon as he had scraped together enough money to enable him to live in decent comfort on his income. He retired to Havre, purchased a boat, and blossomed out into an amateur skipper. His two sons, Pierre and Jean, had remained in Paris prosecuting their studies, and from time to time spent their holidays in sharing their father's amusements.

Pierre was the elder by five years. When his school-days were over he had enthusiastically tried half a dozen professions one after the other, and, disgusted with each in turn, had as hopefully started upon the next. Medicine had been his latest choice, and he had studied with such enthusiasm that he had recently qualified, after an unusually short course of study, by special permission of the authorities. He was ardent and intelligent, changeable but obstinate, full of Utopian dreams and philosophical ideas.

Jean, who was as fair as his brother was dark, as deliberate as Pierre was impulsive, and as gentle as the latter was aggressive, had plodded on through his law studies and had received his diploma as a licentiate at the same time as Pierre had taken his in medicine. Now both were taking a rest at home, and both purposed settling in Havre if the prospects proved inviting.

But a vague jealousy, one of those latent jealousies which, growing up between brothers and between sisters, gradually ripen till they burst,— on the occasion of a marriage perhaps, or of some stroke of good fortune coming to one of them,— kept them in a constant state of fraternal and friendly warfare. They were, no doubt, fond of each other, but each kept his eye on the other.

Pierre was five years old when Jean was born, and had looked with the eyes of a petted animal at that other little creature which had suddenly taken a place in his mother's and father's arms and in their love and affection. Jean, from his birth, had always been a model of sweetness, gentleness, and good nature. Pierre, by degrees, had come to chafe at listening eternally to the praises of this boy, whose sweetness was, in his eyes, indolence, his gentleness, stupidity, and his good nature, blindness. His parents, whose ambition for their sons was some respectable and modest vocation, took him to task for his changeableness, his fits of ardor, his abortive beginnings, and all his useless aspirations after grand ideas and the liberal professions.

Since he had reached man's estate they no longer said in so many words: "Look at Jean and follow his example"; but whenever he heard them say "Jean did this — Jean did that," he understood their meaning and the covert hint their words conveyed.

Their mother, an orderly person, a thrifty and somewhat sentimental woman of the middle class, with the soul of a soft-hearted shopwoman, was for-

ever quieting the little rivalries between her two big
sons, for which the petty occurrences of life give
occasion. Another little circumstance, too, at this
time upset her equanimity, and she was afraid of complications. In the course of the winter, while the
boys were finishing their studies, she had made the
acquaintance of a neighbor, Madame Rosémilly,
the widow of a merchant-ship captain, who had died
at sea two years before. This young widow of
twenty-three was a strong-minded woman, who knew
life as wild animals do — by instinct, as though she
had actually seen, experienced, understood, and
weighed every possible contingency, and judged it
with a healthy, strict, and generous mind. She had
got into the habit of calling to work or chat for an
hour in the evening with these friendly neighbors,
and take a cup of tea with them.

Old Roland, always impelled by his seafaring
hobby, would question their new friend about the
deceased captain; and she would talk about him, his
voyages, and his old-fashioned yarns, without hesitation, like a resigned and sensible woman who enjoys
life and respects the dead.

The two sons, on their return, finding the pretty
widow quite at home in their house, immediately
began to pay her court, not so much from a wish to
charm her as from a desire to cut each other out.
Their mother, practical and prudent, sincerely hoped
that one of them might win the widow, for she was
wealthy. At the same time she would have preferred
that the other should not be grieved thereby.

Madame Rosémilly was fair, with blue eyes, a
mass of light waving hair, which fluttered at the

slightest breath of wind, and had a piquant, dashing, pugnacious manner, which did not in the least indicate the sober bent of her mind.

So far, she appeared to prefer Jean, attracted, doubtless, by natural affinity. She betrayed her preference, however, merely by a scarcely perceptible difference of voice, and also by occasionally asking his opinion. She seemed to know instinctively that Jean's views would coincide with her own, and that Pierre's would inevitably be different. When she referred to the doctor's ideas on politics, or philosophy, or morals, she would sometimes call them "your crotchets." Then he would look at her with the cold glance of a prosecutor drawing up an indictment against women — all women, poor, weak things.

M. Roland had never invited her to join his fishing expeditions till his sons came home, nor had he ever before taken his wife, for he liked to be off before the dawn, with his ally, Captain Beausire, a retired master mariner (whom he had met on the quay at high tide and with whom he had struck up an acquaintance), and the old salt "Papagris," known as Jean Bart, who had charge of the boat.

But one evening, during the week preceding the opening of this story, Madame Rosémilly, after dinner, at which she had been their guest, remarked: "It must be great fun to go out fishing," and the jeweler, flattered by this, and suddenly fired with the wish to make a convert, exclaimed, "Would you like to come?"

"Of course I should," replied Madame Rosémilly.

"Next Tuesday?"

6

"Yes, next Tuesday."

"Are you the woman to be ready to start at five o'clock in the morning?"

"No, indeed; that is too much," she exclaimed in horror.

He was disappointed. He doubted her devotion. However, he said, "At what hour *can* you be ready?"

"Well — at nine."

"Not before?"

"No, not before. Even that is very early."

The old man hesitated; he certainly would catch nothing, for when the sun has warmed the sea the fish bite no more; but the two brothers eagerly urged the arrangement, and organized and arranged everything on the spot.

On the following Tuesday, therefore, the "Pearl" dropped anchor under the white rocks of Cape la Hève; they fished till midday; then they slept a while; then they fished again without success; and then it was that old Roland, perceiving (somewhat late in the day) that all Madame Rosémilly really enjoyed and cared for was the sail on the sea; seeing, too, that his lines hung motionless, had uttered in a spirit of quite unreasonable vexation that vehement "Zut!" which applied as much to the apathetic widow as to the fish that would not be caught.

Now, behold him, contemplating his fishy spoil with the joyful thrill of a miser. And seeing as he looked around the sky line that the sun was sinking, he said:

"Well, boys, suppose we get home."

The young men hauled in their lines, coiled them,

cleaned the hooks, and stuck them into corks, and sat waiting. Old Roland stood up to look out, captain fashion. "No wind," he exclaimed. "You will have to row, young men." And suddenly extending an arm to the northward, he added: "Here comes the Southampton packet."

Far over the level sea, stretched out like a blue sheet, immense and shining and shot with flame and gold, an inky cloud appeared against the red sky in the direction in which he had pointed, and beneath it they could distinguish a steamer's hull, a tiny dot in the distance. To the southward numerous other wreaths of smoke could be seen, all converging upon the pier of Havre, which was at present only just discernible as a white streak,— the lighthouse like a horn upright at the end of it.

"Is not the 'Normandie' due to-day?" asked Roland.

"Yes, it is due to-day," replied Jean.

"Give me my glass. I believe I see her out there."

The father pulled out the telescope, put it to his eye, swept the horizon for the speck, and then, delighted at having seen it, exclaimed:

"Yes, yes, there it is. I know her two funnels. Would you like to look, Madame Rosémilly?"

She took the telescope and pointed it toward the Atlantic horizon, but could distinguish nothing — nothing but blue, with a colored halo round it, a circular rainbow — and then all sorts of curious things, blinking eclipses which made her giddy.

She returned the glass with the remark: "I never *could* see with that thing. It used to make my husband angry. He would stand for hours at the window watching the ships pass."

Old Roland, much put out, retorted: "Then it must be on account of some defect in your eye, for my glass is a very good one."

Next he offered it to his wife. "Would you like to look?"

"No, thank you. I know beforehand that I could not see through it."

Madame Roland, a woman of forty-eight, but who did not look it, seemed to be enjoying the excursion and the closing day more than any other of the party. Her chestnut hair was but faintly streaked with white. Her face was calm and reasonable, and she had a kindly, happy manner which was pleasant to see. Pierre often said that she knew the value of money, but that did not hinder her from enjoying the pleasures of day-dreaming. She was fond of reading novels and poetry, not on account of their value as works of art, but for the sake of the sentimental mood they inspired in her. A line of poetry, often poor, and even bad, would touch the chord, as she expressed it, and give her the feeling of some desire almost realized. In these faint emotions she found delight. They brought a little flutter to her soul, otherwise as strictly kept as a ledger Since they settled at Havre she had become perceptibly stouter, and her figure, once slender and supple, had grown heavier.

This day on the water had been most enjoyable to her. Her husband was harsh to her without being brutal, as a man who is a tyrant in his shop is inclined to be, without real anger or hate. Such men cannot give an order without swearing. He controlled himself in the presence of strangers, but in private he gave himself free vent. In the outside world he was himself afraid of everybody. She, in sheer terror of tumult, scenes, and useless explanations, always gave in; she never asked a favor of him; for a long time she had never dared to ask him to take her out in the boat. So she had joyfully embraced the opportunity, and was greatly enjoying the novel pleasure.

From the start she surrendered herself to the smooth, gliding motion over the water. She was not thinking; her mind was not occupied either with memories of the past or hopes for the future; she simply felt as if she were floating in some soft ethereal heaven which lulled and rocked her into a dreamy state of ecstasy.

When their father gave the command to return, "To the oars!" she smiled to see her two stalwart sons take off their jackets and roll up their shirt-sleeves on their bare arms. Pierre, who was nearest to the two ladies, took the stroke oar, and Jean the other. They sat watching till the skipper should say, "Give way!" for he insisted that everything should be done in seamanlike fashion.

At the same instant they dipped their oars and lay back, pulling with might and main, and then began a struggle to display their strength. They had come out without trouble under sail, but the breeze had died away and the masculine pride of the two brothers was aroused by the prospect of measuring their strength. When they went out with their father only they rowed without anyone steering. Roland would be busy getting the lines ready, and merely kept a lookout on the boat's course, guiding it by a sign or a word, "Easy, Jean; pull, Pierre." And he would say: "Now then, number one; come, number two—a little elbow grease." Then the one who had been dreaming pulled harder, and the one who had got excited slowed down, and the boat's head came round.

But to-day they intended to show their muscle. Pierre's arms were hairy, thin but sinewy; Jean's were round and fleshy, and the knotty biceps moved under the skin. At first Pierre had the advantage. With set teeth, knit brows, rigid legs, and hands clenched on the oar, he made it bend from end to end at every stroke, and the "Pearl" turned landward. Father Roland, seated in the bow, so as to leave the stern seat to the ladies, wasted his breath shouting: "Easy, number one; pull harder, number two!" Pierre pulled harder in his frenzy, and "number two" could not keep time with his wild stroke.

At last the skipper cried "Stop!" The two oars were lifted at the same moment, and then, by his father's orders, Jean rowed alone for a few minutes. But from that moment he had it all his own way; he warmed to his work; Pierre, on the other hand, breathless and exhausted by his first zealous spurt, was soft and panting. Four times in succession old Roland made them stop till the elder recovered his breath, so that the boat could be brought back into her proper course again. Then the doctor, humiliated and angry, the perspiration dripping from his forehead, his cheeks pallid. blurted out:

11

"I don't understand what has come over me. I have a pain in my side. I started all right, but it has strained me."

"Shall I take both oars for a time?" asked Jean. "No, thanks; it will go off."

And their mother, somewhat annoyed, said: "Why, Pierre, what is the sense of getting into such a state? You are not a child." And Pierre shrugged his shoulders and applied himself once more to the oar.

Madame Rosémilly pretended that she neither saw, heard, nor understood. Her fair head was thrown back with a taking little jerk every time the boat moved forward, making her light wayward locks flutter about her temples.

Very soon old Roland called out: "Look, the 'Prince Albert' is overhauling us!"

They all looked round. Long and low in the water, with two raking funnels, her yellow paddle-boxes like two fat cheeks, the Southampton packet plowed along at full speed, crowded with passengers under open parasols. Its hurrying, noisy paddle-wheels beat up the water into foam, giving it the appearance of a hasty courier pressed for time, and its upright stem cut through the water, throwing up two transparent waves which glided off along the hull.

When it approached the "Pearl," old Roland took off his hat, the ladies fluttered their handkerchiefs, and half a dozen of the parasols on board the steamboat waved an answer to this salute as she went on her way, leaving behind a few broad undulations on the calm, glassy surface of the sea.

Other ships there were, each capped with smoke, coming in from all parts of the horizon to the short, white pier, which swallowed them up, one after another, like a mouth. Fishing barks, also, and small craft with broad sails and slender masts, were coming in, stealing across the sky line in tow of insignificant tugs, some fast, some slow, all toward the devouring ogre, which seemed from time to time to have had a surfeit, and vomited out into the open sea a different fleet of steamers, brigs, schooners, and three-masted vessels with their top-weight of tangled rigging. The busy steamers puffed off to right and to left over the smooth bosom of the deep. Sailing ships, cast off by their pilot tugs, lay motionless, arraying themselves from the mainmast to the foretops in canvas, white or brown, all reddened by the setting sun.

Madame Roland, her eyes half shut, murmured, "How beautiful the sea is!"

"Yes," replied Madame Rosémilly, with a long sigh, but without a trace of sadness. "Yes, but it is sometimes very cruel, too."

"Look," exclaimed Roland, "there is the 'Normandie' just going in. Isn't she a big ship?"

Then he pointed out the opposite shore, far away on the other side of the mouth of the Seine,—a mouth extending to more than twenty kilometers, he said,—with Villerville, Trouville, Houlgate, Luc, Arromanches, the little river Caen, and the rocks of Calvados which make the coast dangerous as far as Cherbourg. Then he expatiated on the sand banks of the Seine, which shift at every tide, so much so that even the Quilleboeuf pilots are at fault if they do not survey the channel every day. He pointed out how the town of Havre divides Upper from Lower Normandy; how in Lower Normandy the shore slopes down to the sea in pasture lands, fields, and meadows; how the coast of Upper Normandy, on the other hand, is steep, with a high cliff, cleft by ravines, and forms an immense white rampart all the way to Dunkirk, while a village or port lies hidden in every hollow: Étretat, Fécamp, Saint Valery, Tréport, Dieppe, and so on.

But the two women were not listening. Half dozing and comfortable, impressed by the sight of the sea covered with ships scurrying hither and thither like wild animals about their lair, they sat silent, somewhat awestruck by the soothing, gorgeous sunset. Roland alone talked ceaselessly; he was one of those mortals nothing can impress. Women, whose nerves are more sensitive than men's, sometimes feel, they do not know why, the sound of needless talk to be as irritating as an insult. Pierre and Jean, who had cooled down, were rowing slowly, and the "Pearl" was nearing the harbor, a tiny dot among those huge ships.

Once alongside the quay, Papagris, who was waiting there, gave his hand to the ladies to assist them ashore and they made their way into the town. A great crowd — the same crowd that haunts the pier every day at high water — was also moving homeward. Madame Roland and Madame Rosémilly led the van, followed by the three men. As they walked up the Rue de Paris they stopped now and again before some milliner's or jeweler's shop to examine a bonnet or an ornament and pass their opinion on it:

then on again. Roland paused in front of the Place de la Bourse, as was his custom every day, to gaze at the docks full of ships — the Bassin du Commerce, with other docks beyond it, all closely packed with huge hulks, lying side by side in rows, four or five deep. Masts innumerable rose in the air; for a distance of several kilometers along the quays they gave this great gulf in the center of the town the appearance of a dead forest with their yards and rigging. Above this leafless forest the gulls wheeled, ready to pounce, like a falling stone, on any scraps flung overboard. A sailor boy, fixing a pulley to a cross-beam, looked as if he had gone up there bird-nesting.

"Will you dine with us without any kind of ceremony, so that we may end the day together?" said Madame Roland to her friend.

"Certainly I will, with pleasure, the more as it is without ceremony. It would be dismal to go home and remain alone this evening."

Pierre, who had overheard, and who was beginning to chafe under the young woman's indifference, muttered to himself: "Well, the widow is taking root here now apparently." For some days past he had alluded to her as "the widow." The name, harmless in itself, irritated Jean by the tone in which it was uttered, which sounded to him malicious and offensive.

The three men did not speak another word till they reached the door of their own house. It was a narrow building, consisting of a ground floor and two floors above, in the Rue Belle-Normande. Joséphine, the maid, a girl of nineteen, an ill-paid, rustic maid-of-all-work, endowed to excess with the frightened

15

animal air of the peasant, opened the door, followed upstairs at her master's heels to the drawing-room on the first floor, and then announced:

"A gentleman called three times."

Old Roland, who never spoke to her without shouting and swearing, cried out: "Who do you say called, in the devil's name?"

Her master's roar did not make her wince. "A gentleman from the lawyer's."

"What lawyer?"

"Why, M'sieu' Lecanu—who else would it be?"

"And what did the gentleman say?"

"That M'sieu' Lecanu would call himself in the course of the evening."

Maître Lecanu was M. Roland's lawyer, and in a manner also his friend, who managed his business affairs for him. Something urgent and important must be in the wind to make him send word that he would call in the evening. The four Rolands looked at each other, put out by this intelligence as people of small means are apt to be at any interference of a lawyer, with its suggestion of contracts, inheritance, lawsuits—all kinds of desirable or undesirable contingencies. The father, after a short interval of silence muttered:

"What in the world can it mean?"

Madame Rosémilly began to laugh. "Why, a legacy, of course. I am sure of it. I bring good luck."

But they did not anticipate the death of anybody who was likely to bequeath them anything. Madame Roland, who had a good memory for family histories, began to think over all their relations on her own

16

and her husband's side, and to trace back pedigrees and the ramifications of relationship. Before even taking off her bonnet, she said: "Why, father" (she called her husband "father" at home, and occasionally "Monsieur Roland" before visitors), "do you remember who was Joseph Lebru's second wife?"

"Yes — a little girl called Dumenil, a stationer's daughter."

"Had they any children?"

"I should say so. Four or five at least."

"It is not from that quarter, then."

Already she was eager in the quest; she grasped at the prospect of some additional comfort dropping from the skies. But Pierre, who was very fond of his mother and knew her to be rather visionary, fearing she might be disappointed, grieved, and worried if the news turned out to be bad instead of good, checked her.

"Don't get excited, mother," said he, "there is no rich American uncle. For myself, I rather believe it is about a marriage for Jean."

Everybody was astonished at the suggestion, and Jean was a little irritated at his brother's mentioning such a thing before Madame Rosémilly.

"And why for me any more than for you?" he asked. 'The hypothesis is very open to question. You are the elder; you, therefore, must be the first to be thought of. Besides, I have no desire to marry."

Pierre smiled, and asked with a sneer: "Are you in love, then?"

"Is it necessary," retorted the other, much put out, "that a man should be in love because he does not wish to marry yet?"

17

"Ah, there you are! That 'yet' settles it. You are waiting your time."

"Granted that I am waiting, if you prefer to have it so."

But old Roland, who had been listening and meditating, all at once hit upon the most likely solution of the problem. "Dear me! what fools we are to rack our brains. Maître Lecanu is a great friend of ours. He knows that Pierre is on the lookout for a medical partnership and Jean for a lawyer's office, and he has found something suitable for one of you." This was so obvious and probable that everybody accepted it.

"Dinner is ready," announced the maid, and they all hurried off to their rooms to wash their hands before sitting down to table.

In ten minutes they were at dinner in the little dining-room on the ground floor. At first all were silent, but presently Roland began again in astonishment at this visit from the lawyer.

"After all, why didn't he write? Why should he have sent his clerk three times? And why is he coming himself?"

Pierre thought it quite natural: "No doubt an immediate decision is wanted, and perhaps there are certain confidential conditions which it would not do to express in writing."

All the same, everybody was puzzled, and all four were a little annoyed that a stranger should have been invited, who would be in the way of their discussing and deciding on what course to pursue. They had scarcely gone upstairs to the drawing-room when the lawyer was announced. Roland flew to meet him.

"Good evening, my dear Maître," said he, giving his visitor the title which in France is the official prefix to the name of any lawyer.

Madame Rosémilly rose. "I must go," said she. "I am very tired."

A faint attempt was made to detain her, but she refused to stop and went home without either of the three men offering to escort her, as they had hitherto invariably done. Madame Roland did the honors eagerly to the visitor.

"Will you take a cup of coffee, Monsieur?"

"No, thank you, I have just finished dinner.'

"A cup of tea, then?"

"Thank you, presently I will. First let us attend to business."

The dead silence which followed this remark was only broken by the regular tick of the clock, and downstairs by the clatter of saucepans which the girl was cleaning—too stupid even to listen at the door. The lawyer proceeded:

"Did you, when in Paris, know one M. Maréchal —Léon Maréchal?"

"I should think so!" exclaimed both M. and Mme. Roland in concert.

"He was a friend of yours?"

"Our best friend, Monsieur," replied Roland, "but dreadfully fond of Paris; never to be dragged away from the boulevard. He was a head clerk in the ex-chequer office. I have never seen him since I left the capital, and latterly we have ceased corresponding. When people are far apart, you know—"

The lawyer gravely interposed: "M. Maréchal is dead."

19

Husband and wife both responded with the little start of pained surprise, true or false, but always at command, with which news of this kind is received.

"My Paris correspondent," went on Maître Lecanu, "has just communicated to me the chief clause of his will, by which he makes your son Jean—Monsieur Jean Roland—his sole legatee."

All were too much astonished to say a single word. Mme. Roland was the first to control her emotion.

"Good heavens!" she stammered out. "Poor Léon—our poor friend! Dear me! Dear me! Dead!"

The tears came to her eyes: a woman's silent tears, drops of grief from her very soul, ran trickling down her cheeks. Roland was thinking less of the loss of his friend than of the prospect announced. But he did not dare to inquire at once into the terms of the will and the amount of the fortune. With a view of arriving in a roundabout way at these interesting facts, he asked:

"And what did he die of, poor Maréchal?"

Maître Lecanu had no idea. "All I know is," he said, "that, dying without any direct descendants, he has left the whole of his fortune—about 20,000 francs a year [$3840] in three per cents—to your second son, whom he knew from his birth, and deemed worthy of the legacy. If M. Jean refuses the money, it is to go to the foundling hospitals."

Old Roland could not hide his delight. "Sacristi!" he exclaimed. "It is the thought of a benevolent heart. Had I had no heir I would not have forgotten him. He was a true friend."

The lawyer smiled. "I was very glad," said he,

20

"to announce the event to you myself. It is always a pleasure to be the bearer of good news."

It had not occurred to the lawyer that the good news was that of a friend's death, of Roland's best friend; and the old man himself had suddenly forgotten the friendship he had just been talking about with so much warmth. Madame Roland and her sons, however, still looked sad. Madame Roland, in fact, continued to shed a few tears, wiping her eyes with her handkerchief, with which she afterward covered her lips to smother her deep sobs. .

"He was a good fellow," murmured the doctor; "very affectionate. He often asked my brother and me to dine with him."

Jean, with wide-open, bright eyes, stroked his handsome fair beard, a favorite gesture of his, and drew his fingers down to the tips of the longest hairs, as if he wished to pull it longer and thinner. Twice his lips parted to utter some appropriate remark, but after long cogitation all he said was: "Yes, he was certainly very fond of me. He always embraced me when I went to see him."

But his father's thoughts were off at a gallop round this future inheritance; nay, this inheritance already in hand; this money waiting behind the door, which would walk in very soon, to-morrow, at a word of assent.

"And there is no possible difficulty in the way?" he asked. "No lawsuit—no one to dispute the will?"

Maître Lecanu seemed quite at ease. "No; my Paris correspondent writes that everything is in order. M. Jean has but to sign his acceptance."

"Good! Then — then the fortune is quite assured?"

"Perfectly."

"All the necessary formalities have been gone through?"

"All."

All at once the old jeweler had an impulse of shame — shame of his avidity for information — obscure, instinctive, and momentary.

"You understand," he proceeded, "that when I ask all these questions so soon it is to save my son any disagreeable happenings which he might not foresee. Sometimes there are debts, embarrassing liabilities, lots of things! And a legatee finds himself in an inextricable thicket. To be sure, I am not the heir, but I think first of all for the little one."

They were in the habit of speaking of Jean among themselves as "the little one," though he was much bigger than Pierre. All at once Madame Roland seemed to wake out of a dream, to recollect some far-away event, a thing she had heard of long ago and had almost forgotten, and of which she was not altogether certain. She asked doubtingly:

"Did you not say that our poor friend Maréchal had left his fortune to my little Jean?"

"Yes, Madame."

"I am very pleased to hear it," she resumed. "It proves that he was fond of us." Roland had arisen.

"And do you want, my dear sir, my son to sign his acceptance immediately?"

"No, no, M. Roland. To-morrow, at my office. To-morrow, at two o'clock, if that time will suit you."

"Yes, of course—yes, indeed. I should say so."

Then Madame Roland (who had also risen), smiling after her tears, went up to the lawyer, and laying her hand on the back of his chair, looked at him with the pathetic eye of a grateful mother.

"And now for that cup of tea, Monsieur Lecanu."

"Now I shall take it with pleasure, Madame."

The maid was called, and first brought in some dry biscuits in deep tin boxes, the kind of brittle English biscuits that appear to be meant for a parrot's beak, soldered in metal cases as if they were intended for a voyage round the world. Then she brought little gray linen napkins, folded square, the kind of *serviettes* which economical households never seem to have washed. Another journey produced the sugar basin and the cups; finally she went off to boil the water—and everybody awaited events.

Conversation was impossible; everybody had too much to think about and nothing at all to say. Mme. Roland alone attempted a few vapid nothings. She narrated the events of the fishing party and sounded the praises of the "Pearl" and of Mme. Rosémilly.

"Charming! charming!" said the lawyer again and again.

Roland leaned against the marble mantelpiece as if it had been winter and the fire had been burning, his hands in his pockets and his lips formed to whistle, fidgeting, tortured by the uncontrollable desire to give expression to his delight. Pierre and Jean, in two armchairs, of similar pattern, stared before them from opposite sides of the center table, in identical attitudes and with dissimilar expressions.

Ultimately the tea was brought in. The lawyer

took a cup, sugared it, crumbled into it a piece of biscuit that was too hard for his teeth, and drank the mixture. Then he rose, shook hands with everybody, and took his leave.

"It is understood, then," repeated Roland at parting. "To-morrow, at your office, at two o'clock?"

"Precisely. To-morrow, at two."

Jean was silent. Their guest gone, silence reigned till old Roland clapped his younger son on the back and cried: "Well, you are a lucky dog! Why don't you embrace me?"

Jean smiled and embraced his father with the remark: "It did not appear to me to be necessary."

The old man was crazy with joy. He paraded about the room, drummed on the furniture with his thick finger-nails, pirouetted on his heels, and repeated over and over again:

"What luck! what luck! Now, this is what I really call luck!"

"You used to know this Maréchal well, then?" asked Pierre.

"Rather!" replied his father. "Why, he used to come to our house every night. You must remember how he used to bring you from school on half-holidays, and often took you off with him again after dinner. The very day Jean was born it was he who went for the doctor. He had been our guest at breakfast when your mother was taken ill. Off he set post-haste for the doctor. In his haste he took my hat in mistake for his own. The reason I remember that is that we had a hearty laugh over it afterward. Most likely he thought of that when he was dying, and having no heir he may have reflected: 'I remember

24

helping to bring that boy into the world; now I will leave him my savings.'"

Mme. Roland, seated in a deep chair, appeared buried in memories of the past. As though thinking aloud, she said: "Ah, he was a good, devoted, faithful friend, such as one rarely meets with nowadays."

Jean rose. "I am going for a stroll," said he.

His father was astonished and tried to detain him; they had much to discuss, plans to make, resolutions for the future. But he insisted, pleading an engagement. Besides, there would be ample time to settle everything before he came into possession of his fortune. So off he went. He wished to be alone for reflection. Pierre also said he was going out and followed his brother a few minutes after.

Whenever he found himself alone with his wife, old Roland embraced her, kissed her a dozen times on each cheek, and calling to mind and meeting a reproach which she had often brought against him, said:

"You see, dearest, it would have been of no use staying on longer in Paris and working for the children till I dropped, instead of coming here and recruiting my health, when fortune is so kind to us."

She was very serious. "Fortune is kind to Jean," said she. "But what about Pierre?"

"Oh, Pierre — he is a doctor. He will make lots of money. Besides, his brother will surely help him."

"No, Pierre would not take it. Besides, this legacy is Jean's, and his alone. Pierre will find himself at a great disadvantage."

The old gentleman was apparently puzzled.
"Well, well," he said, "we will leave him a larger
share in our will."

"Oh, no! that would hardly be right."

"Confound it all!" he exclaimed. "What do you
want me to do about it? You always raise up a lot
of uncomfortable notions. You are determined to
spoil all my pleasure. Well, I am off to bed. Good
night. At the same time, I call it good luck, deuced
good luck!"

And off he went, delighted in spite of everything,
and without a single word of regret for the friend
who had been so generous in his death.

Mme. Roland remained seated, still pondering, before a lamp which was burning out.

CHAPTER II.

GERMINATION

THE moment he got out Pierre directed his steps toward the Rue de Paris, the principal street of Havre, which was brilliantly illuminated and full of commotion and gaiety. The somewhat crisp air of the seacoast brushed his face, and he sauntered along, with his cane under his arm and his hands behind his back. He was uneasy, depressed, and gloomy, like the hearer of unpleasant news. No well-defined idea oppressed his mind and he would have been at a loss to account for his dejection and lethargy, on the spur of the moment. He was wounded, but he did not know in what part; somewhere within him there was a painful pin-prick —one of those indescribable wounds we cannot exactly locate, but which are none the less troublesome, depressing, and irritating—a vague, slight pang, like a minute germ of distress.

When he got as far as the square in front of the theater, he was drawn by the illumination of the

Café Tortoni and slowly approached its glittering *façade*. He was about to enter, but just then he reflected that he would be certain to meet friends and acquaintances there to whom he would be obliged to talk, and a strong antagonism swelled in his breast against this good-natured meeting over coffee cups and liqueur glasses. Turning back he regained the principal street leading to the harbor.

"Where shall I go?" he asked himself, striving to think of a favorite spot in accord with his present frame of mind. None occurred to him. Solitude made him feel irritable, but all the same he did not want company. As he emerged upon the Grand Quay he hesitated again; then he turned toward the pier; he had chosen solitude. Going up to a bench on the breakwater he sat down, tired already of walking and displeased with his stroll when it was hardly begun.

"What is the matter with me to-night?" he asked himself. And he began to search his memory for any vexation which had worried him, as a doctor questions a sick man to discover the cause of his feverishness. He was a man whose mind was at one and the same time irritable and calm; he was in the habit of becoming excited, and then examining his impulses and approving or condemning them; but in course of time nature's power always prevailed and the sensitive part of him always got the better of the intellectual. Now he was trying to find out what had caused this irritable mood, this desire to be doing, without wanting to do anything in particular, this wish to meet some one for the sake of arguing with him and at the same moment an aversion for the people he might chance to meet, and a distaste for the things they might talk to him about.

"Can it be Jean's inheritance?" he asked himself. Yes, that was possible, indeed. When the lawyer had told them about it he had felt his heart beat faster. One is not always master of his emotions; sometimes they are so sudden and pertinacious that a man struggles against them in vain.

He began to turn over in his mind the physiological problem of the impressions produced by any occurrence on man's instinct, which give rise to a current of painful and pleasant sensations absolutely antagonistic to those which the intellectual part of the man wishes, aspires to, and regards as just and healthy, when he has mastered himself by the cultivation of his thinking powers. He attempted to portray in his mind's eye the feelings of a son who has fallen heir to a vast fortune, and who, thanks to that fortune, will now experience many long-sighed-for pleasures which the meanness of his father had hitherto forbidden — a father, nevertheless, loved and mourned.

He rose and walked to the end of the pier. He felt better. He was relieved that he now understood — that he had detected himself, that he had unmasked that *other* which lies latent in all of us.

"So it was because I was jealous of Jean," he thought. "That is really horribly mean. I am certain of it now. The first notion that passed through my mind was that he would marry Madame Rosémilly. And this, notwithstanding that I am not in love with that priggish little fool myself, for she is the very woman to disgust a man of good sense and

good behavior. That shows it to be the most gra-
tuitous jealousy, the very essence of jealousy, which
exists merely because it exists! I must watch that!"

He was now in front of the flagstaff from which
the depth of water in the harbor is signaled, and he
struck a match to scan the list of vessels signaled in
the roadstead and coming in with the next high tide.
They came from Brazil, La Plata, Chili, and Japan;
there were two Danish brigs, a Norwegian schooner,
a Turkish steamer—this last amazed Pierre as much
as if it had been a Swiss steamer; and his whimsical
mood drew a picture of a vessel with men in turbans
and loose trousers climbing the shrouds.

"How absurd," thought he. "And yet the Turks
are a maritime people."

He went on a few paces further and stopped
again, looking out over the roads. To the right,
above Sainte-Addresse, the two electric lights of Cape
la Hève, like enormous twin Cyclops, darted their
long powerful beams across the ocean. Starting from
the two centers, side by side, the two parallel beams
of light, like the colossal tails of two comets, poured
in a straight and endless slope from the summit of
the cliff to the furthest horizon. On the two piers,
two other lights, the offspring of these giants, indicated the entrance to the harbor. Far away on the
other side of the Seine numerous others appeared,
some steady, some intermittent, some flashing, some
revolving, opening and shutting like eyes,—they were
indeed the eyes of the ports,—yellow, red, and green,
keeping guard over the night-enshrouded ocean with
its sprinkling of ships; the living eyes of the hos-
pitable shore, which said, by the mere mechanical,

regular movement of their eyelids: "Here I am. I am Trouville; I am Honfleur; I am the Audemer River." And towering above all the others, so that it might have been taken for a planet, the lofty lighthouse of Étouville pointed the way to Rouen across the sand banks at the mouth of the broad river.

Some small stars seemed to have fallen here and there on the illimitable deep, blacker than the sky itself. Close inshore or far in the distance they twinkled through the night haze, also of various colors, white, red, and green. Most of them were motionless; others appeared to be hurrying onward. Here were the lights of ships at anchor; there, those of vessels moving about in search of anchorage. Just then the moon rose behind the town. It, too, looked like some gigantic heavenly pharos stationed in the sky as a beacon for the innumerable fleet of the stars.

"Behold all this!" murmured Pierre, almost thinking aloud. "And we mortals lose our tempers for a few pence!"

Suddenly, close by, a shadow slipped through the wide, black ditch between the two piers, a great fantastically shaped shadow. He leaned over the granite parapet. A fishing boat was gliding in, wafted along by the breeze from the ocean, which filled its broad, brown sail, silently, without the sound of a voice or the splash of a ripple.

"If one could only live on board that boat," thought he, "how peaceful it would be — perhaps!" A few paces further on he saw a man sitting at the extreme end of the breakwater. Was he a dreamer, a lover, a philosopher — was he happy or was he in

31

despair? Who was he? He went on, curious to see the face of this lonely individual. It was his brother!

"What, you here, Jean?"

"Pierre! You? What brought you here?"

"I came out to get some fresh air. And you?"

Jean laughed. "I came out to get some fresh air, too."

Pierre sat down beside his brother. "Lovely — isn't it?"

"Oh, yes, lovely." Pierre was sure from the tone of Jean's voice that he had not looked at anything. He went on:

"For my part, when I come here I am always seized with a wild craving to be off with all these boats, north or south. Only to think that all these little specks of light out there have just arrived from the utmost parts of the earth, — from the lands of flowers and lovely olive and copper-colored girls, the lands of humming-birds, of elephants, of roaming lions, of ebony-colored monarchs, the lands which take the place of fairy tales to us who no longer believe in Puss-in-Boots or the Sleeping Beauty. How splendid it would be to indulge in an expedition to these lands; but then, think of the expense, it would cost no end —"

He interrupted himself, for he remembered that his brother had money enough now; and free from care, from the necessity of laboring for daily bread, unfettered, happy, and light-hearted, he could go wherever he wished, to the lands of the fair-haired Swedish maidens or the dark-skinned damsels of Havana.

Then one of those uncontrollable flashes which came to him so suddenly and quickly that he could neither prevent them, nor stop them midway, nor explain them away, sent to him, he himself imagined, from some different, independent, and violent soul, darted through his brain.

"Bah! he is too great a simpleton. He will marry the little Rosémilly woman." He rose to his feet. "I will leave you now," he said aloud, "to dream of your future. I must be going." He squeezed his brother's, hand and added in a husky voice:

"Well, my dear old fellow, you are now a man of means. I am very glad to have dropped upon you to-night so that I might tell you how delighted I am about it, how sincerely I congratulate you, and how much I love you."

Jean, tender and soft-hearted, was deeply moved. "Thanks, dear brother, thanks!" he stammered.

And Pierre turned away with his heavy step, with his cane under his arm and his hands behind his back. Once more in the town, he resumed his search for something to do. He was cheated out of his walk and out of the companionship of the sea by the presence of his brother. He had an inspiration. "I will go and take a glass of liqueur with old Marowsko," and he turned his steps toward that quarter of the town known as Ingouville.

He had met old Marowsko — "*le père Marowsko*" he called him — in the hospitals in Paris. Marowsko was a Pole — an old refugee, it was whispered, who had gone through terrible experiences out there, and who had come to ply his trade as a chemist and druggist in France, for which he had had to pass a fresh examination. Nobody knew anything of his early life, and all sorts of rumors were afloat among the indoor and outdoor patients of the hospital and afterward among his neighbors. He had a reputation as a dangerous conspirator, as a nihilist, as a regicide, as a patriot ready to dare and do anything and everything and who had escaped death by a miracle.

Pierre Roland's vivid and venturous imagination had been captivated by these tales: he had struck up an intimacy with the old Pole; but he had never been able to draw from him any revelation as to his former life. It was in reliance on the large custom which he expected the rising practitioner would bring him that the old man had left Paris to settle at Havre. In the meantime he made a very poor living in his little shop, vending medicines to the smaller tradesmen and work-people in his quarter of the town.

Pierre often paid him a visit and chatted with him for an idle hour after dinner. He liked Marowsko's quiet demeanor and rare speech, and gave him credit for great depth of character on account of his long periods of silence.

A solitary gas-jet flamed over a counter loaded with phials. Those in the window were not lighted on account of the expense. Behind the counter, seated on a chair, his legs stretched out and crossed, was the old man. He was quite bald, and his large hooked nose, which looked like a prolongation of his bald forehead, gave him a woeful resemblance to a parrot. When Pierre entered he was sound asleep, with his chin resting on his breast. The jangle of the shop bell woke him up, and recognizing the doctor,

34

PIERRE ET JEAN

he stepped forward to meet him, with both hands
extended in welcome.

His black frock coat, stained with acids and
syrups, was far too wide for his slender little figure,
and had the appearance of a shabby old cassock. He
spoke with a strong Polish accent which gave a
childish intonation to his small voice, like the lisping
attempts of an infant learning to speak.

Pierre sat down and Marowsko asked him:
"What news, my dear doctor?"

"None whatever. Everything just as usual, everywhere."

"You are not looking very gay this evening."

"I am not often gay."

"Come, come, you will have to shake off that.
Try a glass of liqueur."

"Thank you, I will."

"I will give you something new to try. For two
months back I have been experimenting to extract
something from currants. Only a syrup has been
made from them, as yet. And I have done it. I
have invented a very good liqueur — very good indeed; very good."

And with great delight he went to a cupboard
which he opened and pulled out a bottle from among
the rest. He moved about and did everything in
jerks. His actions were never quite completed. He
never entirely stretched out an arm, nor put out his
legs to their full extent; in fact he never made any
distinct, complete movement. His ideas were designed to fit his actions; he suggested, promised,
sketched, hinted them, but never fully gave them
voice.

35

His great aim in life seemed to be to concoct syrups and liqueurs. "A good syrup or a good liqueur should make a fortune," he would often say. He had compounded hundreds of these sweet mixtures, but had never succeeded in marketing a single one. Pierre maintained that Marowsko invariably reminded him of Marat.

Two little glasses were brought out of the back shop and placed on the board which he used for compounding his mixtures. Then both men examined the color of the fluid by holding it up to the gas.

"A fine ruby," Pierre declared.

"Is it not?" Marowsko exclaimed, his old parrot face beaming with a satisfied smile.

The doctor sipped, smacked his lips, meditated, sipped again, meditated anew, and spoke:

"Very good—capital! Something quite new as regards flavor. It is a discovery, my dear fellow."

"Really? Well I am very pleased to hear it."

Then Marowsko asked Pierre's advice as to how he should name the new liqueur. He thought of calling it "Extract of Currants" or "Fine Groseille" or "Groselia" or "Groseline." Pierre did not think well of any of these names.

Then the old man had a new idea. "What you said a while ago would do very well, very well: 'Fine Ruby.'" But the doctor doubted the merit of this name, although he was the originator of it. He recommended "Groseillette" and nothing else, and Marowsko thought that excellent.

Then they relapsed into silence and sat under the solitary gas-jet for several minutes without uttering a syllable. At last Pierre broke the silence, almost in spite of himself. "A strange thing happened at our house to-night," he said. "A friend of my father's, who died recently, has left his whole estate to my brother."

The druggist did not at first appear to understand. After thinking it over, however, he said that he hoped that the doctor would have half of the inheritance. When the thing was explained to him he seemed astonished and vexed; and to express his dissatisfaction that his young friend had been left out, he repeated several times:

"It will not look well. It will not look well."

Pierre, who was getting back into his former state of irritation, wanted to know what Marowsko meant by this phrase. Why would it not look well? Why should it look badly that his brother had fallen heir to the money of a friend of the family?

But the cautious old man would not give any further explanation. "In such cases the money is usually left equally to two brothers, and, I tell you, it will not look well."

Out of all patience, the doctor went away, returned to his father's house, and retired to bed. For some time after he could hear Jean softly moving about the next room, and then, after drinking two glasses of water, he fell asleep.

CHAPTER III.

THE BIRTH OF SUSPICION

THE doctor awoke the following morning fully resolved to make his fortune. Several times already he had formed the same resolution without converting it into a reality. The hope of rapidly acquired wealth had sustained his efforts and his confidence at the commencement of all his trials of new careers, till the first check sent him upon a new one. He lay pondering snug in bed between the warm sheets. How many physicians had grown rich in quite a short time! Nothing was needed but a slight knowledge of the world; for in his studies he had learned to criticise at their true value the most eminent physicians and he judged them to be all blockheads. He was assuredly as good as they were, if not better. If he could possibly obtain a practice among the *élite* of Havre, he could easily earn a hundred thousand francs a year.

He calculated with the utmost precision what his profits would certainly amount to. In the mornings he would visit his patients; a very modest average of ten a day, at twenty francs each, would give seventy-two thousand francs a year at least, or even seventy-five, for an average of ten patients was undoubtedly below the mark. In the afternoon he would receive at home, say, other ten patients, at ten francs each — that would be thirty-six thousand francs. In round numbers that made an income of a hundred and twenty thousand francs. Old patients, or personal friends, to whom his charge would be but ten francs a visit, or, at home, five, would probably reduce this total, but consultations with other physicians and sundry incidental fees would equalize matters.

It would be the easiest thing in the world to achieve all this by skillful advertising paragraphs in the "Figaro" to the effect that the scientific faculty of Paris had their eye on him and were interested in the cures effected by the modest young Havre practitioner! Presently he would find himself wealthier than his brother and more famous; and he would have the satisfaction of owing his fortune to his own exertions alone. He would be generous to his old parents and they would be proud of him. He would not marry, would not hamper his career with a wife who would only be in his way, though he might make love.

He felt so certain of success that he jumped out of bed as if he would grasp it on the spot, and dressed to go out and look through the town for apartments to suit him. As he wandered through the streets he reflected how slight are the motives that influence men's actions. He might and ought to have formed this resolution three weeks ago. Now the news of his brother's inheritance had forced it on him.

He stopped before every door which displayed a placard announcing "Fine apartments" or "Handsome rooms" to let; those which had no qualifying adjective he treated with scorn. His inspection of the rooms was made with a high and mighty air; he measured their height, sketched the plan in his notebook, with the passages, the arrangement of the exits, and explained that he was a medical man and had many visitors. He required a broad and well-kept staircase; and he could not go higher than the first floor.

Having written down seven or eight addresses and scribbled some hundred notes, he returned home to breakfast a quarter of an hour late.

In the hall he heard the clatter of plates. They had begun without him! Why? They never used to be so punctual. He was annoyed and put out, for he was rather thin-skinned. As he entered Roland said to him:

"Come on, Pierre, hurry up! You know we have to be at the lawyer's at two. This is not the day to be dawdling."

Pierre seated himself without response, first kissing his mother and shaking hands with his father and brother; and he helped himself from the dish in the middle of the table to the cutlet which had been kept for him. It was cold and dry, probably the worst of the lot. He reflected that they might have left it on the hot plate till he came in and not have lost their heads so entirely as to forget their other son, their eldest born. The conversation, which his com-

ing had interrupted, was resumed at the point where
they had left off.

Said Madame Roland to Jean: "I will tell you
what I should do at once, were I in your place. I
should have handsome rooms so as to attract attention; I should ride on horseback and get one or two
interesting cases to defend and make a name in court.
I should set up as a kind of amateur lawyer and be
very select. Thank goodness, you are out of danger
of want and if you do follow a profession it is, after
all, only to secure the benefit of your studies, and
because a man should never be idle."

Old Roland, who was peeling a pear, exclaimed:
"Christi! If I were in your place I would buy a
fine yacht, a cutter built on the lines of our pilot
boats. You could sail as far as Senegal in a boat
like that."

Pierre, in his turn, gave his opinion. After all,
said he, it was not money that made the moral or
the intellectual worth of a man. To a man of in-
ferior intellect money was only a means of degrada-
tion; in a strong man's hands it was a powerful
lever. And strong men were rare. If Jean were a
really superior man, now was the time to prove it
when want was out of his reckoning. But he would
have to work a hundred times harder than he would
otherwise have done. His care now would be not
to argue for or against the widow and the orphans
and pocket fees for every case he gained, but to
become a really famous legal authority, a legal lumi-
nary.

"If I were wealthy," he added in conclusion, "I
would work hard in the dissecting room!"

Old Roland shrugged his shoulders. "All very fine," said he, "but the wisest plan is to take life easy. We are human beings, not beasts of burden. If you are born poor, you have to work; so much the worse; you work. But when you have an income! you would be a fool if you worked yourself to death."

"Our ideas differ," replied Pierre, haughtily. "I do not respect anything in the world except knowledge and brains; everything else is beneath contempt."

Madame Roland always endeavored to soften the shocks between father and son. She now turned the conversation and began to talk about a murder committed a week or two before at Bolbec Nointot. They all knew the details of the crime and were carried away by the horrible fascination and the mystery by which crime, however low and disgusting, exercises a universal glamour over the curiosity of the world. But every now and then old Roland looked at his watch. "Come," he said at last, "it is time we were off."

Pierre sneered. "It isn't one o'clock yet," he said. "It was really hardly necessary to condemn me to eat a cold cutlet."

"Are you going to the lawyer's?" his mother asked.

"I? No. Why should I?" he replied, brusquely. "My presence is quite unnecessary."

Jean sat silent, as though it did not concern him at all. While they were discussing the Bolbec murder he, in his rôle of legal authority, had given his opinion and put forth some reflections on crime and crim-

inals in general. Now he held his tongue, but the
sparkle in his eye and the color in his cheeks, even
the gloss of his beard, seemed to declare his happiness.

The rest of the family gone, Pierre, alone once
more, resumed his quest for apartments to let. Two
or three hours spent in going up and down stairs
brought him at last to a pretty set of rooms in the
Boulevard François 1ᵉʳ; a commodious *entresol* with
two doors opening on different streets, a glass corridor, where his waiting patients could promenade
among flowers, and a splendid dining-room with a
bow window commanding the sea.

The terms — three thousand francs — caused him to
hesitate before taking it; the first quarter must be
paid in advance, and he did not possess a penny he
could call his own.

The little fortune his father had saved produced
about eight thousand francs a year, and Pierre had
often blamed himself for having put his parents in an
awkward position by his long delay in deciding on a
profession caused by giving up his attempts to begin
new courses of study. He left, therefore, promising
to send an answer in the course of a couple of days;
he reflected that he would ask Jean to lend him the
amount of the first quarter's rent, or even of the first
half year's, which would be fifteen hundred francs, as
soon as Jean should have got possession of his inheritance.

"It will only be a loan for a few months at the
outside," he thought. "I shall most likely pay it back
before the year is out. It is a trifle, and he will be
glad to do it for me."

It was not quite four o'clock, and as he had absolutely nothing to do he went to sit in the public gardens; here he remained a long time on a bench, thinking of nothing, his eyes fixed on the ground, weighed down by a distressing sense of weariness.

And yet he had been living like this ever since his return home, without suffering so acutely from the emptiness and the inaction of his life. He reviewed his days from the time he rose till the time he went to bed.

He had idled on the pier at high tide, idled in the streets, in the *cafés*, at Marowsko's, everywhere. And now, all at once, this mode of life, hitherto endurable, had become disgusting, intolerable. Had he possessed any small change he would have hired a carriage for a long drive in the country, by the farm ditches under the shade of the beech and elm-trees; but such a treat was beyond the reach of a man who had to think twice before venturing on a glass of beer or buying a postage stamp. It suddenly occurred to him how hard it was for a man of more than thirty to be compelled to ask his mother with a blush for a twenty-franc piece now and then.

"Christi!" he muttered, as he drew patterns in the gravel with the ferule of his cane. "If I only had money!" And again the thought of his brother's legacy came into his head like the sting of a wasp; but he drove it out angrily. He would not allow himself to descend to jealousy.

Some children were playing about in the dusty paths — little mites with long, fair hair — making little heaps of sand with the utmost gravity and care, only to stamp them down again when made. It was one of Pierre's gloomy days, those days when we search every cranny of our hearts and shake out every crease.

"All our endeavors are like the labors of these children," thought he. And he wondered if the wisest thing in life would not be to beget two or three such children of his own and watch them growing around him. A longing for marriage now came upon him. A man is not so lost when he is not alone. At least he has some one by his side in moments of trouble or of doubt; and it is at least something to be able to speak on equal terms to a woman in times of suffering.

Then his thoughts turned to women. He did not know much about them. He had not had much to do with them as a medical student, short flirtations begun and broken when his month's allowance was received and spent. Still there must be some kind, gentle, and comforting creatures among them. There was his mother, the good sense and saving grace of his own home. How glad he would be to make the acquaintance of a woman, a true woman!

He jumped up with a sudden determination to go and call on Mme. Rosémilly. But he sat down again as quickly as he had risen. He did not like that woman. Why? She had too much vulgar and mercenary common sense. Besides, she seemed to prefer Jean. This preference, although he would not confess it to himself, had much to do with his poor opinion of the widow's intellect. Though he loved his brother, he could not help thinking him rather mediocre and regarding himself as the better man. However, he could not sit there till nightfall; and as

he had done the evening before, he anxiously wondered, "What am I going to do?"

He felt in his heart the necessity of being made
much of and comforted. Comforted — for what? He
could not have expressed it in language, but he was
in one of those moods of weariness and exhaustion
when the presence of a woman, her kiss, the touch
of a hand, the rustle of a petticoat, a kindly look out
of black eyes or blue, seem the one thing needful at
the moment to our hearts. And all at once he recollected a little barmaid at a beer-shop whom he
had escorted home one evening and had seen again
occasionally.

Once more he rose. He would go and drink a
glass of beer and talk with the girl. What would he
say to her? What would she say to him? Nothing,
in all probability. But what did it matter? He
would amuse himself with her for a second or two.
She seemed to like him. Why then should he not go
to see her oftener?

She was dozing on a chair in the beer-shop,
which was almost empty. Three men were drinking
and smoking with their elbows leaning on the oak
tables. The bookkeeper was reading a novel at her
desk, and the proprietor, in his shirt-sleeves, lay fast
asleep along a bench.

As soon as she saw him the girl rose and eagerly
came to meet him.

"Good day, Monsieur," she said. "How are you?"

"Pretty well — and you?"

"I — oh, very well. What a stranger you are."

"Yes, I have very little spare time. I am a doctor, you know."

"Indeed! You never told me. I was sick last week, and if I had known that, I would have sent for you. What will you take?"

"A bock. And you?"

"A bock, since you are good enough to treat me."

She had at first addressed him with the familiar *tu,* and continued to use it, as if his friendliness had carried with it permission. They talked for a while and every now and then she took his hand familiarly. "Why don't you come here oftener? I am very fond of you, sweetheart," she said.

He was already disgusted with her; he saw how silly and commonplace she was. "A woman," he said to himself, "should appear to us idealized, or at least with her vulgarity veiled by some kind of poetry."

Next she asked him: "You passed the other day with a good-looking man, with a great, fair beard. Is he your brother?"

"Yes, he is my brother."

"He is very nice looking."

"Do you think so?"

"Yes, indeed; and he looks like a man who enjoys himself."

What curious impulse possessed him all at once to tell this barmaid about Jean's legacy? Why should this business which he tried to forget about when alone, which he thrust from him in dread of the pain it caused him, come to his lips now? And why did he allow it to overflow them, as if he must again unbosom his heart to some one, filled as it was with bitterness?

47

He crossed his legs and said: "He has extraordinary luck, that brother of mine. He has just fallen heir to a legacy of twenty thousand francs a year."

The girl opened wide her greedy eyes: "Oh! who left him that? His grandfather perhaps, or his aunt?"

"No! Just an old friend of the family."

"Only a friend! Impossible! And what about you—did he leave you nothing?"

"No, I only knew him slightly."

She sat thoughtful for a while; then, with a strange smile, she said: "Well, he is a lucky dog, that brother of yours, to have friends of that description. My word! no wonder he is so different from you."

He would have liked to slap her, without knowing why, and asked with compressed lips: "What do you mean by that?"

"Oh, nothing. Only that he has better luck than you."

He threw a franc on the table and went away.

He kept on repeating her phrase: "No wonder he is so different from you." What had been her meaning under these words? There was certainly some malice, some spite in the remark. Yes, that girl must have fancied, undoubtedly, that Jean was Maréchal's son. The agitation that overcame him at the idea of such a suspicion was so violent that he stood still, looking around for some place to sit down. Just before him stood another *café*. He entered, sat down, and as the waiter came up he ordered a bock.

He felt his heart beating, his skin creeping. Then the remembrance of Marowsko's words the night before flashed upon him. "It will not look well." Had he had the same thought, the same suspicion as this wench? Bending his head over his glass, and watching the white froth rising into bursting bubbles, he asked himself: "Is it possible that people should imagine such a thing?"

But the reasons that would awaken this awful doubt in the minds of others now crowded upon him, one after the other, clear, obvious, and exasperating. It was the simplest and most natural thing in the world that a childless old bachelor should leave his money to the two sons of his friend; but that he should leave it all to only one of them — of course people would be amazed, and whisper and end by smiling. How could he not have foreseen this? Why had his father not felt it? How was it his mother had not guessed it? No; they had been too overjoyed at this unlooked-for wealth to entertain such an idea. Besides, why should these worthy people have ever dreamed of anything so ignominious?

But the public — their neighbors, the shopkeepers, the tradesmen, everyone who knew them — would they not repeat the horrible thing, laugh at it, enjoy it, make merry over his father and look down on his mother?

The barmaid's remark, too, that Jean was fair and that he was dark, that they did not in the slightest degree resemble each other in face, figure, manner, or intellect, would not that occur to everybody? When anyone spoke about Roland's son, the question would be asked: "Which, the true or the false?" He got up, determined to put Jean on his guard against the terrible danger that imperiled their mother's honor.

But what could Jean do? The easiest thing would no doubt be to give up the inheritance, which would in terms of the will go to the poor, and to inform all friends and acquaintances who had heard of the bequest that the will contained clauses and conditions which it would be impossible to accept — which would have made Jean merely a trustee and not really an heir.

As he turned to go home he reflected that he must see his brother alone, so as not to speak about such a matter before his parents. When he reached the door he heard a great noise of voices and laughing in the drawing-room, and when he entered he found Captain Beausire and Mme. Rosémilly, whom his father had brought home with him and invited to dine with them in honor of the great news. Vermouth and absinthe had been served to whet their appetites, and all had been put into good humor. Captain Beausire was a comical little man, who had become rotund by dint of rolling about at sea, and whose ideas appeared also to have acquired the rotundity of pebbles, who laughed with his throat full of *rs*, and who looked upon life as an excellent thing, in which everything that happened was acceptable. He was clinking glasses with Roland's father, while Jean was offering two freshly filled glasses to the ladies. Mme. Rosémilly refused, till Captain Beausire, who had been a friend of her husband, called out:

"Come, Madame, *bis repetita placent*, as we say in fair Latin, which means that two glasses of vermouth never hurt anybody. Look at me; since I left the sea, I give myself an artificial roll or two every day before dinner in this way; I add a little pitching after my coffee, and that keeps things lively for the remainder of the evening. I never rise to a gale, mind you, never, never. I am too much afraid of hurting myself."

Roland, whose seafaring craze was humored by the old salt, laughed heartily. His face was flushed and the absinthe had made his eyes watery. He had a well-developed stomach which appeared to swallow up the rest of his body,— he was all stomach, indeed,— flabby, like men who spend their existence sitting and who have neither thighs, chest, arms, nor neck; constant sitting having made them develop all in one place. Beausire, on the other hand, though short and stout, was as firm as an egg and as hard as a cannon-ball.

Mme. Roland had not emptied her glass. She was looking at Jean with sparkling eyes; joy had brought the color to her cheeks. In Jean, too, the height of joy was now apparent. The thing was settled, signed, and sealed; he was the possessor of twenty thousand francs a year. The ring of his laughter, his mellower voice, his manner of looking at the others, his greater confidence, bespoke the assurance that money gives. Dinner was announced, and the old man was going to give his arm to Mme. Rosémilly when his wife exclaimed:

"No, no, father. This is Jean's day."

Unaccustomed luxury adorned the table. In front of Jean, who took his father's seat, a great bouquet of flowers mixed with favors — a bouquet for a really great occasion — rose like a cupola arrayed with flags,

51

flanked by four tall dishes. One contained a pyra-
mid of fine peaches; the second, a monumental cake
stuffed with whipped cream and covered with pin-
nacles of sugar—a cathedral of confectionery; the
third, slices of pineapple floating in clear syrup; the
fourth—unheard-of extravagance—black grapes from
the sunny south.

"Heavens!" exclaimed Pierre, as he sat down.
"We are celebrating the accession of Jean the Rich."

After the soup, Madeira circulated, and now all
talked at once. Beausire was giving the history of a
dinner he had eaten at the table of a negro general.
Old Roland was listening and trying to get in, between the sentences, an account of another dinner,
given by a friend of his at Meudon, which made
every guest ill for a fortnight. Mme. Rosémilly,
Jean, and Mme. Roland were scheming an excursion
to breakfast at Saint Jouin, from which they expected
to derive great pleasure; Pierre alone was sorry that
he had not dined by himself in some tavern on the
shore, whereby he would have escaped all this noise
and laughter; it annoyed him. He was wondering
how he could manage to confide his fears to his
brother, and persuade him to give up the fortune he
had already accepted and the intoxicating anticipation
of which he was enjoying. It would be hard on
him, of course, but he could not hesitate. His
mother's reputation hung in the balance.

The appearance of an enormous shadefish drove
Roland back to fishing stories. Beausire spun some
amazing yarns of adventure on the Gaboon, at Sainte-
Marie, in Madagascar, and off the coasts of China and
Japan, where the fish are as strange looking as the

natives. And he described the fishes — their goggle gold eyes, their blue or red bellies, their funny fins like fans, their strange crescent-shaped tails — with such droll gestures that they all laughed till the tears rolled down their cheeks.

Pierre alone appeared incredulous, and muttered to himself: "It is quite true, the Normans are the Gascons of the north!"

A *vol-au-vent* followed the fish; then a roast fowl, a salad, French beans with a Pithiviers lark-pie. Mme. Rosémilly's maid helped to wait on them, and the fun increased with the number of glasses of wine drunk. When the cork of the first champagne bottle was drawn with a pop, old Roland, greatly excited, mimicked the noise with his tongue and declared: "I like that noise better than the report of a pistol."

Pierre, more and more irritable every minute, retorted ironically: "And yet it is probably more dangerous for you."

Roland, on the point of drinking, replaced his untouched glass on the table and asked: "Why?" He had recently been complaining of his health, of languor, giddiness, frequent and inexplicable discomfort. The doctor replied:

"Because a bullet might very easily miss you, but a glass of wine is absolutely certain to hit you in the stomach."

"What then?"

"Then it scorches your stomach, upsets your nervous system, impedes the circulation, and leads to the apoplectic fit which always threatens a man of your constitution."

The jeweler's incipient intoxication vanished like smoke before the wind. He gazed at his son with a fixed, uneasy look, trying to find out if he was making fun of him. But Beausire exclaimed:

"Oh, these precious doctors! They all tell the same story. Eat nothing, drink nothing, never make love, never enjoy yourself; it all ruins your precious health. Well, all I can say is, I have done all these things, sir, in every quarter of the globe, wherever and whenever I have had the chance, and I am none the worse for it."

Pierre replied sharply: "In the first place, captain, you are stronger than my father; and in the next, all good livers talk as you do till the time when —well, when they don't come back to the careful doctor to say, 'You were right.' When I see my father doing what is worst and most dangerous for him to do, naturally I ought to warn him. If I did not I should be a bad son."

Mme. Roland, much disturbed, now interposed: "Come, Pierre, what is the matter with you? For this once it cannot harm him. Think of the occasion it is for him—for us all. You will spoil his pleasure and make us all sad. It is too bad of you to do such a thing."

"He can do as he likes," he muttered, shrugging his shoulders. "I have warned him."

But old Roland did not drink. He sat looking at his glass full of the limpid, luminous liqueur whose light, intoxicating essence rose from its depths to fly off in tiny bubbles on the surface. He scrutinized it with the suspicious eye of a fox smelling at a dead hen and fearing a trap. He asked, doubtfully: "Do

54

you really think it will do me much injury?" Pierre
was touched with remorse for allowing his ill nature
to punish the others.

"No," said he. "This once you may drink it; but
do not take too much or get into the habit of it."

Old Roland raised his glass, but could not yet
make up his mind to put it to his lips. He looked at
it regretfully, with fear and longing; then he smelled
it, tasted it, sipped and swallowed it slowly, his
heart full of terror, weakness, and desire, and, after he
had drained the last drop, regret.

Pierre's eyes all at once met Mme. Rosémilly's;
hers rested on him clear and blue, piercing and hard.
And he read and understood the precise thought that
lurked in that look—the indignant thought of this
simple-minded, right-thinking little woman. It said,
"You are jealous, that is what you are. Shameful!"

He bowed his head and proceeded with his dinner. He was not hungry and found nothing to his
taste. He was troubled with a desire to be off, a
longing to get away from these people, to hear no
more of their talk, their jests, and their laughter.

Old Roland, to whose head the fumes of the wine
were once more rising, had already forgotten his
son's advice and with a tender expression was eye-
ing a champagne bottle which stood nearly full beside his plate. Fear of being lectured again restrained
him from touching it and he was wondering by
what stratagem or trick he could get hold of it without attracting Pierre's notice. He picked up the bottle
with an air of indifference, and holding it by the
neck, stretched his arm across the table to fill the
doctor's glass, which was empty; then he filled all

the other glasses and when he came to his own he talked very loud, so that they might have imagined that it was by inadvertence if he poured anything into it. But no one in fact took any notice.

Pierre, without noticing it, was drinking a good deal. Nervous and irritable, he raised to his lips every minute the tall crystal funnel, where the bubbles danced in the sparkling, living liquid. He allowed the wine to slip very slowly over his tongue, so as to feel the light sweet sting of the gas as it evaporated.

By degrees a pleasant warmth glowed through him. Spreading from the stomach to his chest, it took possession of his limbs, and spread throughout his flesh like a warm, comforting tide, bearing pleasure with it. He felt better, more at ease, less irritable and his resolution to speak to his brother that same evening gradually vanished. He did not for a moment think of giving it up, but merely shrank from disturbing the happy humor in which he found himself. Beausire presently got on his feet and proposed a toast. Bowing to the company, he began:

"Most gracious ladies and gentlemen, we have met to celebrate a happy event which has fallen to the lot of one of our friends. It used to be said that Fortune was blind, but in my opinion she is only short-sighted or playful, and she has recently acquired a good pair of glasses, which have enabled her to discover in the good town of Havre the son of our worthy friend Roland, skipper of the 'Pearl.'"

All cried bravo and clapped their hands, and old Roland rose to reply. Clearing his throat, for it felt choked and his tongue was heavy, he stammered

56

out: "Thank you, captain, thank you—for myself and my son. I shall never forget your behavior on this occasion. Here's good luck to you!" His eyes and nose were moist, and he sat down, thinking of nothing more to say.

Jean, laughing, spoke in his turn: "It is I," said he, "who should thank my friends here, my excellent friends," here he glanced at Mme. Rosémilly, "who have given me such an affecting proof of their esteem. But I cannot prove my gratitude by words. I will prove it to-morrow, every hour of my life, always, for our friendship is not one which can fade away."

His mother, deeply affected, murmured: "Well said, my boy." But Beausire cried out: "Come, Mme. Rosémilly, say something on behalf of the fair sex."

She raised her glass, and in a sweet voice, slightly mingled with sadness, she said: "I will pledge you to the memory of Monsieur Maréchal."

There was a momentary lull, a pause for decent meditation, as after prayer. Beausire, who always possessed a flow of compliment, said: "Only a woman ever thinks of these refinements." Then, turning to old Roland, "By the way, who is this Maréchal? You and he must have been great friends."

The old man, emotional with liqueur, began to weep, and in a broken voice said: "Just like brothers, you know. He was a friend such as one does not make twice—we were inseparable—he dined with us every day—and would treat us to the play —I need say no more—no more—no more. A true friend—a real true friend—wasn't he, Louise?"

His wife merely answered: "Yes, he was a faithful friend."

Pierre looked from his father to his mother, and as the subject changed, he drank some more wine. The rest of the evening he hardly remembered. They had coffee and liqueurs and laughed and joked a great deal. About midnight he retired to bed, with a muddled brain and heavy head, and slept like an animal till nine the next morning.

CHAPTER IV.

IN THE FURNACE OF DOUBT

HIS slumbers, bathed in champagne and *chartreuse*, had apparently soothed him, for he woke in a most amiable mood. While dressing he weighed and summed up his emotions of yesterday and tried to bring into relief clearly and fully their real and occult causes, those from within himself and those from without.

It was possible, it is true, that the girl in the beer-shop had had a sinister suspicion — worthy of such a person — on being told that only one of the Roland brothers had been made heir to a stranger, but do not natures like hers always entertain such ideas, without a shadow of ground, about every honest woman? Do they not calumniate and abuse all those whom they think blameless, every time they speak? If a woman who is above suspicion is spoken of in their presence, they are as angry as if they were insulted, and cry out: "Ah, yes, I know your married women; a nice set they are! Why,

59

they have more lovers than we have, only they are such hypocrites that they hide it. Oh, yes, a nice set indeed!"

Certainly under no other circumstances would he have understood or dreamed of the possibility of such an innuendo against his poor mother, so kind, so simple minded, so good. But his heart was filled with the fermenting leaven of jealousy. His agitated mind, in search, in spite of himself, of all that could injure his brother, had probably even attributed to the pothouse barmaid a gross intention of which she was quite innocent. His unaided imagination had invented this horrible doubt — his imagination which he never restrained, which always evaded his will and roamed, unhindered, audacious, and crafty, into the wide world of fancies, returning now and again with some that were shameless and odious, and burying them deep in his soul, in its most unplumbed recesses, like something stolen. His own heart, most assuredly, held secrets from him; and had that wounded heart not seen in this monstrous suspicion a way of keeping his brother out of the inheritance which had aroused his jealousy? He suspected himself now, cross-examining all the secrets of his mind, as some people search their consciences.

Mme. Rosémilly, though possessed of a limited intelligence, had assuredly a woman's instinct and subtle intuition. Yet such an idea had never entered her head, for she had pledged the memory of the deceased Maréchal with perfect sincerity. She was not the woman to have done this had she had the slightest suspicion. Now he doubted no longer. His involuntary displeasure at his brother's windfall and his deep affection for his mother had exaggerated his scruples—very pious and respectable scruples, but exaggerated. He felt happy as he put this into words in his mind as if he had done a good action, and he determined to be charitable to everybody, beginning with his father, whose crazes, foolish remarks, vulgar ideas, and too evident mediocrity were a continual annoyance to him.

He rose in time for breakfast and amused the whole family by his fun and gaiety. His mother was quite delighted, and said to him:

"My little Pierre, you have no idea how humorous and clever you can be when you like."

He talked away, expressing himself in witty fashion and making them laugh by his clever jests about their friends. He made Beausire his butt and, to some extent, Mme. Rosémilly, too, but very judiciously and not too spitefully. As he looked at his brother he thought to himself: "Stand up for her, you muff! However rich you may be, I can always outshine you when I take the pains."

As they drank their coffee he said to his father: "Are you going out in the 'Pearl' to-day?"

"No, my boy."

"May I have her with Jean Bart?"

"Certainly, as long as you please."

He bought a good cigar at the nearest tobacconist's and went down to the pier with a jaunty step. He looked up at the sky. It was of a clear, luminous, pale blue, freshly swept by the sea breeze.

Papagris, the boatman, popularly known as Jean Bart, was slumbering in the bottom of the boat, which he was required to have ready every day at midday when they had not been out fishing in the morning.

"You and I together, mate," said Pierre. He descended the iron ladder of the quay and jumped into the boat.

"Which way is the wind?" he asked.

"Still due east, M'sieu' Pierre. A capital breeze out on the water."

"Well then, old fellow, let us be off."

They hoisted the foresail and weighed anchor, and the boat, getting under way, slipped slowly down toward the jetty over the smooth water of the harbor. The breath of wind that blew down the streets caught the top of the sail so lightly that it was imperceptible, and the "Pearl" seemed to be gifted with life—the life of a bark driven by some mysterious latent power. Pierre took the tiller, his cigar between his teeth and his legs stretched on the bunk, and with eyes half shut against the glaring sunlight, watched the great tarred beams of the breakwater as they glided past.

When they got to the open sea and skirted the end of the north pier, which had shielded them, a stronger wind blew in the doctor's face and on his hands, like a chilly caress, filled his chest, which drank it in with a long sigh, and, distending the brown sail, sent the "Pearl" scudding along at a lively rate on her beam. Jean Bart quickly hoisted the wing-like triangular jib. Then he took two strides to the stern and let out the spanker, which had been close reefed against its mast.

The boat heeled over and flew at top speed, while along the hull the hissing water rushed past them.

The prow cut up the sea like the share of a plow gone mad, and the yielding water which it turned up rolled over and fell, white with foam, as the plowed land, heavy and brown, rolls over and falls in a ridge. At every wave — there was a short, choppy sea running — the "Pearl" quivered from the end of the bowsprit to the rudder, which trembled in Pierre's hand; when the wind rose in squalls, the swell rose to the gunwale as if it would sweep into the boat. A collier from Liverpool was lying at anchor, waiting for the tide; they swept round her stern and took a look at each of the ships in the roads in succession; then they went further out to scan the unrolling coast line.

For three hours Pierre roamed hither and thither, over the dancing sea, careless, calm, and happy, guiding this thing of wood and canvas which obeyed the touch of his hand as if it had been a winged creature.

He was lost in the day-dreams one has on horseback or on the deck of a boat — dreaming of his future, which he painted in the brightest colors, and full of the joys of living. To-morrow he would ask his brother to lend him fifteen hundred francs for three months, so that he could install himself at once in the pretty rooms on the Boulevard François Ier. Suddenly the sailor exclaimed: "The fog is coming up, M'sieu' Pierre. We must go in."

Pierre glanced up; away to the north he saw a gray, filmy but thick shadow which hid the sky and spread above the water; it drove down upon them like a cloud. He tacked in the direction of the shore and steered for the jetty, flying before the breeze and

followed by the mist, which was rapidly overtaking
them. When it reached the "Pearl," folding her in
a dense shroud, an icy shiver coursed through Pierre's
limbs, and the smoky, earthy smell peculiar to a sea
fog caused him to shut his mouth against the taste
of the cold, damp vapor. Before the boat reached
her wonted anchorage in the harbor the town was
completely buried in this thin fog, which, without
falling, wet everything as if it had been rain, and
swept along the house-tops and the streets like the
flow of a stream. Pierre, whose hands and feet were
half frozen, hurried home, flung himself on his couch
and slept till dinner time. On his entrance into the
dining-room his mother was remarking to Jean:

"The glazed corridor will be splendid. I will put
flowers in it, and will see they are properly attended
to. When you entertain it will be like fairyland."

"What on earth are you talking about?" asked
the doctor.

"About some lovely rooms I have engaged for
your brother — quite a discovery; an *entresol* with
an entrance from two streets; with two drawing-
rooms, a glazed corridor, and a dining-room, — the
very thing for a bachelor."

Pierre grew pale. "Where may this be?" he asked.

"Boulevard François 1ᵉʳ."

There was no longer room for doubt. He sat
down so angry that he wanted to cry out: "This is
past a joke! Is nobody to have anything but him?"

His mother went on gleefully: "And just think,
the rent is only two thousand eight hundred francs a
year. They wanted three thousand, but I got them
to take off two hundred francs by taking the rooms

64

for three, six, or nine years. Your brother will be very comfortable there. An imposing residence makes a lawyer's fortune. It brings clients, pleases them, and holds them, and is a tacit reminder that a man who can afford such style wants to be well paid for his work."

She paused and proceeded: "We must get something to suit you now; much less expensive, of course, for you have no money, but neat and tidy. It will do much for your advancement."

Pierre rejoined with disdain: "For me! Oh! I shall get along by my perseverance and skill."

"Yes," his mother replied, "but to have good rooms will help you all the same."

The meal was about half finished when he suddenly asked: "How did you become acquainted with this Maréchal?" Old Roland tried to recollect:

"Just wait, I hardly remember. It is so long ago, now. Ah, yes, now I have it. It was your mother who became acquainted with him in the shop, wasn't it, Louise? It was as a customer we knew him first."

Pierre, prodding the beans on his plate viciously, went on: "When did you make his acquaintance?"

Roland again thought deeply, but could remember no more, and called his wife's better memory to his aid.

"What year was it, Louise? You remember everything. Let me see, was it in '55 or '56? You should know better than I, your memory is so good."

She thought a moment and replied steadily and with serene conviction:

"It was in '58, when Pierre was three years old. I cannot possibly be mistaken, for he had scarlet

65

fever that year, and Maréchal, though then a comparative stranger, was of great assistance to us."

"Of course," exclaimed Roland, "quite so; we couldn't have done without him. When your mother was half dead with fatigue, and I had the shop to look after, he went to the chemist's for medicine. He was the kindest soul on earth! And when you got better you have no idea how pleased he was and how he petted you. From that time on we became great friends."

Immediately the thought struck Pierre with the force of a cannon-ball: "If he knew me first and was so fond of me, if *I* was the cause of this great friendship for my parents, why did he leave his fortune to Jean and nothing to me?"

He asked no more questions but sat gloomy and absent-minded, nursing a new anxiety as yet indefinite, but which promised to be the germ of a fresh anguish.

He went out presently and roamed about the town again. The streets were shrouded in mist, which made the night densely dark and unpleasant. It was as if a pestilence had fallen upon the world. Wreaths of mist swept past the gas-lamps, blotting them out every now and then. The pavement was slippery as on a frosty night after rain, and vile stenches ascended from the areas — the smells of cellars, drains, sewers, dirty kitchens — and mingled with the abominable odor of the fog.

Pierre, his shoulders up to his ears, his hands in his pockets, made for Marowsko's, glad to get indoors out of the cold. The druggist dozed as usual under the gas-jet which was the only guardian of the premises. When he recognized Pierre, whom he loved as a faithful dog loves his master, he bestirred himself, brought out two glasses, and the groseillette.

"Well," said the doctor, "how is the liqueur getting on?"

The Pole said that four of the principal *cafés* in the town had promised to retail it, and that two newspapers, the "North Coast Pharos" and the "Havre Semaphore," had agreed to advertise it in consideration of a supply of drugs to the editors.

A long silence ensued. Finally Marowsko inquired if Jean had actually got possession of his inheritance; then he asked two or three other questions on the same subject. His affection for Pierre made him jealously rebellious against this preference for Jean. Pierre felt as if he could actually hear his thoughts; he guessed and read in his averted eyes and the hesitation in his voice the words which the druggist felt inclined to speak, but was either too timid or too prudent to utter.

He was convinced that the old man was thinking: "You should not have allowed him to accept an inheritance which will lead people to talk."

And all at once the old desire to be alone returned to Pierre with such force that he got up without drinking his glass of groseillette, bade the astonished druggist good-bye, and hurried into the misty streets again.

"What on earth," he asked himself, "did Maréchal leave all his money to Jean for?"

It was no longer jealousy which made him ask this question, the mean but natural jealousy which he was aware of within himself, and against which he had been fighting for the past three days, but this dread that he should himself come to believe that Jean was the dead man's son. As he wandered through the night he racked his memory and his reason for the truth. That discovered, he would never let it enter his thoughts again.

He reasoned thus: "Let me examine the facts first of all. What do I know about him and his behavior to my brother and to me? Then the probable causes for this preference must be found out. He knew Jean from his birth, that's true. But he had known me before. Why did he not choose me as his heir, since it was through me, my scarlet fever, that he became so intimate with my parents. He ought on that account logically to have had a warmer interest in me,—but perhaps he felt an instinctive liking for my brother as he watched him growing up."

With all the powers of his brain and intellect he tried to reconstruct from what he recollected the picture of Maréchal, to understand and realize what manner of man was this who had passed him by with indifference after all those years in Paris. The exertion of walking dulled and disconnected his ideas, and blurred his memory. To examine the past and the unknown with sufficient penetration he would have to be at rest in some quiet spot. He would go and sit on the jetty where he had been the other night. As he neared the harbor a low, deep roar like the bellowing of a bull, but longer and steadier, came over the waters. It was the moan of a fog-horn, the cry of a vessel which had lost its way in the fog. He shuddered and his blood ran cold; this cry of distress stirred his heart and affected his nerves as deeply as if he had himself uttered it. It was answered by a similar moaning voice further out; then, near at hand, the fog-horn on the pier uttered a mournful sound in reply. Pierre hurried to the pier, with no thought of anything else but to walk on into the ill-omened, booming night.

He sat down at the end of the breakwater and shut his eyes against the two electric lights, dimmed by the fog, which made the harbor accessible in the dark, and the red gleam of the light on the south pier, now scarcely visible. Turning sideways, he leaned his elbows on the granite parapet and hid his face in his hands.

Without pronouncing the words aloud his mind kept repeating, "Maréchal — Maréchal," as if he would summon and challenge a phantom. And suddenly, on the dark background of his closed eyelids, he saw him as he had actually seen him in life; a man of about sixty years old, his white beard trimmed to a point, with heavy white eyebrows. Of medium height, his manners were pleasing, his eyes gray and mild, his motions quiet, his appearance altogether that of a lovable, kindly man. He called Pierre and Jean " my dear children," and had never shown any decided preference for either of them, inviting both of them together to dine with him. Then Pierre, with the perseverance of a dog seeking a lost scent, endeavored to recollect the words, gestures, voice, and looks of the dead man. Gradually he could see him quite plainly in his apartments in the Rue Tronchet, where he had entertained the two brothers at dinner.

Two maids had waited on him, old women who always called the boys "Monsieur Pierre and Monsieur jean." Maréchal would hold out both hands to his young visitors, the right to one, the left to the other, just as they happened to come in.

"How are you, my boys," he would say, "and how are your parents? They never write to me."

The conversation was always about commonplace affairs, as it would naturally be between intimate friends. The old man's mind was by no means original, but very entertaining and gracious. He had certainly been a good friend to them, one of those good friends whom we value the less because we are so sure of their friendship.

Recollections now poured upon Pierre. He remembered how Maréchal of his own accord, seeing that he was troubled occasionally and suspecting that it proceeded from the usual impecuniosity of a student, had lent him money, some few hundred francs, forgotten by both lender and receiver, or never repaid. It was plain that, since he foresaw his wants in this way, Maréchal must have been always fond of him. Well—if so, why did he leave his whole estate to Jean? No, he could not recollect that the old man had ever shown any greater liking for Jean than for himself, or had ever interested himself more in one brother than in the other. Well—if so, he must have had some very strong private reason for leaving all to Jean—all—and nothing to Pierre.

The longer he thought about it, the more he recalled of the past few years, the more amazing and incredible it seemed that Maréchal should have acted in this way. An excruciating pang of anguish pierced his throbbing heart. Its springs seemed broken and the blood coursed through it in an unchecked, surging flood. Then under his breath, as one talks in a dream, he muttered: "I must know, my God! I must know!"

He pierced further back still into the past, to an earlier period of his parents' life in Paris. But the faces he could not decipher and his visions were indistinct. Had Maréchal fair, brown, or dark hair? He could not tell; the later picture, the old man's face, blotted out all the rest. But he remembered that in former days he had been slimmer, softer handed and had often brought flowers on his visits, very often, for his father would always say: "What, more flowers! This is absurd, my good fellow; you will ruin yourself," and Maréchal would reply: "It does not matter. It pleases me."

Then he recalled his mother's voice as she smiled and said: "Thank you, my kind friend." She must have said this often to make him remember it so well.

So Maréchal, the gentleman, the rich man, the customer, brought flowers to the humble shopkeeper. He, an educated and fairly cultured man. Had he not often discussed poets and poetry with Pierre? He was not a critical reader, but appreciated poetry with a sympathetic feeling. The doctor had frequently smiled at the emotion he evinced, which appeared to him silly. Now he felt that this sentimental creature could never have been a friend of his father, who was so commonplace, bigoted, and dull, to whom the very word "poetry" meant imbecility.

Maréchal, at that time young, unattached, and wealthy, must have chanced to go into the shop, purchased something, returned, chatted, smiled at the pretty young wife and shaken hands with the husband.

And then — good God — what then?

He had loved and petted Pierre, the jeweler's firstborn, till the birth of the second; then till his death he had rema'ned silent as the sphinx; then when his flesh was crumbling to dust in his grave and he had nothing now to fear or to conceal, he had bequeathed his whole fortune to this second child. Why? The man must have foreseen the deduction that everyone would draw. He must have understood he was clouding the reputation of a woman. If Jean were not his son how could he have done this?

And suddenly the clear remembrance flashed upon his mind, Maréchal and Jean were both fair. He now recollected a little miniature he had once seen in their Paris house, which had now disappeared. Was it lost or hidden? If he could have it but for one minute! Was it in his mother's secret drawer among treasured love-tokens?

He groaned, and, as if in answer, the pier fog-horn close beside him boomed, with a strident, savage roar, through the dark night across the mist-shrouded ocean. And once more, through the fog, the night gave forth responsive cries, — terrifying cries these, from the throats of the great blinded steamships. Then silence reigned again. Pierre looked about him as if startled out of a bad dream and surprised to find himself in such a place.

"I am crazy," he said, "to suspect my mother." And a tide of love and repentance and sorrow surged up in his heart. Could anyone who knew her or had ever seen her dream that the soul of this loyal,

single-hearted woman was not purer than water?
And yet he, her own son, had suspected her. Could
he have done so at that moment he would have
asked her for pardon on his knees.

His father was no doubt a very worthy man; honest and fair in his dealings, but with a mind whose
horizon was bounded by his shop. How came it
that his mother, who must have been beautiful at one
time — that was still evident — and endowed with a
fine, sensitive, emotional nature, could have married
a man so unlike herself? The answer is plain. She
had married, as young French girls do, a young
man with some means selected for her by her relatives. They had settled down to their shop in the
Rue Montmartre, and the young wife, presiding at
the desk, inspired by the feeling of home and that
fine, sacred sense of a community of interests which
takes the place of love and even of respect at the
hearths of most of the mercantile houses in Paris.
had gone to work with her finer and more active intellect to make the fortune they aspired to. And in
this way had her life been led, monotonous, peaceful,
respectable — and without love.

Without love — was it possible that a young woman
could be without love? Could a good-looking young
woman, living in Paris, reading books, applauding
actresses who died of passion on the stage, exist from
youth to old age without feeling her heart moved?
He would not believe it of any other woman; why
should his mother be different from all others?

She had been young, and she had possessed all
the romantic weaknesses of youth. Imprisoned in the
shop, beside a commonplace husband who talked of

nothing but business, she had had all the poetic dreams of youth. And one day a man had appeared, as lovers do in books, and talked as they talk.

She had loved him. Could he deny that, even though she was his mother? Must a man reject evidence because it concerned his mother? And she had been false. The conclusion must be that this man had remained faithful to her through distance and through old age; and he had left all his money to his son — their son!

Pierre sprang to his feet, trembling with rage, with outstretched arm, eager to strike, to crush somebody. Whom? Everyone; his father, his mother, his brother, the dead man.

He hastened home thinking what he was to do. As he passed a tower beside the signal pole the jarring roar of the fog-horn sounded close to his ear. It startled him so that he almost fell, and retreated to the granite parapet. The steamer which had sounded first was already at the entrance of the harbor.

Pierre turned and saw its red light through the fog. Then its bulky shadow crept between the piers, thrown by the broad light of the electric lanterns. Behind him, the hoarse voice of the lookout, an old, retired sea captain, shouted: "What ship?" and through the fog the equally hoarse voice of the pilot replied: "The 'Santa Lucia.'"

"Where from?"

"Italy."

"What port?"

"Naples."

And Pierre's bewildered eyes saw in fancy the fiery play of Vesuvius, and the fireflies dancing at

74

the foot of the volcano in the orange groves of Sorrento or Castellamare. Often had he dreamed of those familiar names as if he knew the spot. Oh, if he could only go away immediately, no matter where, and never return, never write, never let anyone know what had become of him! But he must go home to his father's house. No, he would not go in, on any account; he would remain there till dawn. He liked the roar of the fog-horns. Collecting himself, he paced up and down like an officer on deck.

Another ship followed the first, huge and mysterious; an English Indiaman, homeward bound. Several more he saw arrive in rapid succession, out of the dense mist. Then, the dampness becoming unbearable, he made for the town. He felt so cold that he went into a sailor's tavern for a glass of grog. When he felt the hot, stinging liquid burn his mouth and throat, he felt hope revive.

He might be mistaken. He knew his own vagrant unreasonableness well. Doubtless he was mistaken. He had argued like the prosecutor of a charge against an innocent person, whom it is always easy to convict in our own mind, when we have an object in finding him guilty. After sleeping over it he would think differently. He went in and to bed, and by force of will at last fell asleep.

CHAPTER V.

THE PORTRAIT

THE doctor rested but an hour or two in troubled slumber. When he woke in the darkness of his warm room, he felt, even before his thoughts began to awake, that disagreeable oppression and weariness of spirit that the sorrow we have slept with leaves behind. The catastrophe which at the first shock merely jarred us seems, during our sleep, to have burned into our very flesh, exhausting it like a fever. Memory came back to him like a blow and he sat up in bed. Slowly and consecutively he went through all the reasonings which had caused him so much anguish on the jetty amid the roaring fog-horns. Thought seemed to dispel doubt. He felt his logic dragging him along to absolute certainty, as if by a relentless, strangling hand.

He was hot and thirsty and his heart beat furiously. He rose to open his window and inhale the fresh air, and as he stood by the open window a low sound came through the wall. Jean was peacefully

sleeping and snoring gently. He could actually sleep!
He had no doubt, no suspicion! He took this money
and thought it quite fair and natural! He slept, rich
and contented, never dreaming that his brother was
tortured with bitterness and distress. Wrath boiled
up within him against this careless, happy sleeper.
Yesterday he would have knocked at his brother's
door, entered, seated himself by the bedside, and said
to him, surprised by his sudden waking:

"Jean, you should not keep this legacy which
may bring suspicion and dishonor upon our mother."

To-day his lips were sealed, and he could not tell
Jean that he did not believe he was their father's
son. He must guard this secret from every eye, especially his brother's. He could no longer stay in
the room. This house crushed him! The very roof
seemed to weigh on his head and the walls to suf-
focate him. To relieve his thirst he went with a
lighted candle to fetch a glass of fresh water from
the filter in the kitchen.

He descended the two flights of stairs. Reascend-
ing with the water-bottle filled, he sat down, in his
nightshirt, on a step of the stairs, in a draft, and
drank like a runner out of breath. The silence of the
house affected him; and he began to listen for the
faintest sounds. First the tick of the clock in
the dining-room seemed to grow louder every second.
Then he heard another snore, an old man's snore —
short, hard, and labored, his father's, doubtless. The
idea that these two men — father and son — were
nothing to each other revolted him! Not a single tie
bound them together and they did not know it. All
their daily intercourse was based on the assumption

that the same blood flowed in the veins of both. Yet two strangers, born continents apart, could not have been more alien to each other. They thought they loved each other, but their love was the outcome of a lie, of which he alone would ever possess the secret.

But if he were mistaken! Oh! if only one of those slight resemblances, which run from ancestor to remote descendant, could be traced between his father and Jean. The mere curve of a nostril, the breadth of the forehead, the color of the hair, a gesture, or a habit,—any sign which an expert eye could mark as characteristic,—would suffice for him, a medical man.

But he could not, after long thought, remember anything. Still, he had only looked carelessly, being at the time without cause for suspicion.

He rose to return to his room, and ascended the stairs slowly, deep in thought. Passing the door of his brother's room he stopped, his hand extended to open it. An invincible desire had seized him to see Jean at once, to look at him at leisure, to catch him asleep, with the countenance calm and the relaxed features at rest, and all the mask of life put off. In this way he might seize the latent secret of his physiognomy, and any appreciable resemblance would not escape his notice.

But if Jean were to wake, what was he to say? How explain his intrusion? He stood still; his hand on the door handle, trying to make up a reason, an excuse. Suddenly he remembered that he had a week before lent Jean a phial of laudanum to cure his toothache. He might have been in pain himself to-night and have come for the drug. He entered with the stealthy step of a burglar. Jean was sunk in a deep animal sleep, with his mouth open; he did not wake but he stopped snoring.

Pierre, bending over him, gazed at him eagerly. No, this youngster did not resemble Roland in the slightest; and for the second time the remembrance of the little portrait of Maréchal, which had disappeared, came back to his mind. He must find it! When he saw that his doubts would probably be set at rest.

His brother moved, doubtless conscious of some one near him, or disturbed by the light of the candle on his eyelids. The doctor retreated on tiptoe to the door, closed it noiselessly behind him, and returned to his room, but not to bed.

Day was long in dawning. One after the other the hours struck on the dining-room clock, with deep and solemn tone, as if the little piece of clockwork had swallowed the chime of a cathedral. The sound came up the empty staircase, pierced walls and doors, and died away in the rooms, where it fell on the unhearing ears of the slumbering household. Pierre began to walk to and fro between his bed and the window. What was he to do? He was too agitated to spend the day at home. He still wished to be alone, at all events till next day, to consider, to compose himself, to strengthen himself for the everyday life he must face once more.

He resolved to go over to Trouville and watch the people upon the sands. That would amuse him, change the complexion of his thoughts, and give him time to harden himself to the terrible thing he had discovered. When morning broke he dressed himself. The cold fog had disappeared and it was a beautiful day. The Trouville boat did not start till nine, so it occurred to him to say good morning to his mother before he started.

He waited till her usual hour for rising and went downstairs. His heart beat so violently as he reached her door that he stopped for breath. His hand was weak and trembling as it lay on the handle, which he could hardly turn to open the door. He knocked. His mother's voice asked:

"Who is there?"

"I — Pierre."

"What do you want?"

"Only to say good morning. I am going to Trouville to spend the day with friends."

"But I am still in bed."

"Well, don't disturb yourself. I shall see you this evening when I return."

He trusted he could get away without seeing her, without imprinting on her cheek the false kiss it made his heart sick to think of. But she replied:

"No, wait a moment. I will let you in. Wait till I get into bed again."

He heard the sound of her bare feet on the floor and of the bolt being drawn. Then she called out: "Come in."

He entered. She was sitting up in bed. Roland, a silk handkerchief serving him for a nightcap, lay sleeping beside her with his face to the wall. Nothing would wake him but a shaking hard enough to pull his arm off. When he went fishing, the maid Joséphine, rung up by Papagris at the hour agreed on, had to rouse her master from his heavy slumbers.

As he approached his mother Pierre looked at her with a sudden feeling of never having seen her before. She held up her face, which he kissed on each cheek and then sat down in a low chair.

"Did you decide on your excursion last night?" she asked.

"Yes, last night."

"Will you come back to dinner?"

"I don't know; at all events don't wait for me."

He gazed at her with amazement and curiosity. This woman was his mother! All those features, seen every day from childhood, from the time when his eyes could first see, her smile, her voice—so well known and familiar, to him appeared different from what they had always been hitherto. Although it was really she and he knew every detail of her face, this was the first time he had identified them all. Scrutinizing closely the face he loved so well, he perceived a physiognomy new and strange.

He rose to go, but, giving way to the unconquerable desire for information which had pursued him since the day before, he said:

"By the way, I remember you once had a little portrait of Maréchal in the drawing-room in Paris."

She hesitated, or he thought she hesitated, for a second or two, then she said, "Certainly."

"What has become of it?"

Again she hesitated: "That portrait—wait a moment; I don't quite know—perhaps it is in my desk."

"I wish you would be so kind as to get it out."

"Certainly, I will look for it. Why do you want it?"

"Oh, not for myself. I thought it would make an appropriate gift for Jean, and that he would like to have it."

"Yes, that is so; a good idea. I will look for it when I get up." And Pierre went out.

It was a calm, azure day. In the streets everybody seemed in good spirits, the tradesmen going to business, the clerks to their offices, and the girls to their shops, singing, some of them, as they went along, under the influence of the fine weather. The passengers were embarking on the Trouville boat. Pierre took his seat aft on a wooden bench.

"Now," he asked himself, "was my mother ill at ease when I asked for the portrait or only astonished? Has she lost or has she hidden it? Does she or does she not know where it is? If it is hidden—why?"

And following up his train of thought from one deduction to another he made up his mind to this: that portrait—friend or lover—had remained in the drawing-room in a conspicuous position till one evening she had removed the dangerous little picture and hidden it.

Pierre remembered now that it was a very long time before they left Paris that it had disappeared, about the time, he thought, when Jean's beard began to grow.

The motion of the boat putting off put an end to his meditations. He turned his attention to the water. Outside the piers the little steamer, puffing, snorting, and quivering, turned to the left and steered for a point distantly visible through the morning mist. The brown sail of a clumsy fishing-smack, which lay motionless on the expanse of water, resembled a great rock rising out of the sea. The Seine, flowing down from Rouen, looked like a wide gulf of the sea. In less than an hour they were in the harbor of Trouville. It was the universal hour for bathing, and Pierre sought the beach.

At a distance it was like a garden of gay flowers. Right along the yellow sand stretching from the pier to the Roches Noues, sunshades of every color, hats of every shade, dresses of every hue, grouped outside the bathing machines, ranged in long lines along the water's edge, scattered here and there, looked like huge bunches of flowers on a wide meadow. And the babel of sounds — voices ringing clear through the thin air, the uproar of children being bathed, the clear laughter of women — made a harmonious, constant noise, borne on the careless breeze, and mingling with the air itself.

Pierre picked his way through this crowd, more lost and isolated than if he had been thrown overboard from the deck of a vessel a hundred miles out at sea. He heard, unheeding, snatches of sentences as he passed; he saw, without looking, men and women talking and smiling together. Then all at once he became conscious of them as if he had just awoke, and hatred of them all filled his heart, for they seemed happy and contented.

As he went along he studied the groups, threading his way around them full of a new set of ideas. All these gorgeous gowns which covered the sands like bouquets of flowers, these flaming parasols, the fictitious grace of the tight waists, the ingenious inventions of fashion, from the neat little shoe to the bizarre hat, the graceful gesture, voice, and smile, the coquettish airs, appeared to him but extraordinary attributes of feminine depravity. Without exception, the aim of all these bedizened women was the charming and deluding of some man. They had tricked themselves out for all men except the husband they no longer needed to conquer — for the lover of yesterday and of to-morrow, for the stranger that might come under their notice, or for whom they were perhaps looking.

And beside them sat these same men hunting them like game which was shy and cunning, notwithstanding it looked so near and easy of capture. This wide beach, in fact, was but a love market, where some bargained for their kisses, others only promised them. All over the world, he reflected, it was always the same.

His mother had only been like the others. Like the others? Not at all. There were exceptions — many of them. The wealthy, giddy, pleasure-seeking women he saw around mainly belonged to the fashionable and showy class and their less respectable sisters. On these sands, trampled by the idle crowds, the virtuous, home-keeping women were not to be found.

The rising tide was gradually driving the foremost pleasure seekers back. The different groups every now and then jumped up and fled with their chairs before the yellow waves which rolled up with a lacelike edge of foam. The bathing machines were being hauled by horses, and along the boarded promenade which lined the shore, the fashionably dressed people, jostling and mingling, flowed in two opposite streams, slow and dense. Pierre, whom the bustle made nerv-

ous and irritable, escaped to the town, where he
went to breakfast in a little tavern on the edge of
the country.

His coffee finished, he extended his legs on a
couple of chairs under a lime-tree in front of the
house, and as he had hardly slept the previous night
he fell into a slumber. He slept for several hours,
woke, shook himself, and finding it was time to get
on board again he departed, plagued by the stiffness
which had attacked him during his long sleep. He
was anxious to be home again; to learn if his mother
had found Maréchal's portrait. Would she mention it
first, or would he have to ask for it again? If she
awaited further questioning that would show she had
some secret reason for concealing it.

But when he reached home and got to his room
he hesitated about going down to dinner. He was
too miserable. His soul was still in revolt. However, he resolved to go through with it, and appeared
in the dining-room as the rest were sitting down to
table.

They were all beaming with pleasure.

"Well," Roland was saying, "how are you getting on with your purchases? I don't want to see
anything till it is all in place."

His wife replied, "Oh, we are getting along
nicely. But it takes a lot of consideration to buy
things which will match. The question of furniture
is an engrossing one."

She had spent all day with Jean seeing cabinet-
makers and upholsterers. She preferred rich, gaudy
materials, to attract the eye. Jean, on the other
hand, wanted simplicity and elegance. This meant a

repeated argument upon everything put before them. She held that a client must be impressed with a sense of wealth the moment he was shown into his counsel's waiting-room. Jean, on the contrary, who only cared to attract a refined, wealthy class, aimed at captivating persons of refinement by a quiet and perfect taste. The discussion, maintained all day, was again taken up with the soup.

Roland had no opinion on the subject. "I do not want to hear anything about it," he replied. "I will go and see it when it is quite finished."

Mme. Roland appealed to Pierre's judgment: "And what do you think about it, Pierre?"

His nerves were so agitated that he would have liked to swear. However, he merely replied dryly in a voice shaking with vexation: "Oh, I am of Jean's opinion. I like nothing so well as simplicity, which, in matters of taste, is the same as correctness in matters of conduct."

"You must recollect," his mother went on, "that we are living in a commercial city, where good taste is not met with everywhere."

"What does that matter?" replied Pierre. "Is that a reason for living like the stupid people? If my fellow-citizens are stupid and ill mannered, must I follow their example? A woman's conduct is not based on her neighbor's lightness."

Jean began to laugh: "You seem to borrow your arguments from the maxims of a moralist."

Pierre was silent, and his mother and brother returned to the question of materials and armchairs. He sat watching them, as he had watched his mother that morning before he started for Trouville—as a

86

stranger would study them; and he really felt as if
he had suddenly come into a family to whom he was
a complete stranger. His father, above all, was an
astonishment to his eye and his mind. That flabby,
hulking man, happy and foolish, was his father!

His family! In the last two days an unknown
malicious hand, that of a dead man, had rent and
shattered, one after another, the ties which had bound
these four human beings together. It was all at an
end, forever. He had no mother any longer—for he
could no longer love her since he could not reverence
her with that absolute, pious respect which filial love
demands; no brother, nothing but his father, that
vulgar man whom in spite of himself, he could not
love. And he suddenly burst out: "By the way,
have you found that portrait?"

She opened her eyes in astonishment: "What
portrait?"

"Maréchal's."

"No—that is—yes—I have not found it, but I
know where it is."

"What is that?" asked Roland.

"A little portrait of Maréchal," replied Pierre,
"which used to be in the drawing-room in Paris. I
thought Jean would like to have it."

Roland exclaimed: "Why, certainly, I remember
it distinctly. I saw it again last week. Your mother
found it in her desk when she was arranging her papers. It was on Thursday or Friday. Don't you remember, Louise? I was shaving when you found it and
laid it on a chair beside you along with a bundle of
letters half of which you burned. Is it not strange
that you should have discovered that portrait only

two or three days before Jean heard of his legacy? If I believed in presentiments I should set that down as one."

Mme. Roland calmly replied: "Yes, I know where it is. I will bring it presently."

So she had not told the truth! When she had said that morning to her son in reply to his question as to what had become of the miniature, "I don't quite know — perhaps it is in my desk" — it was a lie! She had seen, touched, and handled it a few days ago; and then she had hidden it again in the secret drawer along with *his* letters.

Pierre looked at the mother who had lied to him with the concentrated anger of a son who had been cheated, plundered of his most sacred affection, and with the wrath of a jealous man who discovers, after being long blind, that he has been shamefully betrayed. Had he been her husband instead of her child he would have seized her by the wrists, the shoulders, or the hair and flung her to the ground, struck her, hurt her, crushed her! And he must do nothing, say nothing, show nothing! He was her son; vengeance did not belong to him. It was not he who had been deceived.

Yet had she not deceived his affection, his pious respect? Like all mothers, she owed it to her son to be without reproach. If the rage that boiled within him touched on hatred it was because he felt her to be still more guilty toward him than toward his father.

The love of husband and wife is a contract in which the one who breaks it is guilty merely of treachery; but when the wife is also a mother her

88

duty is a higher one, for nature has intrusted the mothers with a race. If she falls then she is cowardly, worthless, infamous.

"I don't care," said Roland, suddenly, extending his legs under the table, according to his nightly custom, while he sipped his glass of black-currant brandy. "You may do worse than live idle when you have a nice little income. I hope Jean will invite us to dinner in style now. If I have dyspepsia occasionally it can't be helped."

Then, turning to his wife, he added: "Go and get that portrait, little woman, now that you have finished your dinner. I should like to see it again myself."

She rose, took a taper, and obeyed. Then after an absence which Pierre thought long, though she was not away more than three minutes, she came back smiling with an antique gilt frame in her hand.

"There it is," she said. "I found it without any trouble."

The doctor was the first to take the portrait, which he examined, holding it at some distance from him. Conscious that his mother was watching him, he slowly raised his eyes and looked at his brother to compare the faces. He could scarcely restrain himself from saying: "Dear me! How like Jean!" Though he did not dare to speak the terrible words, his manner of comparing the two faces betrayed his thought.

There were certainly features common to both; there were the same beard and forehead; yet there was nothing positive enough to justify his saying: "This is the father and that is the son." It was rather a kinship of physiognomies that was shown. But what appeared to Pierre more significant was the fact that his mother rose, turned her back, and was pretending to replace the sugar basin and liqueur bottle in a cupboard.

"Hand it to me," said Roland.

Pierre handed the miniature to his father, who drew the candle nearer him to examine it better; then he murmured in a voice of pity:

"Poor fellow! So he was like that when we first knew him! How time flies! He was a good-looking man then, and had such a pleasant manner, had he not, Louise?"

His wife making no reply, he proceeded:

"And what a calm temper! I never saw him angry. And now it is all over—nothing is left of him—except what he bequeathed to Jean. Well, you can at least be sure that he was a faithful friend to the last. He did not forget us even on his death-bed."

Jean next held out his hand for the portrait. After looking at it for some time he said sorrowfully:

"I don't recognize it at all. I remember him only when his hair was white."

He returned the picture to his mother, who glanced at it hastily and said, in even tones:

"It is yours now, my little Jean, since you are his heir. We will put it in your new apartments," and when they adjourned to the drawing-room she put it on the mantelpiece beside the clock, where it used to stand.

Roland filled his pipe; Pierre and Jean lighted cigarettes. As usual when they smoked them after dinner, Pierre walked to and fro about the room. Jean buried himself in a deep armchair, his legs crossed. Their father commonly sat astride on a chair and expectorated across the room into the fireplace.

Mme. Roland occupied a low seat beside a small table on which the lamp stood, engaged in her sewing. This evening she was knitting something for Jean's new rooms. It was a complicated piece of work and demanded her whole attention. But every now and then her eye, counting the stitches, glanced quickly and stealthily at the little picture leaning against the timepiece. The doctor, pacing the little room in four or five steps, met her glance at every turn.

It seemed as if they were spying on each other; and keen, unbearable uneasiness devoured Pierre. He said to himself, at the same time distressed and glad: "She must be in torture if she knows that I suspect!" and every time he approached the fireplace he paused to look at Maréchal's picture and to show the haunting idea that possessed him. And this little picture, no bigger than the palm of one's hand, became like a malicious, threatening living being for this little family. Suddenly the street door bell rang. Mme. Roland, usually so self-possessed, started violently, betraying to her doctor son the agitation of her nerves. "That must be Mme. Rosémilly" she said, and her gaze returned anxiously to the mantelpiece.

Pierre could see, or imagined he did, her fears and distress. A woman's eye is sharp, her wits quick, her instincts suspicious. When the woman who was about to enter saw the miniature, she might at the first glance discover the likeness. That meant that the world would know everything.

He was seized with dread, and, turning as the door opened, he took the painting and slipped it under the timepiece without being perceived by his father and brother. When next he met his mother's eyes they seemed to him changed and dim.

"Good evening," said Mme. Rosémilly. "I have come to ask you for a cup of tea."

While they were busy greeting her, Pierre made off. Everyone was surprised when they discovered his absence. Jean, annoyed for the young widow's sake, muttered: "What a bear!"

Mme. Roland replied: "You must not be angry with him; he is not well to-day. He is tired out with his trip to Trouville."

"That does not matter," said Roland, "that is no excuse for going off like a barbarian."

Mme. Rosémilly tried to smooth matters by saying:

"Not at all. He has gone off in the English fashion; people always go away like that in polite society when they want to leave early."

"Oh, in polite society, I dare say," replied Jean. "But a man is not supposed to treat his family à l'Anglaise, and my brother has done nothing else for some time."

CHAPTER VI.

Gehenna and Hymen

Nothing happened at the Rolands' for a week or two. The father fished, Jean went on with his furnishing, with the assistance of his mother, and Pierre, very disconsolate, appeared no more except at the meal hours.

His father sharply asked him one evening:

"Why the deuce do you carry about such a glum face? This is not the first time I have remarked it."

The doctor replied: "It is because I feel the burden of life weigh so heavy upon me."

The honest man could not understand him at all, and replied with a grieved air:

"This is really too much. Since we have had the good fortune to receive this inheritance everyone seems unhappy. It is as if we had met with an accident, as if we were lamenting somebody!"

"I am indeed lamenting somebody," said Pierre.

"You! Whom?"

"Oh! some one you did not know and whom I loved very much."

Roland supposed it concerned a flirtation, some young woman his son had fallen in love with and demanded:

"A woman, no doubt?"

"Yes, a woman."

"Dead?"

"No, worse, ruined."

"Ah!"

Although astonished at this unforeseen confidence, made in his wife's presence, and at the strange tone of his son, the old man did not insist on an explanation, for he was of the opinion that third parties had no concern with such matters.

Mme. Roland seemed not to have heard this conversation. She looked ill and was very pale. Several times already her husband, surprised to see her sitting as if she would collapse in her chair, and to hear her gasp as if she had difficulty in breathing, had said to her:

"Really, Louise, you look quite ill, you fatigue yourself too much getting Jean's furniture together! Rest yourself a little! He is not pushed for time, now that he is rich."

She would shake her head without reply. Her pallor to-day was so evident that Roland remarked again:

"Come," said he, "this will not do at all, my poor old girl, you must take care of yourself."

Then, turning to his son:

"You see quite well that your mother is suffering. Have you not attended to her?"

Pierre replied:

"No, I have not noticed that there was anything the matter with her."

"But, good heavens!" said Roland, "that is perfectly patent. What use is it your being a doctor if you do not see when your mother is indisposed? Just look at her, there, look at her!"

Mme. Roland began to gasp and grew so pale that her husband cried:

"But she is going to be ill."

"No — no — it is nothing — it will pass off — it is nothing."

Pierre came near and looked at her steadily.

"Let us see what ails you," said he.

She repeated hurriedly in a low voice:

"Nothing — nothing — I assure you — nothing."

Roland had gone to get some vinegar; he returned and holding out the bottle to his son, said:

"There, see to her, now. Have you sounded her heart, at least?"

As Pierre stooped to feel her pulse she withdrew her hand with a movement so abrupt that she hit it against a chair which stood beside her.

"Come," said he in a cold tone, "let me advise you since you are ill."

Then she rose and held out her arm to him. Her skin was burning, the beatings of her heart violent, and he murmured:

"Indeed, it is serious enough. It will be necessary to take a composing draught. I will give you a prescription."

And as he wrote, bent over his paper, a low noise of smothered sighs, of short, suppressed sobs, made him suddenly turn round again. She was weeping, her face in her hands.

Roland, astounded, demanded:

"Louise, Louise, what ails you? What ails you?"

She did not reply and seemed torn by a deep and terrible grief. Her husband attempted to take her hands and draw them from her face. She resisted, repeating:

"No, no, no."

He turned to his son:

"What ails her? I have never seen her like this before."

"It is nothing," said Pierre. "She is only a little hysterical."

And it seemed to him that his heart was solaced to see her so tortured, that this sorrow alleviated his resentment, diminished the weight of opprobrium for his mother. He gazed at her like a judge satisfied with the punishment he has inflicted. But suddenly she rose, rushed to the door, with an impetus so swift that it was impossible to prevent or stop her, and ran to shut herself up in her room. Roland and the doctor remained face to face.

"Do you understand anything of all this?" asked the first.

"Yes," replied the other, "this comes from a simple nervous ailment which often shows itself at mother's age. It is probable that she will still have many spasms like this."

She had others, indeed, nearly every day; and they appeared to be excited by a word from Pierre, as if he had the secret of her curious, unknown malady. He guessed by her face her intervals of calmness, and by wily ruses awoke with a single word the anguish a moment before calmed. And he himself suffered as much as she did. He suffered frightfully from the fact that he could love and respect her no more — do nothing but torment her.

When he had exposed the bleeding wound, opened by him in this womanly and motherly heart, when he felt how miserable and desperate she was, he went out alone through the town, so stung by remorse, so crushed by pity, so distressed by having bruised her under his filial scorn, that he wanted to throw himself into the sea, to drown himself and end it all.

Oh! how he had wanted to forgive her! But he could not, being unable to forget. If only he had been able to stop making her suffer, — but he could not, because he suffered so much himself. He returned at the meal hours, full of relenting resolutions, then, whenever he came within sight of her, whenever he caught her eye, hitherto so clear and so frank, and now so nervous and afraid, he spoke in spite of himself, unable to restrain the perfidious phrase that rose to his lips. The terrible secret, known to them alone, embittered him against her. And there was now nothing to hinder him reading that secret. Jean lived almost constantly in his new rooms and only came home to dine and sleep in his father's house.

Jean often noticed his brother's bitterness and anger, which he put down to jealousy. He determined that he would some day show him his place and teach him a lesson. Life at home was growing very unpleasant on account of these continual scenes. But now that he spent his days from home he did not feel this unkind conduct so much, and his desire for peace inspired him with patience. His good luck, too, had turned his head, and he hardly thought of anything but his own immediate interests. He would come in full of new little worries, about the style of a morning coat, the shape of a felt hat, or the correct size of visiting cards. His talk was full of the details of his house — the linen-shelves in his bedroom cupboard, the pegs for the entrance hall, the electric bells to keep out unwelcome visitors.

An excursion had been planned for the day when he was to go into his new quarters. They were to go to Saint Jouin, dine there, and return to tea in his rooms. Roland, of course, wanted to go by sea, but the uncertainty of making the distance in a sailing boat in the face of a head wind caused his plan to be discarded and a coach was hired for the occasion.

They started at ten o'clock so as to arrive in time for lunch. The dusty highway lay across the plain of Normandy, whose gentle undulations, sprinkled with farmhouses, peeping out from among trees, give it the appearance of a vast park. The four Rolands, Mme. Rosémilly, and Captain Beausire all sat silent in the vehicle as it rumbled on, drawn by a pair of heavy horses, the ears of the occupants deafened by the noise of the wheels and their eyes shut to keep out the clouds of dust.

It was harvest time. The dark clover and the bright green beet-root alternated with the yellow corn, which lighted up the landscape with its pale golden hues; the fields seemed to have absorbed the sunshine which poured down on them. The reapers were at work in some places, and the men were swaying to and fro in the spots cleared by the scythes, as they swept clean the level land with the wing-like blades.

A two hours' drive brought them to a point where they turned to the left, past a whirling windmill — a sad, hoary wreck, rotting, and in its last stages, the sole survivor of its race; then the coach turned in at a pretty innyard and drew up at the door of a neat little hostelry well known in the district.

The hostess, *la belle Alphonsine,* appeared smiling at the threshold and Jean gave his hand to the two ladies, as they hesitated at the carriage step.

Several visitors were already lunching in a tent beside a grass plot under the shade of some apple-trees — Parisians who had come from Étretat; from the house came the sound of talking and the noise of plates and pans. The outer dining-rooms were full, so they were shown into a room inside the house. Roland's eye was caught by some shrimping nets hanging against the wall.

"Ah, ha!" he cried, "they catch prawns here, do they?"

"Oh, yes," replied Beausire. "It is the most famous place for them on the coast."

"Capital! Suppose we try to catch some after breakfast."

It happened to be low tide at three o'clock, so they resolved to spend the afternoon hunting prawns among the rocks.

They breakfasted lightly, a precaution against the tendency of blood to the head after wading. They wished, besides, to keep an appetite for dinner, which had been ordered on a large scale for their return at six o'clock.

Roland's impatience would not allow him to sit still. He wanted to buy the prawn nets, which are rather like those used for catching butterflies in the country. They are called on the French coast *lanets,* and consist of netted bags fixed at the end of a pole. Alphonsine, always smiling, was delighted to help them. Then she aided the ladies to make an impromptu change of toilette, to preserve their dresses from harm. She offered them skirts, rough worsted stockings, and hempen shoes. The men doffed their socks and went to the shoemaker's to buy wooden shoes to put on.

At last they set out, the nets slung over their shoulders and creels on their backs. Mme. Rosémilly looked charming in this guise, with an air of countrified audacity. Her skirt, lent by Alphonsine, tucked up and stitched in place to allow her to run and leap on the rocks without danger, displayed the ankle and lower calf of a strong and nimble little woman. The loose dress gave her movements freedom and an enormous broad-rimmed garden hat, of coarse yellow straw, covered her head; to crown all, a bunch of tamarisk pinned into it on one side lent her an extremely dashing and military air.

Jean had asked himself every day since he came into his fortune if he should marry her. Every time he saw her he resolved to ask her to be his wife; and then, as often as he found himself alone again he came to the conclusion that waiting would give him time for reflection. Now she was not as rich as he was, for she had only twelve thousand francs a year; but it was invested in real estate, in farms and lands near the Havre docks, and this would in the near future greatly increase in value. Their wealth was therefore nearly equal and the young widow certainly attracted him very much.

As he watched her walking before him to-day he said to himself:

"I must really make up my mind to it. I cannot do better, I am sure."

They descended a little ravine which sloped from the village to the cliff. The cliff at the end of the dell rose to a height of about eighty meters above the sea level. Framed between its green banks on either side, a great triangle of silvery blue water was visible in the distance. A sail on the horizon looked like an insect. The pale blue sky was so identically like the water that it was impossible to see where one ended and the other began. The two ladies, walking in front of the men, stood out against this brilliant background, their figures clear cut against the sky.

Jean watched with a sparkling eye Mme. Rosémilly's neat ankle, the slender waist, and the coquettish broad hat as they sped before him. His ardor was aroused, and urged him on to the sudden resolution which takes hold of hesitating and timid natures. The soft air, fragrant with the odors of the seacoast — of the gorse, the clover, and the thyme, mingling with the salt smell of the uncovered rocks — mounted to his brain. At every step and every glance he cast on the trim figure before him he felt more and more determined to delay no longer, to tell her that he loved her and hoped to marry her. The

prawn fishing would give him the necessary opportunity; and it would be a pretty spot for love making,
too — their feet in a pool of water while they watched
the shrimps taking cover under the seaweed.

At the edge of the cliff they observed a little footpath zigzagging down its face; beneath them, half-
way down, an extraordinary mass of enormous rocks
were huddled and piled one above the other on a
kind of grassy undulating plateau which stretched as
far as they could see to the south, apparently formed
by some old landslip. On this shelf of brushwood
and grass, thrown up, to all appearance, by the throes
of a volcano, the fallen rocks resembled the ruins of
some ancient city which had at one time looked out
over the ocean, under the shelter of the long white
wall of the overhanging cliff.

"That is lovely!" exclaimed Mme. Rosémilly,
standing still. Jean had come up to her side and,
his heart beating, offered his hand to help her down
the narrow steps cut out of the rock.

They went on before; Beausire, steadying himself
on his little legs, offered his arm to Mme. Roland,
who felt giddy at the sight of the abyss beneath her.

Roland and Pierre brought up the rear, and the
doctor had to help his father down the steps, for
Roland's head was so giddy that he could only slide
in a sitting posture from step to step.

The two young people led the way at a great rate
till they saw all at once beside a wooden bench which
offered a resting place halfway down the incline, a
spring of clear water welling from a crevice in the
cliff. It fell into a hollow the size of a washing basin,
which it had worn in the rock; then, tumbling in a

tiny cascade about a couple of feet high, it trickled across the footpath, carpeting it with cresses on its way, and disappeared among the briers and grass on the plateau where the rocks lay piled.

"I am so thirsty!" cried Mme. Rosémilly.

But how was she to drink? She tried to catch the water in her hands, but it trickled through her fingers. Jean was equal to the occasion. He placed a stone on the path, on which she kneeled and put her lips to the spring itself.

When she raised her head, covered with innumerable tiny drops, which were showered all over her face, her hair, her eyelashes, and her dress, Jean stooped over her and murmured: "How pretty you look!"

She replied as if she were scolding a child: "Will you be quiet?"

These were the first words in the nature of a flirtation they had ever exchanged.

"Come," said Jean, quite agitated. "Let us get on before they overtake us."

For they could see quite close to them now Captain Beausire's back as he descended backwards, giving both his hands to Mme. Roland. Further behind, Roland was letting himself slide down with the speed of a tortoise, squatting on the steps and clinging with hands and elbows, Pierre in front watching his progress.

The path, less steep, now became almost a road, zigzagging between the huge bowlders which had rolled from the top of the cliff. Mme. Rosémilly and Jean began to run and soon reached the beach. They crossed it to the rocks, which extended in a long, flat solitude covered with seaweed and sprinkled with innumerable glistening pools. The ebb-tide flowed beyond far away, on the other side of this expanse of slimy, black, and olive-green weed.

Jean rolled up his trousers to his knees and his sleeves to his elbows; then with a shout of "Forward!" he boldly leaped into the nearest pool left by the tide.

The lady, more cautious, but fully intending to go in too, by and by, edged round the little pool, stepping carefully, for she slipped on the shining weed.

"Do you see anything?" she asked.

"Yes, I see your face reflected in the water."

"If that is all you see, you will not have good fishing."

He murmured softly in reply: "Of all fishing it is that in which I should prefer to succeed."

She laughed: "Try then; you will find it will slip through your net."

"Still—if you will— "

"I will see you catching prawns—nothing else in the meantime."

"You are cruel. Let us go on a little further; there are none here."

He gave her his hand to help her over the slippery rocks. She leaned on him somewhat timidly, and he suddenly felt himself overwhelmed by love and passion, as if the fever gathering within him had only been waiting till to-day to declare itself.

They came by and by to a deeper cleft in the rocks. Here the long, thin weeds, many hued, in green and rose-colored tangles, were floating and swaying beneath the surface of the water as it

104

trickled away to the far-off sea through some unseen cranny in the rocks.

"Look, look," cried Mme. Rosémilly. "I see one, a big one, just there!" Jean saw it too and leaped boldly into the pool up to his waist. But the creature slowly retreated before the net, waving its long whiskers. He drove it in the direction of the seaweed, and made sure of his quarry. When it found itself hedged in, it darted over the net, shot across the pool, and disappeared.

The young lady, who had followed the chase in the greatest excitement, could not help ejaculating: "Clumsy!"

He was annoyed and thoughtlessly drew his net over a hole full of seaweed. As he brought it to the surface he saw in it three large transparent prawns, caught napping in their hiding place.

He triumphantly presented them to Mme. Rosémilly, who was afraid to touch them on account of the sharp saw-like crest on their heads. However, she at last took them up by the ends of their long whiskers and dropped them one by one into her creel, adding a little seaweed to keep them alive. Then, finding a shallower pool, she stepped in hesitatingly, for the sudden cold on her feet took her breath away, and began fishing on her own account. She was skillful and cunning, with the needful light touch and fisherman's instinct. With nearly every dip she brought up some prawns, taken by surprise by her quick and noiseless pursuit.

Jean caught none now; he contented himself with following her, step by step, touching her now and then, bending over her, pretending to be greatly distressed by his awkwardness, and beseeching her to give him a lesson.

"How do you manage it?" he kept saying. "Show me."

And as both their faces were reflected side by side in water so clear that the black weeds at the bottom formed a mirror, Jean smiled at the face which looked up to him from beneath, and now and then blew it a kiss with his finger tips.

"Oh! how tiresome you are," she exclaimed. "My dear fellow, you should never do two things at one time."

He replied: "I am only doing one—loving you."

She drew herself up and said seriously: "What has come over you these last ten minutes; have you lost your senses?"

"No, I have not. I love you and at last I dare to tell it."

They were both standing in the salt pool wet half-way up to their knees and holding their nets with dripping hands. They looked into each other's eyes.

"How very stupid to tell me so at such a time and place. Could you not wait till some other day and not spoil my fishing?"

"Forgive me," he murmured, "but I could no longer keep silent. I have loved you a long time. To-day you intoxicated me."

She seemed all at once to have resigned herself to exchange pleasure for business.

"If we sit down on that rock," said she, "we can talk more comfortably."

They perched themselves upon a high bowlder, side by side in the warm sunshine. She began again:

106

"My good friend, you are no longer a child, nor am I. We both know quite well what we are doing and what will be the consequences of our actions. If you have seriously resolved to make love to me to-day, I naturally infer that you want to marry me."

He was hardly prepared for this business-like statement of the case, and answered naïvely:

"Why, yes."

"Have you talked about it to your parents?"

"No, I wanted first of all to know whether you would accept me."

She gave him her hand, still wet, which he eagerly clasped.

"I am ready and willing," she said. "I think you are a kind, true-hearted man. But I should not like to displease your father and mother."

"Do you suppose my mother has not expected this, or that she would like you so well if she did not hope that you and I would marry?"

"True. I feel somewhat anxious."

No more was said. For his part, he was surprised that she was so sensible about the matter. He had looked forward to little flirtations, refusals which meant yes, and a whole love comedy mingled with prawn fishing in the sparkling water. But it was all over; he was pledged—married—in a score of words. As they were agreed about it there was no more to be said, and they both sat, a little embarrassed by the sudden event; puzzled, in fact, without daring to speak, to fish, or knowing what to do.

Roland's voice released them from their predicament.

"Come here, children. Come and see Beausire. The fellow is positively emptying the sea of prawns!"

The captain had indeed had an amazing haul. Wet to the waist, he waded from pool to pool, picking out the likeliest spots at a glance, and scouring all the holes covered with seaweed, with a slow, steady sweep of the net. And the pretty, transparent gray prawns jumped about in his hand as he jerked them sharply out of the net and put them into his creel. Mme. Rosémilly, astonished and delighted, stuck to his side, apparently almost forgetting her promise to Jean, who followed them in a dream, devoting himself to the childish amusement of plucking the animals from among the waving weeds.

Suddenly Roland exclaimed: "Ah, here is Mme. Roland come to join us."

She had at first kept to the beach with Pierre. Neither of them had any desire to play at paddling about among the rocks and the tide pools. Yet they had both felt the peril of staying together. She was afraid of her son, and he feared both her and himself; he was afraid of his own cruel temper. But they sat down side by side on the pebbles. And each of them gazing at the vast beautiful expanse of blue water shot with silver, under the warmth of the sun, fanned by the sea breeze, had the same thought: "How delightful this would have been — once."

She did not dare to speak to Pierre, knowing well that she would receive some harsh answer; and he did not dare to address her, knowing that in spite of himself he would speak harshly. He sat digging up and turning over the rounded pebbles with the end of his cane. She, with a weary look on her face, had picked up three or four little stones and slowly and mechanically passed them from one hand to the other. Then her idle gaze, roaming over the scene before her, saw among the weed-covered rocks her son Jean fishing with Mme. Rosémilly. She watched their movements, half understanding, with maternal instinct, that they were talking of something unusual. She saw them bending side by side over the pools, standing face to face as they talked, and then scrambling up and seating themselves on the rock. Their forms stood out against the sky in sharp relief; they looked as if they were alone in the center of the wide expanse and acquired a kind of symbolic dignity in the vast extent of sky and sea and cliff.

Pierre was also watching them and a hoarse laugh burst all at once from his lips. Without turning her head Mme. Roland asked:

"What is it?"

He sneered and replied: "I am learning how a man lays himself out to be managed by his wife."

She flushed with anger at the supposed insinuation: "To whom are you referring?"

"To Jean, by Jove! It is excruciatingly funny to watch these two."

She murmured in a low tone, trembling with emotion: "Oh, Pierre! how cruel you are. That woman is honesty itself. Your brother could not find a better."

He laughed a harsh, sarcastic laugh: "Ha! ha! Honesty itself! All wives are honesty itself," and he shouted with laughter.

She did not reply, but rising, hurried down the shelving beach, and at the risk of falling into one of the seaweed-hidden crevices and of breaking a leg or an arm, she hastened, almost running, plunging through the pools, straight to her other son.

At her approach Jean called out:

"Well, mother? So you have made the attempt?"

Without replying, she seized him by the arm. He saw her agitation and said in astonishment: "How pale you are; what ails you?"

She stammered: "I nearly fell; I was afraid of the rocks."

Then Jean took her under his care and explained the sport to her. But she paid hardly any attention, and he himself was full of the desire to confide in some one. He therefore drew her aside and said in a low voice:

"Guess what I have just done!"

"But—I cannot."

"But guess."

"I cannot. I don't know."

"I have asked Mme. Rosémilly to marry me."

She made no reply. Her brain was in such a whirl that she could not realize what he said.

"Marry?" she echoed.

"Yes. Have I not done well? Don't you think she is charming?"

"Yes, charming, of course. You have done very well."

"Then you approve?"

"Yes."

"But what a strange manner you have of saying so. I could almost fancy you were not pleased."

110

"Oh, yes, indeed, I am very glad."

"Really and truly?"

"Really and truly."

And in proof of what she said she flung her arms around him and kissed him with maternal warmth. When she had wiped the tears from her eyes, she saw a man lying on the beach at full length, his face against the stones; it was her other son, Pierre, lost in thought and despair. She drew her little Jean further away, to the edge of the water, and there they discussed for a long time his proposed marriage.

The rising tide forced them at last to rejoin the fishers, and soon they all made their way to the shore. Pierre pretended to be asleep. They roused him and went to dinner.

CHAPTER VII.

DENUNCIATION

O N THEIR way home in the carriage, all the men except Jean slept. Beausire and Roland every five minutes dropped their heads on a neighboring shoulder and were repelled with a shove. Then they sat up, stopped snoring, opened their eyes, muttered that it was a lovely night! and repeated the maneuver on the other side.

Their sleepiness was so heavy when they got to Havre that they could hardly shake it off, and Beausire went the length of refusing to go to Jean's apartments, where tea was waiting for them, and had to be put down at his own door.

The young lawyer was going to spend his first night in his new abode, and he was full of boyish delight at being able to show his *fiancée* the apartments in which she was soon to dwell. The maid had gone to bed, Mme. Roland declaring that she would make the tea. She did not approve of servants being kept up late, for fear of fire. No one had as yet been admitted to the rooms except herself, Jean, and the tradesmen, so that their attraction might be heightened.

Jean requested them to wait in the anteroom for a moment. He wished to light the lamps and candles. This done he called out, "Come in!" and opened the door to its fullest extent. The glazed corridor lighted by a chandelier and little colored lamps, concealed among palms, india-rubber plants, and flowers, was first seen. This caused a thrill of surprise like the sight of a scene on the stage. Roland, dazzled by such splendor, swore under his breath, and felt inclined to clap his hands. They entered next the first drawing-room, a small room hung in dull gold and furnished to match. The larger drawing-room — the lawyer's consulting-room, was very simply hung with light salmon color and was dignified in style.

Jean seated himself before the book-laden writing table and in solemn, forensic tones, began:

"Yes, Madame, the law is explicit, and assuming the consent you promised me, I am perfectly certain that the affair we discussed will reach a happy consummation within three months."

He looked at Mme. Rosémilly, who smilingly turned to Mme. Roland. The latter took her hand and squeezed it. Jean, in great glee, jumped about like a schoolboy, exclaiming: "Hah! the acoustics of this room are splendid; it would be a famous room to speak in." And he continued: "Gentlemen of the jury, if the natural instincts of humanity and benevolence which we feel for the unfortunate were the motive of the acquittal which we confidently look for from you, I should appeal to your hearts as fathers and as men; but law is on our side, and it is the point of law alone which we intend to submit to your judgment."

Pierre, looking round upon this home which he felt might have been his, became restless under his brother's fooling, which he deemed altogether too absurd. Mme. Roland opened a door on the right and showed the bedroom. All her motherly love had been lavished on its decoration. It was hung with Rouen cretonne in imitation of old Normandy chintz, and the Louis XV. design, a shepherdess in a medallion held in the beaks of two doves, lent the walls and furniture a pretty rustic air.

"Charming!" exclaimed Mme. Rosémilly, growing serious as they entered the room.

"Do you admire it?" asked Jean.

"Very much."

"You cannot think how pleased I am."

They looked tenderly at each other. She felt somewhat constrained in this room, soon to be her own. She observed that the bed was quite a family one, evidently chosen by Mme. Roland in the expectation that her son would soon marry, and this foresight pleased her, as if she had been expected to become a member of the family.

When they had returned to the drawing-room Jean threw open the door to the left, exhibiting the round dining-room with three windows, decorated in imitation of a Chinese lantern. Its bamboo furniture, mandarins, silk hangings shot with gold, fans, screens, swords, masks, and a thousand trifles in china, wood, paper, iron, mother-of-pearl, and bronze had a pretentious and bizarre appearance which stamped it as the work of unpractical hands and uncultured eyes. It was, however, the most admired. Pierre alone made some rather ironical remarks which jarred on his brother's feelings. On the table stood fruits arranged in pyramids and cakes in monuments.

Hardly anyone was hungry; they tasted the fruit and nibbled at the pastry Then, in about an hour, Mme. Rosémilly asked permission to take leave. It was decided that father Roland should escort her home and they began to get ready, while Mme. Roland, in the absence of the maid, glanced in motherly fashion around the rooms to see that her son wanted for nothing.

"Shall I come back for you?" asked Roland.

She hesitated, then replied: "No, dear, go to bed. Pierre will see me home."

When they had gone she extinguished the candle, put the cakes, sugar, and liqueurs in a cupboard of which Jean kept the key; then she went into his bedroom, prepared the bed, saw that the *carafe* was full of fresh water, and the window firmly closed.

Jean and Pierre had remained in the little drawing-room, the former still hurt by the criticism on his taste, the latter more and more exasperated to see his brother in these rooms. They both sat sulking without speaking. Pierre suddenly rose:

"Christi!" said he, "the widow had a very jaded air this evening. These excursions do not agree with her."

Jean felt himself shaken by one of those sudden and furious rages which attack easy-going natures

115

wounded to the heart. Such was his emotion that his breath failed him, and he stammered out:

"I forbid you to say 'the widow' when you speak of Mme. Rosémilly."

Pierre turned toward him haughtily.

"I believe you are giving me orders. Have you become mad?"

Jean immediately sat up: "I have not become mad, but I have had enough of your manners toward me."

Pierre sneered: "Toward you? Do you make common cause with Mme. Rosémilly?"

"Understand that Mme. Rosémilly is soon to become my wife."

The other laughed louder.

"Ah, ah! very well. I understand now why I should no longer call her 'the widow,' but you have taken a strange way to announce your engagement."

"I forbid you to jest — you hear? — I forbid it."

Jean had walked up to him, with trembling voice, exasperated by this irony directed at the woman of his love and choice. But Pierre suddenly became as furious as he. All that had been gathering within him of impotent rage, suppressed malice and revolt, and of silent despair, mounted to his head, bewildering him.

"You dare? — you dare? Well, I command you to be silent then, — you understand? I command you."

Jean, surprised by this violence, thought for several seconds, seeking, in this wrath-produced frame of mind the thing, the phrase, the word which could wound his brother to the heart. He replied, forcing himself to calmness, the better to strike — to soften his voice, the bitterer to make his words:

"I have known for a long time that you were jealous of me, ever since the day when you commenced to say 'the widow' because you saw that displeased me."

Pierre gave one of these hoarse and scornful laughs habitual to him.

"Ah! ah! my God! Jealous of you! I?—I? I? of what?—of what, my God?—of your looks or of your intellect?"

But Jean could feel that he had touched his wound.

"Yes, jealous of me from our childhood up. And it burst into fury when you saw this woman prefer me and ignore you."

Pierre, wounded to the heart by this supposition, stammered out: "I? Jealous of you. And on account of that fool, that silly woman?"

Jean saw that his shaft had hit its mark and went on: "What about that day you tried to pull me round in the 'Pearl'? And think of everything you have said in her hearing to impress her? Why, you are bursting with jealousy! When this fortune was left me you positively began to hate me, showed it in every way you could, and made everybody about you uncomfortable over it; every hour of the day you have let out some of your venom."

Pierre, his fist clenched in his passion, barely could resist his impulse to seize his brother by the throat.

"Hold your tongue," he cried, "at all events about this money."

117

Jean proceeded: "Why, your jealousy oozes out of the pores of your skin. You cannot say a word to our father, our mother, or to me which does not betray it. It is because of your jealousy that you pretend to look down on me. Because of that, you must quarrel with everybody. Now that I am rich, you have become doubly venomous; you torment our poor mother as if she were to blame!"

Pierre had gradually retreated to the fireplace, panting and glaring, furious with the passion that leads to unpremeditated crime.

He repeated, in a subdued tone, gasping for breath: "Hold your tongue — for God's sake, hold your tongue!"

"No! I have long waited for an opportunity to tell you all that was on my mind, and I have it now — so much the worse for you. I love this woman. You know that, and deride her to my face — again so much the worse for you. I warn you I will break your viper's fangs, and make you treat me with respect."

"With respect — you?"

"Yes, I."

"Respect you? Who have brought disgrace on us all by your avarice?"

"What is that? Say it again — again."

"I mean that it is not right to accept a fortune from one man so long as another has the repute of being your father."

Jean stood transfixed, hardly understanding, but stupefied by the insinuation he half guessed at.

"What? Repeat that once more."

"I repeat, what everyone is whispering, every

118

busybody circulating—that you are the son of the man who left you his fortune. What then,—a respectable man will not accept a fortune which brings disgrace upon his mother."

"Pierre! Pierre! Think what you say. Is it you who publish this infamous lie?"

"Yes, I. It is I. Have you not seen me stricken with grief for a month past, with sleepless nights and solitary days? I am so wretched, so crazy with shame and sorrow that I hardly know what I am doing or going to do; first I but guessed—now I know the truth!"

"Pierre! Hold your tongue. Mother is in the next room and may hear, she cannot help hearing."

But Pierre insisted upon telling Jean all his suspicions, his doubts, his assurance, culminating with the history of the portrait,—which had again disappeared,—all in broken incoherent sentences, as if he talked in his sleep. He appeared to have forgotten his listener and his mother in the next room. He talked as if he had no listener, but merely for the sake of relieving the suffering he had endured from closing his wound so tightly that it had festered like an abscess and was now splashing everyone in its outburst. He paced the room, gazing on vacancy, gesticulating in despair, choking with sobs; he spoke as if he were confessing his own transgression and casting his misery to the deaf, unseen winds.

Jean, driven to distraction and almost convinced by his brother's denunciation, leaned against the door on the other side of which he knew his mother must have heard everything. She could not get out with-

out coming through this room; and as she had not
opened the door it must have been because she dared
not.

At last Pierre stamped his foot:

"I am a brute to have told you all this," he
cried, and rushed bareheaded down the stairs.

Jean had fallen into a deep stupor, from which he
was awakened by the sound of the outer door slamming behind Pierre. He was alive to the fact that
he would have to make up his mind to do something, but weakness and cowardice kept him in a
torpid state of inaction. He was an inveterate pro-
crastinator; when he was forced to come to an immediate decision about anything he still tried to seize
a few minutes' respite.

But the complete stillness that succeeded Pierre's
shouting struck him with such terror that he suddenly wanted to escape, too. He forced himself to
think. He had never before had to face a difficulty.
Some men allow themselves to glide through life like
running water. Fear of punishment had made him a
diligent scholar, and an existence free from care had
taken him through his legal studies creditably. By
nature he loved order and peace; and confronted
with this calamity, he felt like a drowning man who
cannot swim.

At first he attempted incredulity. His brother had
lied, from hatred and jealousy. But how could he
have been so malicious as to accuse his mother of
such a thing had he not been himself distracted by
despair? Moreover, certain words and tones of bitter
distress, certain gestures of Pierre's, so eloquent of
suffering that they were irresistibly convincing, were

stamped on Jean's ear, his sight, his nerves, and inmost being with a force that carried incontrovertible certainty. He was too cast down to move; his will power was gone. His misery became unendurable; and behind that door he knew his mother was waiting, that she had heard everything.

Not a sound of a movement, not a breath, not a sigh proclaimed the presence of a living being. Had she run away? She could not without jumping from the window. A sudden terror seized him, so violent that he burst the door in rather than opened it and bounded into the bedroom. It appeared to be empty. A lighted candle stood on the chest of drawers. He rushed to the window; the shutters were bolted. Then he saw that the bed curtains were drawn. Opening them he found his mother lying on the bed with her face buried in the pillow.

At first he thought she had smothered herself. He turned her round, the pillow still gripped in her teeth to prevent herself from crying out. The mere touch of her rigid body told him of her unutterable torture. Torn with pity, he forgot all that his brother had told him, and unable to pull the pillow away, he exclaimed, kissing her dress:

"Mother, my poor mother, look up."

Only a slight shiver running over her limbs like the vibration of a taut cord, told that she was alive.

"Mother, mother," he repeated, "listen to me. It is not true. I know it is not true."

A spasm of choking came over her; then she began to sob into the pillow. Her rigid frame relaxed, her fingers released the linen, and he uncovered her face. It was perfectly colorless and from her closed

121

eyes the tears were trickling. He threw his arms around her neck, kissed her tear-laden eyes, and repeated again and again:

"Mother, dear mother, I know it is not true. Do not weep; I know it."

She sat up and, looking him in the face with a degree of courage which would be required to nerve a suicide's hand, said:

"No, my child; it is true."

And each remained speechless. She gasped for breath some little time, till, having once more mastered herself, she went on:

"It is true, my child. Why lie about it? You would not believe me if I denied it."

Her looks were wild. Overcome by terror he kneeled by her bedside, murmuring:

"Hush, mother, hush." She rose with an awful determination.

"Indeed, I have nothing more to say, my child. Good-bye." She was about to leave the room, but he flung his arms around her, exclaiming:

"What are you doing, mother; where would you go?"

"I don't know. How should I? There is nothing left for me to do now that I am alone."

She struggled in his arms, but he held her tight and could only repeat: "Mother, mother, mother!" She kept saying amid her struggles: "No, no. I am no longer your mother. I am nothing to you or to anyone — nothing. You have neither father nor mother now, poor boy — good-bye."

He saw clearly that if he allowed her to go now, it would be forever. Lifting her, he carried her to an

armchair into which he placed her and kneeled in
front of it barring her egress with his arms.

"You shall not leave this spot, mother. I love
you and I will keep you—keep you always—I love
you and you are mine."

She murmured dejectedly: "Impossible, my poor
boy. To-night you weep, but to-morrow you would
turn me out. Even you could not forgive me."

"I? I? How little you know me!" he answered
with such an outburst of real affection that with a
cry of joy she took his head between her hands and
kissed him passionately all over the face.

Then she sat still, with her cheek against his
warm face, and whispered in his ear: "No, my little
Jean, you would not be so forgiving to-morrow.
You may think so but you only deceive yourself.
Your forgiveness to-night has saved my life, but you
must never see me again."

"Do not say that, mother," he repeated, embracing her.

"Yes, my child, I shall go away. Where, I do
not know, nor how, nor what I shall do; but go I
must. I could never look at you, nor kiss you again.
Do you not understand?"

And he in his turn, whispered: "My little mother,
you must stay because I want you; and you must
give me your promise to obey me now,—at once."

"No, my child."

'Yes, mother, you must; do you hear?"

"Impossible, my child. That would be to condemn us all to the torments of hell. What these are
I know; I have known this month past. Your feelings are moved now, but, that over, when you see

123

me with Pierre's eyes, and remember what I have told you — I, Jean, think! your mother!"

"I will not allow you to leave me, mother. I have no one but you."

"But consider, my boy, that we can never again see each other without blushing, without my feelings being overwhelmed with shame. I could never meet your eyes with mine."

"That is not so, mother."

"Yes, yes, it is! Oh, believe me, I have comprehended all your poor brother's struggles. Yes — from the very first day. Now his very step in the house sets my heart beating, and I am ready to faint at the sound of his voice. But I still had you; now I have you no longer. Oh, my little Jean! How do you suppose I could live between both of you?"

"I would love you so much that you would never think of that."

"Impossible!"

"But it is possible."

"How do you suppose that I could forget it, between you? Would you cease to think of it?"

"I swear I would."

"Why, you would think of it every hour of the day."

"No, I swear it. Listen! If you leave me I will enlist and get killed."

This childish threat was too much for her. She clutched him in a passionate embrace. He went on: "I love you more than you suppose — ever so much more. Be reasonable. Try staying for one week only. Will you promise me that? You cannot refuse."

124

She laid a hand on each of Jean's shoulders and held him at arm's length.

"My child," she said, "let us try to be calm and not give way to emotion. First, listen to me. Should I ever hear from your lips what I have heard this past month from Pierre, were I ever to see in your eyes what I have read in his, could I fancy from a word or look of yours that I was as odious to you as I am to him—within one hour I should be gone forever."

"Mother, I swear—"

"Hear me out. For a month past I have endured all that mortal can endure. From the moment I saw that your brother, my other son, suspected me, that he guessed the truth as the moments passed, my life has been a constant martyrdom, indescribable in words."

The contagion of her grief brought the tears to Jean's eyes. He tried to kiss her, but she prevented him.

"Do not touch me, but listen; I have still so much to tell you before you can understand. But that you never can do. If I were to stay, you see, I must—no, no, I cannot."

"Go on, mother, go on."

"I will, for at least I shall not have deceived you. You wish me to stay with you? Why? So that we might see and speak to and meet each other at any hour at home. But I dare not open a door without dreading to find your brother behind it. If I am to stay you must not forgive me, nothing is so hurtful as forgiveness. You must simply bear me no grudge for the past. You must be so strong and so far unlike the world at large as to own to yourself the fact that you are not Roland's son without a blush and without despising me. I have suffered enough—too much. I could bear no more. This is not a thing of yesterday, remember, but of long, long years. That, however, you can never understand, how should you?

"If you and I are to live together, my little Jean, you must be convinced that while I was your father's mistress I was still really his wife; that I was not ashamed of it in my heart; that I have no regrets now; that I never loved any other man; that I shall ever love him, even in death; that he was everything to me for so long! Listen, my boy! I declare, before God, that I should never have known a joy in life had I not met him; nothing—not a touch of love or kindness, not an hour which would have made me regret growing old. To him I owe everything! I had but him and you two boys. But for you three, all would have been empty and dark as the night. I should never have known love or affection —should never even have wept—for I have wept bitter tears since we came to Havre. I belonged to him forever; for ten years we were husband and wife before God, who made us for each other. And then I saw he began to care less for me. Kind and gentle he always was, but things became different. All was over! How I have wept!

"How horribly hollow life is! Nothing but change. After we came here I never saw him again; he never came, though he promised in every letter. I always expected him, but I never saw him again—now he is dead! But his remembrance of you showed that he still cared. I shall never cease to love him, and will never deny him, and I love you because you are his son. I could never be ashamed of him before you. If you want me to stay you must accept the situation, and we can talk of him sometimes. You must love him a little. If you cannot do this, then good-bye, my child; for it is impossible we could live together. I will act as you decide."

"Stay, mother," replied Jean, softly.

She embraced him tearfully and with her face against his proceeded: "But Pierre; what shall we do about him?"

"We will find some way," murmured Jean. "You cannot live beside him any longer."

The thought of her elder son smote her with fear: "No, I cannot, no, no!" and, throwing herself into Jean's arms, she cried in despair:

"Save me from him, little one. Save me, do something — think of something, I don't know what, but save me."

"Very well, mother, I will think of something."

"But now. This minute. Do not leave me. I fear him so much."

"Yes, yes, I will find some way. I promise you I will."

"But at once, quick! You cannot think what I feel when I see him."

Then she whispered in his ear: "Let me stay here, with you."

He reflected, and his common sense pointed out immediately the danger of such a course. But it took long argument to overcome her terror-smitten persistence.

"Only for to-night," she urged, "and in the morning you can send word to Roland that I was taken ill."

"That is impossible, since Pierre left you here. Courage. To-morrow I will arrange everything; I will come to see you by nine o'clock. Come, put on your bonnet, I will see you home."

"Whatever you think best," she replied with an infantile impulse of timid gratitude.

The shock had been so much for her that she could not stand on her feet till he had made her smell some salts and had bathed her forehead with vinegar. When she was able to walk she took his arm. The town clock was striking three as they paused outside her door. Jean kissed her, saying: "Good night, mother, and keep up your courage."

She crept up the stairs to her room and slipped into bed with a long-forgotten feeling of guilt. Roland was snoring. Only Pierre was awake and had heard her come in.

CHAPTER VIII.

A Three-Cornered Council

WHEN Jean returned to his rooms, he dropped helpless upon a sofa, for the grief and anxiety which made his brother want to be in motion and to flee like a hunted quarry, had a different effect upon his lethargic nature, and quite took the strength from his limbs. He was too unstrung to move a finger, even to get to bed, physically and mentally crushed and broken-hearted. He had not, like Pierre, been injured in the purity of his filial love or in his moral dignity — that refuge of a haughty spirit; he was crushed by a stroke of fate which imperiled his nearest worldly interests.

When his mind grew calmer and his thoughts had settled, like water which has been lashed into turmoil, he could comprehend the situation. The heartrending emotion of his mother's confession made him powerless to rebel, especially after the quarrel with his brother, and the latter's brutal betrayal of his secret had already shaken his nerves, though had he learned the truth from any other source he would have been bitterly angry and deeply pained. The shock of his feelings had swept away all prejudice and the sacred delicacy of morality.

He was not the man to resist. He disliked contention, especially against himself, so he at once resigned himself; and his instinctive tendency, his congenital love of peace and of a quiet life made him anticipate the agitation which must overwhelm and ruin him by resistance. That they were inevitable he foresaw, and he decided on superhuman efforts of energy and activity to avert them. The knot must be cut this very day; for even he felt occasionally that imperious demand for a speedy solution which is the sole strength of weak spirits, incapable of a continued effort of the will. His lawyer's mind, accustomed to study and disentangle complex situations and domestic difficulties in families, at once saw the more immediate consequences of his brother's mood.

He could not help, in spite of himself, looking at the question from an almost altogether professional point of view. Continual friction with Pierre had really become past endurance. He could avoid that, it was true, by keeping to his own lodgings; but still his mother could not possibly live in the same house with her elder son. He sat for a long time on the cushions, motionless, pondering, planning, and throwing aside various possibilities without finding one that satisfied him. But all at once the thought broke upon him: this fortune which had come to him. Would an honest man keep it?

"No," was the first prompt answer, and he decided that it would have to go to the poor. It was

hard, no doubt, but unavoidable. He would dispose
of his furniture and work like any other beginner.
His courage was spurred by this manly and stern resolve; he rose and leaned his forehead against the
windowpane. He had been poor; he could be poor
again. He would not die of it, at all events.

The gas-lamp burning across the street riveted
his gaze. A woman, very late, passed at the
moment; and all at once he thought of Mme. Rosémilly with the heart pang, the deep emotion, which a
cruel suggestion produces. All the dread results of
his determination came before his mind at once. He
must give up his marriage, his happiness, everything.
Could he do that, now that he had pledged himself
to her? She had accepted him in the knowledge
that he was rich. No doubt she would take him
still if he were poor; but had he a right to ask such
a sacrifice of her? Would it not be better to hold
this money in trust, to be given up to the poor at
some future time?

All these plausible reasonings were contending
and striving in his soul, where selfishness hid itself
under the mask of honesty. His first scruples gave
way to ingenious arguments, then conquered again,
and again disappeared.

He sat down once more looking for some definite
motive, some soul-satisfying pretext to disarm his
hesitation and convince his natural probity. Twenty
times he asked himself the question: "Since I am
this man's son, and know it and acknowledge it, is
it not natural I should accept the inheritance?" But
even this reasoning could not quell the "No" of his
inmost conscience.

131

Then the thought struck him: "Since I am not the son of the man I have always believed to be my father, I can take nothing from him, either during his lifetime or after his death. That would be neither dignified nor just. I should be robbing my brother."

His conscience being relieved and quieted by this new view of the matter, he approached the window again.

"Yes," he said to himself, "I must give up my share of the family inheritance. Pierre must have the whole of that, as I am not his father's son. That is only just. Is it not just therefore that I should keep my father's money?"

Having decided that he could take no share of Roland's savings, he resigned himself to keeping Maréchal's; for if he gave both up he would find himself a beggar.

This delicate question disposed of he returned to the consideration of Pierre's presence in the family. How could he be got rid of? He was about to give up the search for a solution of that problem when the whistle of a steamer coming into port seemed to blow him the answer. He flung himself on his bed, dressed as he was, and slept and dreamed till daylight.

Shortly before nine o'clock he went out to see if the plans he had made were feasible. After making various inquiries and calls, he went to the old home. His mother was expecting him in her room.

"Had you not come," she said, "I should never have dared to go downstairs."

Roland's voice was heard on the stairs: "Confound it! Are we to have nothing to eat all day?"

132

Receiving no answer he roared out, with an oath, "Josephine; what the deuce are you about?"

The girl's voice came up from the basement: "Yes, M'sieu'—what is it?"

"Where is your mistress?"

"Madame is upstairs with M'sieu' Jean."

Then he shouted up at the upper floor: "Louise." Mme. Roland half opened her door and replied: "What is the matter, my dear?"

"Are we to have nothing to eat to-day?"

"Yes, dear, I am coming."

And she went down, Jean following. Roland, when he saw him, shouted:

"Hello! You there! Tired of your new home already?"

"No, father, but I had something to talk to mother about this morning."

Jean held out his hand, and when he felt the old man's fatherly grasp, a curious emotion suddenly went through him, a sense of parting forever.

Mme. Roland asked: "Is Pierre not coming down?"

Her husband shrugged his shoulders. "No, but never mind him; he is always late. We will begin without him."

She turned to Jean: "You had better go and call him, dear; it hurts his feelings if we do not wait for him."

"Yes, mother, I will go."

The young man went up the stairs with the feverish resolution of a man going, in a fright, to fight a duel. When he knocked at the door, Pierre said:

"Come in."

He entered. The elder was bending over the table, writing. "Good morning," said Jean.

Pierre rose. "Good morning," said he, and they shook hands as if nothing had happened.

"Are you not coming down to breakfast?"

"Well — you see — I have a great deal to do." The elder brother's voice trembled, and his eyes anxiously asked his brother what he intended to do.

"They are waiting for you."

"Oh, there is — is my mother there?"

"Yes, it was she who sent me up to fetch you."

"Ah, very well; then I will come down."

At the door of the dining-room he stopped, in doubt as to going in first; then he opened the door and saw his father and mother sitting at opposite sides of the table.

He went up to his mother without looking at her or saying a word, and, leaning over her, offered his forehead to be kissed as he had done recently, instead of kissing her on both cheeks as he had been accustomed to do. He supposed she must have put her lips near his brow, but he did not feel them, and he drew himself up with a beating heart after this pretense of a kiss. And he wondered: "What did they say to each other after I left?"

Jean always addressed her tenderly as "mother" or "dear mother," when he spoke to her, tended on her, watched over her, and poured out her wine.

Then Pierre saw they had wept together, but he could not read their minds. Did Jean believe in his mother's guilt or did he think his brother a vile wretch? All his self-reproach for having spoken came

134

upon him once more, and he could neither eat nor speak, choked by emotion.

He was now the victim of an unbearable longing to flee from this house, his home no longer, those persons to whom he was united by such slender bonds. He would willingly have escaped that very instant, no matter where, for he felt that all was over, that their torturing presence would entail upon him constant suffering too hard for him to bear. Jean was talking to Roland. Pierre was not listening and their conversation drifted by him, but by and by he became aware of a pointed tone in his brother's voice and turned his ear to what he was saying.

"She will be the finest ship in their fleet," Jean was saying. "They say she is 6500 tons burden. Her first trip is to be made next month."

Roland expressed amazement: "So soon? I thought she was not to be ready to sail this summer."

"Yes, but the work has been pushed forward so as to get her first voyage before autumn. I called at the Company's offices this morning and had a talk with one of the directors."

"Oh, which of them?"

"M. Marchand, a great friend of the Chairman of the Board."

"Indeed! Do you know him?"

"Yes, I went to ask a favor of him."

"And you will obtain permission for me to go over the whole of the 'Lorraine' as soon as she comes into port?"

"Certainly, nothing will be easier."

Then Jean appeared to hesitate, to weigh his

words, as if he wished to lead up to a difficult subject. He proceeded:

"Altogether, life is very pleasant on board these
large transatlantic liners. More than half the time is
spent ashore in two great cities—New York and
Havre, and the rest at sea, in agreeable company.
Very pleasant acquaintances are often struck up among
the passengers, very useful in after life,—very useful.
Just think, the captain, with his coal perquisites,
makes as much as twenty-five thousand francs a
year, sometimes more."

Roland first swore, then whistled, thus testifying
to his high respect for the sum and for the captain.

Jean proceeded: "The purser makes as much as
ten thousand francs, and the doctor has a salary of
five thousand, with board, light, fire, service, and
so on, which brings it up to ten thousand at the
least. That is excellent pay."

Pierre raised his eyes to his brother's and understood. After hesitating a few moments, he asked:

"Is it very difficult to get a position as doctor on
board a transatlantic liner?"

"Yes, and no. It all depends on circumstances,
and one's recommendations."

A long pause ensued, broken by the doctor.

"The 'Lorraine' is to sail next month, you say?"

"Yes, on the 7th."

No more was said. Pierre was considering. To
get a position as doctor on board this steamship
would certainly be one way out of his many difficulties. After trying it he could give it up. In the
meantime, he would be earning a livelihood and asking his parents for nothing. Only two days before

he had sold his watch so that he might not have to ask for money from his mother. No alternative was left, no opportunity to eat the bread of any other house than this, now uninhabitable for him, or to sleep under any other roof. With some hesitation he said by and by:

"If I could I should like to sail in her."

"What is to prevent you?" asked Jean.

"I don't know anyone in the Transatlantic Shipping Company."

But Roland was thunderstruck: "And what about all your grand schemes for getting on?"

Pierre replied in a low tone: "There are times when we must sacrifice all and give up our fondest dreams. After all it is merely to make a beginning; it is only a way of saving a few thousand francs to start with afterward."

It did not take long to convince his father: "That is quite true. In a couple of years you will have saved six or seven thousand francs, and that, well invested, will go a long way. What is your opinion, Louise?"

She replied in a scarcely audible voice: "I think Pierre is right."

"I will go and see M. Poulin about it. I know him intimately. He is the assessor of the Chamber of Commerce, and takes an interest in the Company's affairs. There is M. Lenient, the shipowner, also, who is a great friend of one of the vice-chairmen."

Jean asked his brother: "Would you care about my approaching M. Marchand at once?"

"I should be very glad if you would," answered Pierre, and he added after thinking a little:

137

"Probably the best thing I can do is to write to my professors at the College of Medicine, in whose regard I stand well. Very mediocre men are often shipped on these liners. Good letters of recommendation from professors like Mas-Roussel, Rémusot, Flache, and Borriquel would effect more for me in one hour than any number of doubtful introductions put together. If your friend M. Marchand would submit them to the Board that would settle the matter."

Jean heartily approved. "A capital idea," he said, and smiled with new assurance, almost happy again, certain of the outcome and incapable of anxiety for long.

"Will you write to-day?" he asked.

"Immediately. I will go and do so now. I am too nervous for any coffee this morning," and he rose and left the room.

Then Jean said to his mother: "And you, mother, what are you going to do?"

"I don't know. Nothing."

"Will you call with me on Mme. Rosémilly?"

"Why, yes — certainly."

"You know I must go to see her to-day."

"Yes, yes, of course."

"Why, of course?" asked Roland, who never by any chance understood what was said in his presence.

"Because I promised I would."

"Oh, that alters the case," and he started to fill his pipe, while mother and son went to get ready.

In the street Jean said: "Will you take my arm, mother?"

It was not his custom to offer it as they walked together. She accepted and leaned on his arm. For some time neither spoke; presently Jean said:

"You see Pierre is ready and willing to be off."

"Poor boy," she murmured.

"Why 'poor boy'? He will not be unhappy on board the 'Lorraine.'"

"I know, but I was thinking of so many things."

And for a long time she pondered, her head bent, and her step keeping pace with her son's; then in the abrupt tone of one giving voice to the fruit of long thought, she exclaimed:

"How horrible life is! If by any chance we find any pleasure in it, we sin by enjoying it, and pay a heavy penalty afterward."

"Do not say any more about that, mother," he whispered.

"Is it possible not to do so? I think of nothing else."

"You must forget it."

After a moment's silence she said with deep regret: "How happy I might have been had I married another man."

She was throwing all the responsibility of her fault on Roland now, on his ugliness, stupidity, clumsiness, dullness, and vulgarity. It was due to these that she had driven one son to despair and been forced to make to the other the most bitter confession that could wound a mother's heart. "It is so horrible for a young girl to have to marry such a husband," she muttered.

Jean did not reply. He was thinking of Roland, and perhaps the undefined idea he had long formed of his inferiority, which had brought down Pierre's continual sarcasms, and the scornful indifference of others, the very servant girl's contempt, had prepared his mind for his mother's confession. All this had made his discovery less dreadful for him; and if after last night's shock and agitation he had not felt the reaction of anger and rebellion which Mme. Roland had dreaded, it was because he had for long unconsciously chafed under the sense of being the son of this well-meaning boor.

They had now reached Mme. Rosémilly's. She lived on the road leading to Sainte-Adresse, on the second floor of a large tenement of which she was the owner. Her windows looked out over the whole roadstead.

On seeing Mme. Roland, she threw her arms around her and kissed her, for she guessed the purpose of their visit.

The furniture of the drawing-room, in stamped velvet, was always kept carefully covered. The walls, with its flowered paper, were adorned by four engravings, bought by her late husband. They represented scenes illustrative of a seafaring life. In the first a fisherman's wife was waving a handkerchief from the shore, while her husband's boat was disappearing on the horizon. In the second she was on her knees in the same spot, the lightning playing around her, wringing her hands as she gazed at her husband's boat sinking amidst impossible waves.

The third dealt with a higher rank of society. A young fair-haired damsel, leaning her elbows on the gunwale of a large steamer leaving the shore, gazed

at the receding coast with tearful looks of regret.
Whom was she leaving behind?

In the fourth, the same young lady seated beside
an open window, within view of the sea, had fainted;
an open letter had dropped at her feet. So he was
dead! Behold her despair!

Visitors were usually greatly touched and charmed
by the commonplace pathos of these two works of
art. They needed no explanation and the poor
women portrayed were certainly to be pitied, though
the reason for the grief of the more elegant of the
two was hardly obvious. But that very uncertainty
lent its aid to the sentiment. It was, no doubt, her
lover.

These four pictures riveted and fascinated everyone who entered the room. The eye returned again
and again to contemplate the expression on the two
faces, as like each other as those of sisters. The
shining frames, matching the elegant fashion-plate
style of the works, suggested notions of cleanliness
and propriety confirmed by the rest of the furniture.
The seats were always ranged in the same order
against the wall or round the center table. The spotless white curtains hung so straight that one felt a
desire to rumple them a little; and no grain of dust
was ever allowed to rest on the glass shade which
covered the gilt clock, in the style of the first Empire — Atlas Supporting the World on his Knees — a
world which looked like a melon set there to ripen.

The two women turned their chairs round toward
each other.

"You have not been out this morning?" asked
Mme. Roland.

"No, I must confess I am rather tired."

She spoke in a tone of gratitude for her enjoyment of the excursion and the prawn-fishing.

"I ate my prawns this morning," she added, "they were very nice. If you care to, we might go again some day soon."

The young man broke in: "Before we undertake a second fishing excursion, let us complete the first."

"Complete it? It appears to me to be quite finished."

"Nay, Madame, for I caught something on the rocks of Saint Jouin which I am anxious to take home with me."

She assumed an innocent and coy expression.

"You? What can that be? What can you have found?"

"A wife. And my mother and I have come to ask her if she has changed her mind this morning."

She smiled: "No, Monsieur. I never change my mind."

He held out his hand, into which she put hers with a steady, resolute movement. Then he said: "As soon as possible, I trust."

"Whenever you like."

"In six weeks?"

"I have no opinion on the subject. What is my future mother-in-law's?"

Mme. Roland replied with a somewhat sad smile: "Oh, I cannot say anything. I can only thank you for accepting Jean. I know you will make him happy."

"We will do our best, mamma."

For the first time showing emotion, Mme. Rosémilly rose and, embracing Mme. Roland, kissed her like a child of her own; and the poor woman's sore heart swelled with emotion. Her feeling was beyond her power of expression; it was at the same time melancholy and sweet. In return for the son, the big boy she had lost, she had found a grown-up daughter. Seating themselves again *vis-à-vis* they remained hand in hand smiling at each other, Jean for the moment forgotten.

Then they talked of all the things which had to be considered in view of an early marriage, and when all was settled and arranged Mme. Rosémilly suddenly remembered another detail and asked: "You have told M. Roland, I suppose?"

Both mother and son blushed. It was Mme. Roland who replied:

"Oh, no, that is not necessary!" Then feeling that she owed some explanation, she added: "We never consult him about anything we do. It is time enough to tell him when we have decided on it."

Mme. Rosémilly was not a bit surprised. She only smiled, taking it as a matter of course that the good man counted for so little.

When Mme. Roland and her son reached the street again she said:

"Let us go to your rooms for a little. I should like to rest."

She felt herself homeless,— her own house a terror to her. They went to Jean's rooms.

She heaved a heavy sigh when the door closed behind them, as if she had reached a place of safety, but, instead of resting, she proceeded to open the

cupboards, to count the piles of linen, pocket handkerchiefs, and socks. She changed their arrangement
to please her housekeeper's mind; and when she was
satisfied with her inventory and rearrangements she
drew back and complacently looked at the result,
calling out:

"Come here, Jean, and see how nice everything
looks."

He went and admired it to please her. When he
sat down again she suddenly stole softly behind his
armchair and putting her right arm round his neck
while she kissed him, she with her other hand placed
on the mantelpiece a small packet wrapped in white
paper.

"What is that?" he asked. Receiving no reply,
he understood. He recognized the shape of the
frame.

"Give it to me," he said.

She pretended she did not hear and returned to
the linen cupboards. He got up hurriedly, took the
sad relic, and, crossing the room, placed it in the
drawer of his writing desk, which he locked. She
wiped away a tear with her finger tips and said in a
trembling voice: "Now I will go and see if your
new servant keeps your kitchen in proper order. She
is out, so I can look into everything and make certain."

CHAPTER IX.

EXPATRIATION

ONSIEUR MARCHAND had submitted to the directors of the Trans-atlantic Shipping Company most flattering letters of recommendation from Professors Mas-Roussel, Rémusot, Flache, and Borriquel with regard to their pupil Dr. Pierre Roland, and these had been backed up by M. Poulin, president of the Chamber of Commerce, M. Lenient, a large ship-owner, and M. Marival, Deputy Mayor of Havre and a great friend of Captain Beau-sire. As no medical officer proved to have been appointed to the "Lorraine," Pierre had the good luck to receive the appointment in a few days.

Josephine handed him the letter announcing this one morning. His first feeling was akin to that of a convict condemned to death, whose sentence has been commuted. The thought of his approaching departure, and of the peaceful existence on board ship, ever in motion, ever wandering over the rolling waters, gave him an instant sense of relief. His existence at home was now that of a silent, distant stranger. Ever since the evening when he uttered his terrible secret before his brother, he had had a feeling that the last ties with his family were sundered. Although remorse troubled him for revealing this thing to Jean, and he felt the brutality of the act, yet it was a relief to have done it.

He always avoided the eyes of his mother and brother, and they had become adept in avoiding his. It was the cunning of foes who dread joining battle. He was ever wondering, "What can she have said to Jean? Was it a confession or a denial? And does he believe? What does he think of her — and of me?" The fact that he could not guess made him furious. Except to avoid questions when Roland was within hearing, he hardly ever spoke to them.

He at once showed the letter announcing his appointment to his family. His father, apt to rejoice over everything, clapped his hands. Jean, though secretly overjoyed, spoke soberly: "I sincerely congratulate you," he said, "for I am aware there were several competitors for the appointment. You undoubtedly owe it to the recommendations of your professors."

His mother bowed her head and murmured: "I am delighted that you have been successful."

After breakfast he called at the Company's offices for information on various points, and asked the name of the doctor of the "Picardie," which sailed next day, to obtain from him any details of his new life likely to be of use to him. Doctor Pirette had gone on board, so Pierre went to the ship, where he found him, a fair young man, not unlike Jean, in his little stateroom, and they had a long conversation.

They could hear from the hollow hold the confused, constant din of bales and casks being thrown into it, and the mingled sounds of footsteps, voices, creaking machinery lowering the freight, the boatswain's whistle, and the jangle of the chains drawn round the capstans by the snorting, panting engine, which sent a vibration through the huge vessel.

But when Pierre found himself in the street again, a fresh sadness seized him, settling round him like a fog from the sea, laden with the impure, pestilential breath of a distant, malarial land.

Never had he felt himself in such a pit of misery in his greatest suffering. He had given the last wrench to the fibers of his attachment. There was none left. The distress of a forlorn and homeless animal, the anguish of a creature without a roof for shelter, exposed to the pitiless elements, took the place of his torturing human pain. His flesh had revolted against the insecurity of all his future as he set foot in the rocking vessel. Till now a solid wall, a roof, and the certainty of a shelter from the gale, had protected him. Now the winds, defied with equanimity in the warmth of home, threatened constant danger and discomfort. No solid earth under foot, but only the greedy, heaving sea; only a few yards of planks to pace like a convict; no trees, no gardens, no streets, no houses; nothing but sea and sky and the everlasting rolling of the ship. In bad weather he must cling to the nearest support; in calm he would hear but the throb of the screw and watch but the swift flight of the ship, unceasing, monotonous, exasperating. And for this vagrant convict's life he must blame his mother's sin.

He walked on with the despair of a doomed exile. His haughty contempt and scornful hatred of all strangers gave way to a pitiful impulse to stop them, to tell them he had to leave France, to be listened to and consoled. The shameful need of a beggar filled his heart — the need to feel that some one regretted his departure.

He thought of Marowsko, the only person who loved him enough to feel real grief, and he resolved to go and see him. The druggist started as he entered the shop and left his work of pounding powders in a marble mortar.

"You are invisible, nowadays," said he.

Pierre, without giving the reason, said he had had a great number of important matters to attend to, and took a seat, adding:

"Well, how is business?"

There was no business doing at all. Competition was terrible and wealthy people rare in that workpeople's district. Only cheap drugs would sell, and the doctors would not prescribe the more expensive remedies, which netted a profit of 500 per cent. The old man finished up by saying: "Three months more of this and I shall give up business. Did I not rely on you, my dear doctor, I would have turned shoeblack by this time."

Pierre winced and resolved to deal the blow at once and have done with it.

"I — oh, I shall not be able to be of any service to you. I leave Havre early next month."

Marowsko in his agitation pulled off his spectacles:
"You! You! What do you tell me?"

"I say I am going away, my poor friend."

The old man was dumfounded. He felt his only
hope sinking from under him and all at once he
turned against this man whom he had followed,
loved, and so completely trusted and who now for-
sook him in this way.

"You will surely not play me false—you?"

Pierre was so affected that he could hardly resist
the inclination to embrace the old man.

"I am not playing you false. I have not been
able to find anything to do here, and I am leaving as
doctor of a transatlantic liner."

"Oh, Monsieur Pierre! And you always promised
you would assist me to make a living!"

"What can I do? I have to make a living for
myself. I have not a penny in the world."

"It is wrong," said Marowsko. "It is very wrong
of you. Nothing is left me but to die of hunger.
At my time of life that will be the end of it. It is
wrong to desert a poor old man who came here
only to be with you. It is wrong."

Pierre tried explanations, protestations, arguments,
to show that he could not help doing as he did.
The Pole was too angry at his desertion to listen,
and finished up by an allusion to politics: "You
French—you never keep your promises!"

Pierre rose, offended at this, and assuming a haughty
tone said:

"You are unjust, Marowsko; you ought to understand that a man must have very strong reasons for
acting as I have done. *Au revoir*—I hope I shall

find you more reasonable another day," and he departed.

"Well, well," thought he, "I shall not be sincerely missed by a single soul."

He searched his recollection for all the faces he knew or had known, and among them he recalled that of the tavern girl who had aroused his suspicions of his mother. His instinctive grudge against her made him pause; then suddenly reflecting: "After all, she was right," he looked around him for the turning leading to the tavern. The beer-shop chanced to be crowded and full of smoke. It was a holiday, and tradesmen and laborers were shouting and laughing, the proprietor himself was serving them, hurrying from table to table, removing empty glasses and bringing them back frothing to the brim.

Pierre seated himself near the desk and waited in the expectation that the girl would see and recognize him. But she repeatedly passed him unnoticed with a smart, busy, little strut. At last he attracted her attention by rapping on the table with a coin, and she hurried up.

"What will you have, sir?"

She never looked at him; she was preoccupied with calculations of her sales of liquor.

"Well," he said, "this is a nice way to receive a friend."

She scanned his face: "Ah!" she said hastily. "Is it you? Hope you are well? I have but a minute to spare to-day. A bock, do you want?"

"Yes, a bock!"

When she brought it, he said: "I have come to bid you good-bye. I am going away."

"Indeed," she replied, indifferently. "Where to?"
"To America."
"A splendid country, they say."
And that was all! To be sure, he had been very stupid to attempt to talk to her on such a busy day, when she had so many customers to attend to.

He went down to the shore. Nearing the jetty he made out the "Pearl," with his father and Beausire, coming inshore. Papagris was rowing, and the couple sitting in the stern smoked their pipes with an air of perfect contentment. As they passed Pierre said to himself: "Blessed are the simple-minded!" And he seated himself on a bench on the breakwater, and tried to lull himself into oblivious drowsiness.

In the evening when he returned home his mother said with averted eyes: "You will want a lot of things to take with you. I have ordered your underclothing and seen the tailor about your clothes; but is there nothing else that you need that I don't know about?"

He was about to say: "No, nothing," but he reflected that he must accept the only means available to get a proper outfit, and he replied calmly: "I hardly know yet. I will inquire at the office."

He did so and they furnished him with a list of indispensable things. As his mother took it out of his hand, she gazed up at him for the first time for long, with her eyes full of the humble, beseeching expression of a dog which has been beaten and seeks forgiveness.

On the first of October the "Lorraine" arrived at Havre from Saint-Nazaire, to sail on the seventh for

New York, and Pierre Roland took possession of the little floating home in which his life was hereafter to be confined.

As he was going out the following day he met his mother waiting for him on the stairs. She murmured in a low voice:

"Would you not like me to assist you to put your things to rights on board?"

"No, thank you. That is all done," he replied.

"I should like very much to see your cabin," said she.

"There is nothing to see about it. It is very small and very ugly," and he went downstairs, leaving her leaning against the wall with a pallid, stricken face.

Roland, who had that same day gone over the ship, talked of nothing else all dinner time but this magnificent vessel, and wondered that Mme. Roland did not want to see it, especially as their son was to sail in it. Pierre hardly spoke to any of the family during the following days. Excited, irritable, and harsh, his rough tongue lashed everyone without regard for persons. Only on the day before he was to leave did he soften. As he embraced his parents before leaving to sleep on board, he said:

"You will come on board to bid me good-bye, will you not?"

Roland exclaimed: "Why, of course — certainly we will, Louise?"

"Certainly, certainly," she assented in low tones.

"We sail at eleven precisely," proceeded Pierre. "You will have to be there by half past nine at the latest."

"Ha!" cried his father. "I have a good idea! When we have bid you good-bye, we will hurry on board the 'Pearl' and wait for you outside the jetty, so as to see you again; eh, Louise?"

"Certainly."

"And in that way," Roland went on, "you will not lose sight of us in the crowd that always lines the breakwater when the liners sail. You cannot pick out your friends in the mob. Will that suit you?"

"Assuredly; that is settled."

In an hour he was lying in his berth—a little bunk like a coffin. For a long time he kept his eyes wide open, turning over in his mind all that had elapsed within the last two months, especially within his own soul. His aggressive and vindictive agony, after suffering and causing others to suffer, had become blunted, like a sword. He had hardly spirit enough left in him to bear anyone or anything a grudge; he allowed his rebellious anger to float idly down stream like his future life. Weary of struggling, fighting, hating, everything, he was quite used up and tried to drug his heart into oblivion. All around him the unaccustomed faint noises of the ship were barely audible to his ear on this quiet night in the harbor. He no longer felt the terrible wound which had been tormenting him, but only the discomfort and inconvenience of its healing.

The noise made by the crew woke him out of a sound sleep. It was daylight, and the tidal train had arrived at the pier with the passengers from Paris. He roamed about the ship among these bustling people, all inquiring for their cabins, asking questions and answering each other at random, in the hurry and bustle of a voyage just begun. He greeted the captain and his comrade the purser, and then went into the saloon, in the corners of which several Englishmen had already fallen asleep.

The great, low room, its marble panels picked out with gold, was decked with mirrors, which gave an endless perspective to the long tables and their red velvet-covered pivot seats. It was indeed fit to be the floating cosmopolitan common dining-room of the wealthy of two continents. Its luxury was that of vast hotels, theaters, and public rooms; the commonplace, gilded luxury which pleases the eye of the millionaire.

The doctor was about to enter the second-class saloon, when he recollected that a great number of emigrants had come on board the night before, and he proceeded to the lower deck. In a kind of basement, low and dark as the galley of a mine, Pierre could see hundreds of men, women, and children lying on shelves or in heaps on the floor. He could not discern their faces, but could only see a squalid, tattered crowd, worsted in the battle of life, with starving wives and ailing children, setting out for an unknown country, in the hope, perhaps, of not absolutely dying of hunger. He thought of their wasted work and useless effort, a struggle with death vainly renewed with every succeeding day, of the energy put forth by this ragged crew, on their way to take up again, they knew not where, their miserable existence. He desired to cry out to them:

"Rather pitch yourselves into the sea, with your wives and little ones." And his heart bled so that he

154

left the spot, unable to endure the sight. His father, mother, Jean, and Mme. Rosémilly were waiting for him in his cabin.

"You are early!" he exclaimed.

"Yes," said Mme. Roland in a shaking voice. "We wanted to have a little time to see you."

He looked at her. She was dressed in black, as if in mourning, and her somber garments displayed the fact that her hair, which but a month before had been gray, was now almost white. There was not much room for five persons to sit down in the little cabin, and he himself sat on the bed. Through the open door they could see a great crowd hurrying past, as if it were a street on a holiday, for friends of passengers and curious visitors had invaded the large vessel and thronged the passages, saloons and every corner of it; heads occasionally looked in at the open doorway and voices outside whispered: "That is the doctor's cabin."

Pierre shut the door; but immediately wanted to open it again, for the outside turmoil concealed the nervousness and speechlessness of the little party.

Mme. Rosémilly felt at last that she must break the silence.

"Not much air comes through these little windows."

"These are portholes," said Pierre. He pointed out how thick the glass was, so as to resist the most violent shocks, and occupied a long time in explanation of the fastenings. By and by Roland asked: "Do you keep your doctor's shop here?"

Pierre, opening a cupboard, revealed a range of phials labeled with Latin names. He took out one after another and explained their contents, delivering quite a therapeutic harangue, to which everybody listened most attentively. Roland, nodding his head, repeated over and over again: "How interesting." A tap came at the door. "Come in," said Pierre, and Captain Beausire entered.

"I am late," he said, as he shook hands. "I did not want to be *de trop*." He also seated himself on the bed, and silence reigned once more.

Suddenly the captain got up to listen. He could hear orders being given, and said: "We must be off if we want to get out in the 'Pearl' to see you and bid you good-bye on the open sea."

Old Roland was very anxious about this, doubtless with the object of impressing the voyagers on board the "Lorraine," and rose hastily.

"Good-bye, my boy," said he, as he kissed Pierre on the whiskers, and opened the door.

Mme. Roland had not moved. She sat silent, pale, her eyes downcast. Her husband touched her arm.

"Come," said he, "we must hurry, there is not a minute to spare."

She drew herself up, offered Pierre first one white, waxen cheek and then the other, which he silently kissed. Then he shook hands with Mme. Rosémilly and his brother, asking the latter: "When is the wedding to be?"

"I don't quite know. We will fix it for one of your return voyages."

At last they were all up on deck among the throng of visitors, workmen, and sailors. The snorting steam in the interior of the ship made it seem to quiver with impatience.

156

"Good-bye," said Roland, fussily.

"Good-bye," replied Pierre, standing on one of the landing planks, and he shook hands all round again, and they went off.

"Quick, jump into the carriage," cried old Roland.

A waiting cab took them to the outer harbor, where Papagris waited with the "Pearl" to take them out to sea.

The air was breathless; it was one of those sharp, calm autumn days when the silvery water looks as cold and hard as polished steel.

Jean took one oar, the sailor the other, and they rowed away. The thronging crowd lined the breakwater, the piers, even the granite parapet, pushing and noisy, waiting to see the "Lorraine" come out. The "Pearl" floated down between the two waves of humanity, and was soon outside the mole. Captain Beausire, sitting between the two ladies, took the tiller and said:

"You will see, we shall be close to her, very close."

The two oarsmen pulled with might and main to get out as far as possible. Suddenly Roland exclaimed:

"Here she comes! I can see the masts and her two funnels! She is coming out of the inner harbor."

"Give way, boys!" cried Beausire.

Roland stood up, clinging to the mast, and announced:

"She is now working round in the outer harbor. She is standing still now. Now she is moving again.

Taking the tow-rope on board, very likely. There
she goes. Bravo! Now she is between the piers.
Do you hear the crowds hurrahing? Bravo! The
'Neptune' has taken her in tow. Now I can see
her bows. Here she comes! Good heavens! what a
ship! Look! Look!"

Mme. Rosémilly and Beausire looked behind, the
oarsmen stopped rowing; Mme. Roland alone did
not move.

The towering steamship, in the wake of a powerful tug, which looked like a caterpillar, came slowly
and majestically out of the harbor. The good people
of Havre, crowding the piers, the beach, the windows, called out with patriotic enthusiasm: "*Vive la
'Lorraine'!*" accompanied by acclamations for this
auspicious birth of the graceful daughter given to the
sea by the great maritime town.

As soon as she had passed the granite portals
of the harbor, she cast off her tow-ropes, and went
off alone, like a huge creature, free at last, walking
on the water.

"Here she comes straight down upon us!" Roland kept shouting; and Beausire, delighted, exclaimed:
"Didn't I promise you? Eh? Don't I know how to
do it?"

Jean whispered to his mother: "Look, mother,
she is close on us, now!" And Mme. Roland uncovered her eyes, full of tears.

The "Lorraine" bore down swiftly from the harbor, in the bright, calm sunshine. Beausire, his glass
to his eye, cried out:

"Look out! M. Pierre is at the stern, alone, easily visible! Look out!"

The vessel almost touched the "Pearl" now, as high as a mountain and swift as a train. Mme. Roland held out her arms to it in distraction and despair; she saw her Pierre, her son, with his officer's cap, blowing kisses to her.

He was flying from her, disappearing, a mere speck already on the huge vessel. She could no longer distinguish his form.

Jean took her hand: "You saw him?" said he.

"Yes, I saw him. How good he is!"

And they turned homeward.

"Christi! How fast she goes!" cried Roland with enthusiasm.

The steamer, in fact, shrank with every instant, as if she were melting away in the ocean. Mme. Roland, turning round to look at her, watched her vanishing on the horizon, on her way to an unknown land on the other side of the globē.

In that ship, which nothing could stop, which would soon be out of her sight, was her son, her poor son. She felt as if he had taken with him half of her heart, as if her life were at an end; and she felt too as if she would never see her elder boy again.

"Why do you cry?" asked her husband, "when you know he will be back in a month."

She blurted out: "I don't know; I cry because I am hurt."

The moment they had set foot on shore Beausire left them to go to breakfast with a friend. Jean then led the way with Mme. Rosémilly, and Roland said to his wife:

"A very handsome fellow is our Jean, all the same."

"Yes," replied the mother.

Her mind was too dazed to think of what she was saying, and she went on:

"I am very glad he is to marry Mme. Rosémilly."

The good man was thunderstruck.

"Eh? What? To marry Mme. Rosémilly?"

"Yes, we intended to seek your opinion about it to-day."

"Dear me! And has this engagement been long in the wind?"

"No, only a few days. Jean wanted to be sure that she would have him before asking your advice."

Roland rubbed his hands.

"Good. Very good. Capital. I quite approve."

As they turned off the quay to go down the Boulevard François Ier, his wife looked back once more at the high seas, but nothing was now visible but a whiff of gray smoke, so distant and so faint that it resembled a shred of mist.

BALL-OF-FAT

FOR many days now the fag-end of the army had been straggling through the town. They were not troops, but a disbanded horde. The beards of the men were long and filthy, their uniforms in tatters, and they advanced at an easy pace without flag or regiment. All seemed worn-out and back-broken, incapable of a thought or a resolution, marching by habit solely, and falling from fatigue as soon as they stopped. In short, they were a mobilized, pacific people, bending under the weight of the gun; some little squads on the alert, easy to take alarm and prompt in enthusiasm, ready to attack or to flee; and in the midst of them, some red breeches, the remains of a division broken up in a great battle; some somber artillery men in line with these varied kinds of foot soldiers; and, sometimes the brilliant helmet of a dragoon on foot who followed with difficulty the shortest march of the lines.

Some legions of free-shooters, under the heroic names of "Avengers of the Defeat," "Citizens of the

161

Tomb," "Partakers of Death," passed in their turn with the air of bandits.

Their leaders were former cloth or grain merchants, ex-merchants in tallow or soap, warriors of circumstance, elected officers on account of their escutcheons and the length of their mustaches, covered with arms and with braid, speaking in constrained voices, discussing plans of campaign, and pretending to carry agonized France alone on their swaggering shoulders, but sometimes fearing their own soldiers, prison-birds, that were often brave at first and later proved to be plunderers and debauchees.

It was said that the Prussians were going to enter Rouen.

The National Guard who for two months had been carefully reconnoitering in the neighboring woods, shooting sometimes their own sentinels, and ready for a combat whenever a little wolf stirred in the thicket, had now returned to their firesides. Their arms, their uniforms, all the murderous accoutrements with which they had lately struck fear into the national heart for three leagues in every direction, had suddenly disappeared.

The last French soldiers finally came across the Seine to reach the Audemer bridge through Saint-Sever and Bourg-Achard; and, marching behind, on foot, between two officers of ordnance, the General, in despair, unable to do anything with these incongruous tatters, himself lost in the breaking-up of a people accustomed to conquer, and disastrously beaten, in spite of his legendary bravery.

A profound calm, a frightful, silent expectancy had spread over the city. Many of the heavy citizens, emasculated by commerce, anxiously awaited the conquerors, trembling lest their roasting spits or kitchen knives be considered arms.

All life seemed stopped; shops were closed, the streets dumb. Sometimes an inhabitant, intimidated by this silence, moved rapidly along next the walls. The agony of waiting made them wish the enemy would come.

In the afternoon of the day which followed the departure of the French troops, some uhlans, coming from one knows not where, crossed the town with celerity. Then, a little later, a black mass descended the side of St. Catharine, while two other invading bands appeared by the way of Darnetal and Boisguillaume. The advance guard of the three bodies joined one another at the same moment in Hotel de Ville square and, by all the neighboring streets, the German army continued to arrive, spreading out its battalions, making the pavement resound under their hard, rhythmic step.

Some orders of the commander, in a foreign, guttural voice, reached the houses which seemed dead and deserted, while behind closed shutters, eyes were watching these victorious men, masters of the city, of fortunes, of lives, through the "rights of war." The inhabitants, shut up in their rooms, were visited with the kind of excitement that a cataclysm, or some fatal upheaval of the earth, brings to us, against which all wisdom, all force is useless. For the same sensation is produced each time that the established order of things is overturned, when security no longer exists, and all that protect the laws of man and of nature find themselves at the mercy of unreasoning, ferocious brutality. The trembling of the earth crushing the houses and burying an entire people; a river overflowing its banks and carrying in its course the drowned peasants, carcasses of beeves, and girders snatched from roofs, or a glorious army massacring those trying to defend themselves, leading others prisoners, pillaging in the name of the Sword and thanking God to the sound of the cannon, all are alike frightful scourges which disconcert all belief in eternal justice, all the confidence that we have in the protection of Heaven and the reason of man.

Some detachments rapped at each door, then disappeared into the houses. It was occupation after invasion. Then the duty commences for the conquered to show themselves gracious toward the conquerors.

After some time, as soon as the first terror disappears, a new calm is established. In many families, the Prussian officer eats at the table. He is sometimes well bred and, through politeness, pities France, and speaks of his repugnance in taking part in this affair. One is grateful to him for this sentiment; then, one may be, some day or other, in need of his protection. By treating him well, one has, perhaps, a less number of men to feed. And why should we wound anyone on whom we are entirely dependent? To act thus would be less bravery than temerity. And temerity is no longer a fault of the commoner of Rouen, as it was at the time of the heroic defense, when their city became famous. Finally, each told himself that the highest judgment of French urbanity required that they be allowed to be polite to the strange soldier in the house, provided they did not show themselves familiar with him in public. Outside they would not make themselves known to each other, but at home they could chat freely, and the German might remain longer each evening warming his feet at their hearthstones.

The town even took on, little by little, its ordinary aspect. The French scarcely went out, but the Prussian soldiers grumbled in the streets. In short, the officers of the Blue Hussars, who dragged with arrogance their great weapons of death up and down the pavement, seemed to have no more grievous scorn for the simple citizens than the officers or the sportsmen who, the year before, drank in the same *cafés*.

There was nevertheless, something in the air, something subtle and unknown, a strange, intolerable atmosphere, like a penetrating odor, the odor of invasion. It filled the dwellings and the public places, changed the taste of the food, gave the impression of being on a journey, far away, among barbarous and dangerous tribes.

The conquerors exacted money, much money. The inhabitants always paid and they were rich enough to do it. But the richer a trading Norman becomes the more he suffers at every outlay, at each part of his fortune that he sees pass from his hands into those of another.

Therefore, two or three leagues below the town, following the course of the river toward Croisset, Dieppedalle, or Biessart, mariners and fishermen often picked up the swollen corpse of a German in uniform from the bottom of the river, killed by the blow of a knife, the head crushed with a stone, or perhaps thrown into the water by a push from the high bridge. The slime of the river bed buried these obscure vengeances, savage, but legitimate, unknown heroisms, mute attacks more perilous than the battles of broad day, and without the echoing sound of glory.

For hatred of the foreigner always arouses some intrepid ones, who are ready to die for an idea.

Finally, as soon as the invaders had brought the town quite under subjection with their inflexible discipline, without having been guilty of any of the horrors for which they were famous along their triumphal line of march, people began to take courage, and the need of trade put new heart into the commerce of the country. Some had large interests at Havre, which the French army occupied, and they wished to try and reach this port by going to Dieppe by land and there embarking.

They used their influence with the German soldiers with whom they had an acquaintance, and finally, an authorization of departure was obtained from the General-in-chief.

Then, a large diligence, with four horses, having been engaged for this journey, and ten persons having engaged seats in it, it was resolved to set out on Tuesday morning before daylight, in order to escape observation.

For some time before, the frost had been hardening the earth and on Monday, toward three o'clock, great black clouds coming from the north brought the snow which fell without interruption during the evening and all night.

At half past four in the morning, the travelers met in the courtyard of Hotel Normandie, where they were to take the carriage.

They were still full of sleep, and shivering with cold under their wraps. They could only see each other dimly in the obscure light, and the accumulation of heavy winter garments made them all resemble fat curates in long cassocks. Only two of the men were acquainted; a third accosted them and they chatted: "I'm going to take my wife," said one. "I too," said another. "And I," said the third. The first added: "We shall not return to Rouen, and if the Prussians approach Havre, we shall go over to England." All had the same projects, being of the same mind.

As yet the horses were not harnessed. A little lantern, carried by a stable boy, went out one door from time to time, to immediately appear at another. The feet of the horses striking the floor could be heard, although deadened by the straw and litter, and the voice of a man talking to the beasts, sometimes swearing, came from the end of the building. A light tinkling of bells announced that they were taking down the harness; this murmur soon became a clear and continuous rhythm by the movement of the animal, stopping sometimes, then breaking into a brusque shake which was accompanied by the dull stamp of a sabot upon the hard earth.

The door suddenly closed. All noise ceased. The frozen citizens were silent; they remained immovable and stiff.

A curtain of uninterrupted white flakes constantly sparkled in its descent to the ground. It effaced forms, and powdered everything with a downy moss. And nothing could be heard in the great silence. The town was calm, and buried under the wintry frost, as this fall of snow, unnamable and floating, a sensation rather than a sound (trembling atoms which only seem to fill all space), came to cover the earth.

The man reappeared with his lantern, pulling at the end of a rope a sad horse which would not come willingly. He placed him against the pole, fastened the traces, walked about a long time adjusting the harness, for he had the use of but one hand, the other carrying the lantern. As he went for the second horse, he noticed the travelers, motionless, already white with snow, and said to them: "Why not get into the carriage? You will be under cover, at least."

They had evidently not thought of it, and they hastened to do so. The three men installed their wives at the back and then followed them. Then the other forms, undecided and veiled, took in their turn the last places without exchanging a word.

The floor was covered with straw, in which the feet ensconced themselves. The ladies at the back having brought little copper foot stoves, with a carbon fire, lighted them and, for some time, in low voices, enumerated the advantages of the appliances, repeating things that they had known for a long time.

Finally, the carriage was harnessed with six horses instead of four, because the traveling was very bad, and a voice called out:

"Is everybody aboard?"

And a voice within answered: "Yes."

They were off. The carriage moved slowly, slowly for a little way. The wheels were imbedded in the snow; the whole body groaned with heavy cracking sounds; the horses glistened, puffed, and smoked; and

168

the great whip of the driver snapped without ceasing, hovering about on all sides, knotting and unrolling itself like a thin serpent, lashing brusquely some horse on the rebound, which then put forth its most violent effort.

Now the day was imperceptibly dawning. The light flakes, which one of the travelers, a Rouenese by birth, said looked like a shower of cotton, no longer fell. A faint light filtered through the great, dull clouds, which rendered more brilliant the white of the fields, where appeared a line of great trees clothed in whiteness, or a chimney with a cap of snow.

In the carriage, each looked at the others curiously, in the sad light of this dawn.

At the back, in the best places, Mr. Loiseau, wholesale merchant of wine, of Grand-Pont street, and Mrs. Loiseau were sleeping opposite each other. Loiseau had bought out his former patron who failed in business, and made his fortune. He sold bad wine at a good price to small retailers in the country, and passed among his friends and acquaintances as a knavish wag, a true Norman full of deceit and joviality.

His reputation as a sharper was so well established that one evening at the residence of the prefect, Mr. Tournel, author of some fables and songs, of keen, satirical mind, a local celebrity, having proposed to some ladies, who seemed to be getting a little sleepy, that they make up a game of "Loiseau tricks," the joke traversed the rooms of the prefect, reached those of the town, and then, in the months to come, made many a face in the province expand with laughter.

Loiseau was especially known for his love of farce of every kind, for his jokes, good and bad; and no one could ever talk with him without thinking: "He is invaluable, this Loiseau." Of tall figure, his balloon-shaped front was surmounted by a ruddy face surrounded by gray whiskers.

His wife, large, strong, and resolute, with a quick, decisive manner, was the order and arithmetic of this house of commerce, while he was the life of it through his joyous activity.

Beside them, Mr. Carré-Lamadon held himself with great dignity, as if belonging to a superior caste; a considerable man, in cottons, proprietor of three mills, officer of the Legion of Honor, and member of the General Council. He had remained, during the Empire, chief of the friendly opposition, famous for making the Emperor pay more dear for rallying to the cause than if he had combated it with blunted arms, according to his own story. Madame Carré-Lamadon, much younger than her husband, was the consolation of officers of good family sent to Rouen in garrison. She sat opposite her husband, very dainty, petite, and pretty, wrapped closely in furs and looking with sad eyes at the interior of the carriage.

Her neighbors, the Count and Countess Hubert de Breville, bore the name of one of the most ancient and noble families of Normandy. The Count, an old gentleman of good figure, accentuated, by the artifices of his toilette, his resemblance to King Henry IV., who, following a glorious legend of the family, had impregnated one of the De Breville ladies, whose husband, for this reason, was made a count and governor of the province.

A colleague of Mr. Carré-Lamadon in the General Council, Count Hubert represented the Orléans party in the Department.

The story of his marriage with the daughter of a little captain of a privateer had always remained a mystery. But as the Countess had a grand air, received better than anyone, and passed for having been loved by the son of Louis Philippe, all the nobility did her honor, and her salon remained the first in the country, the only one which preserved the old gallantry, and to which the *entrée* was difficult. The fortune of the Brevilles amounted, it was said, to five hundred thousand francs in income, all in good securities.

These six persons formed the foundation of the carriage company, the society side, serene and strong, honest, established people, who had both religion and principles.

By a strange chance, all the women were upon the same seat; and the Countess had for neighbors two sisters who picked at long strings of beads and muttered some *Paters* and *Aves*. One was old and as pitted with smallpox as if she had received a broadside of grapeshot full in the face. The other, very sad, had a pretty face and a disease of the lungs, which, added to their devoted faith, illumined them and made them appear like martyrs.

Opposite these two devotees were a man and a woman who attracted the notice of all. The man, well known, was Cornudet the democrat, the terror of respectable people. For twenty years he had soaked his great red beard in the *bocks* of all the democratic *cafés*. He had consumed with his friends and *con-*

frères a rather pretty fortune left him by his father, an old confectioner, and he awaited the establishing of the Republic with impatience, that he might have the position he merited by his great expenditures. On the fourth of September, by some joke perhaps, he believed himself elected prefect, but when he went to assume the duties, the clerks of the office were masters of the place and refused to recognize him, obliging him to retreat. Rather a good bachelor, on the whole, inoffensive and serviceable, he had busied himself, with incomparable ardor, in organizing the defense against the Prussians. He had dug holes in all the plains, cut down young trees from the neighboring forests, sown snares over all routes and, at the approach of the enemy, took himself quickly back to the town. He now thought he could be of more use in Havre where more entrenchments would be necessary.

The woman, one of those called a coquette, was celebrated for her *embonpoint,* which had given her the nickname of "Ball-of-Fat." Small, round, and fat as lard, with puffy fingers choked at the phalanges, like chaplets of short sausages; with a stretched and shining skin, an enormous bosom which shook under her dress, she was, nevertheless, pleasing and sought after, on account of a certain freshness and breeziness of disposition. Her face was a round apple, a peony bud ready to pop into bloom, and inside that opened two great black eyes, shaded with thick brows that cast a shadow within; and below, a charming mouth, humid for kissing, furnished with shining, microscopic baby teeth. She was, it was said, full of admirable qualities.

As soon as she was recognized, a whisper went around among the honest women, and the words "prostitute" and "public shame" were whispered so loud that she raised her head. Then she threw at her neighbors such a provoking, courageous look that a great silence reigned, and everybody looked down except Loiseau, who watched her with an exhilarated air.

And immediately conversation began among the three ladies, whom the presence of this girl had suddenly rendered friendly, almost intimate. It seemed to them they should bring their married dignity into union in opposition to that sold without shame; for legal love always takes on a tone of contempt for its free *confrère*.

The three men, also drawn together by an instinct of preservation at the sight of Cornudet, talked money with a certain high tone of disdain for the poor. Count Hubert talked of the havoc which the Prussians had caused, the losses which resulted from being robbed of cattle and from destroyed crops, with the assurance of a great lord, ten times millionaire whom these ravages would scarcely cramp for a year. Mr. Carré-Lamadon, largely experienced in the cotton industry, had had need of sending six hundred thousand francs to England, as a trifle in reserve if it should be needed. As for Loiseau, he had arranged with the French administration to sell them all the wines that remained in his cellars, on account of which the State owed him a formidable sum, which he counted on collecting at Havre.

And all three threw toward each other swift and amicable glances.

173

Although in different conditions, they felt themselves to be brothers through money, that grand freemasonry of those who possess it, and make the gold rattle by putting their hands in their trousers' pockets.

The carriage went so slowly that at ten o'clock in the morning they had not gone four leagues. The men had got down three times to climb hills on foot. They began to be disturbed, because they should be now taking breakfast at Tôtes and they despaired now of reaching there before night. Each one had begun to watch for an inn along the route, when the carriage foundered in a snowdrift, and it took two hours to extricate it.

Growing appetites troubled their minds; and no eating-house, no wine shop showed itself, the approach of the Prussians and the passage of the troops having frightened away all these industries.

The gentlemen ran to the farms along the way for provisions, but they did not even find bread, for the defiant peasant had concealed his stores for fear of being pillaged by the soldiers who, having nothing to put between their teeth, took by force whatever they discovered.

Toward one o'clock in the afternoon, Loiseau announced that there was a decided hollow in his stomach. Everybody suffered with him, and the violent need of eating, ever increasing, had killed conversation.

From time to time some one yawned; another immediately imitated him; and each, in his turn, in accordance with his character, his knowledge of life, and his social position, opened his mouth with carelessness or modesty, placing his hand quickly before the yawning hole from whence issued a vapor.

174

Ball-of-Fat, after many attempts, bent down as if seeking something under her skirts. She hesitated a second, looked at her neighbors, then sat up again tranquilly. The faces were pale and drawn. Loiseau affirmed that he would give a thousand francs for a small ham. His wife made a gesture, as if in protest; but she kept quiet. She was always troubled when anyone spoke of squandering money, and could not comprehend any pleasantry on the subject. "The fact is," said the Count, "I cannot understand why I did not think to bring some provisions with me." Each reproached himself in the same way.

However, Cornudet had a flask full of rum. He offered it; it was refused coldly. Loiseau alone accepted two swallows, and then passed back the flask saying, by way of thanks: "It is good all the same; it is warming and checks the appetite." The alcohol put him in good-humor and he proposed that they do as they did on the little ship in the song, eat the fattest of the passengers. This indirect allusion to Ball-of-Fat choked the well-bred people. They said nothing. Cornudet alone laughed. The two good sisters had ceased to mumble their rosaries and, with their hands enfolded in their great sleeves, held themselves immovable, obstinately lowering their eyes, without doubt offering to Heaven the suffering it had brought upon them.

Finally, at three o'clock, when they found themselves in the midst of an interminable plain, without a single village in sight, Ball-of-Fat bending down quickly drew from under the seat a large basket covered with a white napkin.

At first she brought out a little china plate and a

silver cup; then a large dish in which there were two whole chickens, cut up and imbedded in their own jelly. And one could still see in the basket other good things, some *pâtés*, fruits, and sweetmeats, provisions for three days if they should not see the kitchen of an inn. Four necks of bottles were seen among the packages of food. She took a wing of a chicken and began to eat it delicately, with one of those little biscuits called "Regence" in Normandy.

All looks were turned in her direction. Then the odor spread, enlarging the nostrils and making the mouth water, besides causing a painful contraction of the jaw behind the ears. The scorn of the women for this girl became ferocious, as if they had a desire to kill her and throw her out of the carriage into the snow, her, her silver cup, her basket, provisions and all.

But Loiseau with his eyes devoured the dish of chicken. He said: "Fortunately, Madame had more precaution than we. There are some people who know how to think ahead always."

She turned toward him, saying: "If you would like some of it, sir? It is hard to go without breakfast so long."

He saluted her and replied: "Faith, I frankly cannot refuse; I can stand it no longer. Everything goes in time of war, does it not, Madame?" And then casting a comprehensive glance around, he added: "In moments like this, one can but be pleased to find people who are obliging."

He had a newspaper which he spread out on his knees, that no spot might come to his pantaloons, and upon the point of a knife that he always carried

176

in his pocket, he took up a leg all glistening with jelly, put it between his teeth and masticated it with a satisfaction so evident that there ran through the carriage a great sigh of distress.

Then Ball-of-Fat, in a sweet and humble voice, proposed that the two sisters partake of her collation. They both accepted instantly and, without raising their eyes, began to eat very quickly, after stammering their thanks. Cornudet no longer refused the offers of his neighbor, and they formed with the sisters a sort of table, by spreading out some newspapers upon their knees.

The mouths opened and shut without ceasing, they masticated, swallowed, gulping ferociously. Loiseau in his corner was working hard and, in a low voice, was trying to induce his wife to follow his example. She resisted for a long time; then, when a drawn sensation ran through her body, she yielded. Her husband, rounding his phrase, asked their "charming companion" if he might be allowed to offer a little piece to Madame Loiseau.

She replied: "Why, yes, certainly, sir," with an amiable smile, as she passed the dish.

An embarrassing thing confronted them when they opened the first bottle of Bordeaux: they had but one cup. Each passed it after having tasted. Cornudet alone, for politeness without doubt, placed his lips at the spot left humid by his fair neighbor.

Then, surrounded by people eating, suffocated by the odors of the food, the Count and Countess de Breville, as well as Madame and M. Carré-Lamadon, were suffering that odious torment which has preserved the name of Tantalus. Suddenly the young wife of the manufacturer gave forth such a sigh that all heads were turned in her direction; she was as white as the snow without; her eyes closed, her head drooped; she had lost consciousness. Her husband, much excited, implored the help of everybody. Each lost his head completely, until the elder of the two sisters, holding the head of the sufferer, slipped Ball-of-Fat's cup between her lips and forced her to swallow a few drops of wine. The pretty little lady revived, opened her eyes, smiled, and declared in a dying voice that she felt very well now. But, in order that the attack might not return, the sister urged her to drink a full glass of Bordeaux, and added: "It is just hunger, nothing more."

Then Ball-of-Fat, blushing and embarrassed, looked at the four travelers who had fasted and stammered: "Goodness knows! if I dared to offer anything to these gentlemen and ladies, I would—" Then she was silent, as if fearing an insult. Loiseau took up the word: "Ah! certainly, in times like these all the world are brothers and ought to aid each other. Come, ladies, without ceremony; why the devil not accept? We do not know whether we shall even find a house where we can pass the night. At the pace we are going now, we shall not reach Tôtes before noon to-morrow—"

They still hesitated, no one daring to assume the responsibility of a "Yes." The Count decided the question. He turned toward the fat, intimidated girl and, taking on a grand air of condescension, he said to her:

"We accept with gratitude, Madame."

It is the first step that counts. The Rubicon passed,

one lends himself to the occasion squarely. The basket was stripped. It still contained a *pate de foie gras,* a *pâté* of larks, a piece of smoked tongue, some preserved pears, a loaf of hard bread, some wafers, and a full cup of pickled gherkins and onions, of which crudities Ball-of-Fat, like all women, was extremely fond.

They could not eat this girl's provisions without speaking to her. And so they chatted, with reserve at first; then, as she carried herself well, with more abandon. The ladies De Breville and Carré-Lamadon, who were acquainted with all the ins and outs of good-breeding, were gracious with a certain delicacy. The Countess, especially, showed that amiable condescension of very noble ladies who do not fear being soiled by contact with anyone, and was charming. But the great Madame Loiseau, who had the soul of a plebeian, remained crabbed, saying little and eating much.

The conversation was about the war, naturally. They related the horrible deeds of the Prussians, the brave acts of the French; and all of them, although running away, did homage to those who stayed behind. Then personal stories began to be told, and Ball-of-Fat related, with sincere emotion, and in the heated words that such girls sometimes use in expressing their natural feelings, how she had left Rouen:

"I believed at first that I could remain," said she. "I had my house full of provisions, and I preferred to feed a few soldiers rather than expatriate myself, to go I knew not where. But as soon as I saw them, those Prussians, that was too much for me!

they made my blood boil with anger, and I wept for very shame all day long. Oh! if I were only a man! I watched them from my windows, the great porkers with their pointed helmets, and my maid held my hands to keep me from throwing the furniture down upon them. Then one of them came to lodge at my house; I sprang at his throat the first thing; they are no more difficult to strangle than other people. And I should have put an end to that one then and there had they not pulled me away by the hair. After that, it was necessary to keep out of sight. And finally, when I found an opportunity, I left town and — here I am!"

They congratulated her. She grew in the estimation of her companions, who had not shown themselves so hot-brained, and Cornudet, while listening to her, took on the approving, benevolent smile of an apostle, as a priest would if he heard a devotee praise God, for the long-bearded democrats have a monopoly of patriotism, as the men in cassocks have of religion. In his turn he spoke, in a doctrinal tone, with the emphasis of a proclamation such as we see pasted on the walls about town, and finished by a bit of eloquence whereby he gave that "scamp of a Badinguet" a good lashing.

Then Ball-of-Fat was angry, for she was a Bonapartist. She grew redder than a cherry and, stammering with indignation, said:

"I would like to have seen you in his place, you other people. Then everything would have been quite right; oh, yes! It is you who have betrayed this man! One would never have had to leave France if it had been governed by blackguards like you!"

Cornudet, undisturbed, preserved a disdainful, superior smile, but all felt that the high note had been struck, until the Count, not without some difficulty, calmed the exasperated girl and proclaimed with a manner of authority that all sincere opinions should be respected. But the Countess and the manufacturer's wife, who had in their souls an unreasonable hatred for the people that favor a Republic, and the same instinctive tenderness that all women have for a decorative, despotic government, felt themselves drawn, in spite of themselves, toward this prostitute so full of dignity, whose sentiments so strongly resembled their own.

The basket was empty. By ten o'clock they had easily exhausted the contents and regretted that there was not more. Conversation continued for some time, but a little more coldly since they had finished eating.

The night fell, the darkness little by little became profound, and the cold, felt more during digestion, made Ball-of-Fat shiver in spite of her plumpness. Then Madame de Breville offered her the little foot-stove, in which the fuel had been renewed many times since morning; she accepted it immediately, for her feet were becoming numb with cold. The ladies Carré-Lamadon and Loiseau gave theirs to the two religious sisters.

The driver had lighted his lanterns. They shone out with a lively glimmer showing a cloud of foam beyond, the sweat of the horses; and, on both sides of the way, the snow seemed to roll itself along under the moving reflection of the lights.

Inside the carriage one could distinguish nothing. But a sudden movement seemed to be made between

Ball-of-Fat and Cornudet; and Loiseau, whose eye penetrated the shadow, believed that he saw the big-bearded man start back quickly as if he had received a swift, noiseless blow.

Then some twinkling points of fire appeared in the distance along the road. It was Tôtes. They had traveled eleven hours, which, with the two hours given to resting and feeding the horses, made thirteen. They entered the town and stopped before the Hotel of Commerce.

The carriage door opened! A well-known sound gave the travelers a start; it was the scabbard of a sword hitting the ground. Immediately a German voice was heard in the darkness.

Although the diligence was not moving, no one offered to alight, fearing some one might be waiting to murder them as they stepped out. Then the conductor appeared, holding in his hand one of the lanterns which lighted the carriage to its depth, and showed the two rows of frightened faces, whose mouths were open and whose eyes were wide with surprise and fear.

Outside beside the driver, in plain sight, stood a German officer, an excessively tall young man, thin and blond, squeezed into his uniform like a girl in a corset, and wearing on his head a flat, oilcloth cap which made him resemble the porter of an English hotel. His enormous mustache, of long straight hairs, growing gradually thin at each side and terminating in a single blond thread so fine that one could not perceive where it ended, seemed to weigh heavily on the corners of his mouth and, drawing down the cheeks, left a decided wrinkle about the lips.

In Alsatian French, he invited the travelers to come in, saying in a suave tone: "Will you descend, gentlemen and ladies?"

The two good sisters were the first to obey, with the docility of saints accustomed ever to submission. The Count and Countess then appeared, followed by the manufacturer and his wife; then Loiseau, pushing ahead of him his larger half. The last-named, as he set foot on the earth, said to the officer: "Good evening, sir," more as a measure of prudence than politeness. The officer, insolent as all-powerful people usually are, looked at him without a word.

Ball-of-Fat and Cornudet, although nearest the door, were the last to descend, grave and haughty before the enemy. The fat girl tried to control herself and be calm. The democrat waved a tragic hand and his long beard seemed to tremble a little and grow redder. They wished to preserve their dignity, comprehending that in such meetings as these they represented in some degree their great country, and somewhat disgusted with the docility of her companions, the fat girl tried to show more pride than her neighbors, the honest women, and, as she felt that some one should set an example, she continued her attitude of resistance assumed at the beginning of the journey.

They entered the vast kitchen of the inn, and the German, having demanded their traveling papers signed by the General-in-chief (in which the name, the description, and profession of each traveler was mentioned), and having examined them all critically, comparing the people and their signatures, said: "It is quite right," and went out.

183

Then they breathed. They were still hungry and supper was ordered. A half hour was necessary to prepare it, and while two servants were attending to this they went to their rooms. They found them along a corridor which terminated in a large glazed door.

Finally, they sat down at table, when the proprietor of the inn himself appeared. He was a former horse merchant, a large, asthmatic man, with a constant wheezing and rattling in his throat. His father had left him the name of Follenvie. He asked:

"Is Miss Elizabeth Rousset here?"

Ball-of-Fat started as she answered: "It is I."

"The Prussian officer wishes to speak with you immediately."

"With me?"

"Yes, that is, if you are Miss Elizabeth Rousset."

She was disturbed, and reflecting for an instant, declared flatly:

"That is my name, but I shall not go."

A stir was felt around her; each discussed and tried to think of the cause of this order. The Count approached her, saying:

"You are wrong, Madame, for your refusal may lead to considerable difficulty, not only for yourself, but for all your companions. It is never worth while to resist those in power. This request cannot assuredly bring any danger; it is, without doubt, about some forgotten formality."

Everybody agreed with him, asking, begging, beseeching her to go, and at last they convinced her that it was best; they all feared the complications that might result from disobedience. She finally said:

"It is for you that I do this, you understand."

The Countess took her by the hand, saying: "And we are grateful to you for it."

She went out. They waited before sitting down at table.

Each one regretted not having been sent for in the place of this violent, irascible girl, and mentally prepared some platitudes, in case they should be called in their turn.

But at the end of ten minutes she reappeared, out of breath, red to suffocation, and exasperated. She stammered: "Oh! the rascal! the rascal!"

All gathered around to learn something, but she said nothing; and when the Count insisted, she responded with great dignity: "No, it does not concern you; I can say nothing."

Then they all seated themselves around a high soup tureen whence came the odor of cabbage. In spite of alarm, the supper was gay. The cider was good, the beverage Loiseau and the good sisters took as a means of economy. The others called for wine; Cornudet demanded beer. He had a special fashion of uncorking the bottle, making froth on the liquid, carefully filling the glass and then holding it before the light to better appreciate the color. When he drank, his great beard, which still kept some of the foam of his beloved beverage, seemed to tremble with tenderness; his eyes were squinted, in order not to lose sight of his tipple, and he had the unique air of fulfilling the function for which he was born. One would say that there was in his mind a meeting, like that of affinities, between the two great passions that occupied his life — Pale Ale and Revolutions; and assuredly he could not taste the one without thinking of the other.

Mr. and Mrs. Follenvie dined at the end of the table. The man, rattling like a cracked locomotive, had too much trouble in breathing to talk while eating, but his wife was never silent. She told all her impressions at the arrival of the Prussians, what they did, what they said, reviling them because they cost her some money, and because she had two sons in the army. She addressed herself especially to the Countess, flattered by being able to talk with a lady of quality.

When she lowered her voice to say some delicate thing, her husband would interrupt, from time to time, with: "You had better keep silent, Madame Follenvie." But she paid no attention, continuing in this fashion:

"Yes, Madame, those people there not only eat our potatoes and pork, but our pork and potatoes. And it must not be believed that they are at all proper — oh, no! such filthy things they do, saving the respect I owe to you! And if you could see them exercise for hours in the day! They are all there in the field, marching ahead, then marching back, turning here and turning there. They might be cultivating the land, or at least working on the roads of their own country! But no, Madame, these military men are profitable to no one. Poor people have to feed them, or perhaps be murdered! I am only an old woman without education, it is true, but when I see some endangering their constitutions by raging from morning to night, I say: When there are so many people found to be useless, how unnecessary it is for others to take so much trouble to be nuisances! Truly, is it not an abomination to kill people, whether they be Prussian, or English, or Polish, or French? If one man revenges himself upon another who has done him some injury, it is wicked and he is punished; but when they exterminate our boys, as if they were game, with guns, they give decorations, indeed, to the one who destroys the most! Now, you see, I can never understand that, never!"

Cornudet raised his voice: "War is a barbarity when one attacks a peaceable neighbor, but a sacred duty when one defends his country."

The old woman lowered her head:

"Yes, when one defends himself, it is another thing; but why not make it a duty to kill all the kings who make these wars for their pleasure?"

Cornudet's eyes flashed. "Bravo, my country-woman!" said he.

Mr. Carré-Lamadon reflected profoundly. Although he was prejudiced as a Captain of Industry, the good sense of this peasant woman made him think of the opulence that would be brought into the country were the idle and consequently mischievous hands, and the troops which were now maintained in un-productiveness, employed in some great industrial work that it would require centuries to achieve.

Loiseau, leaving his place, went to speak with the innkeeper in a low tone of voice. The great man laughed, shook, and squeaked, his corpulence quivered with joy at the jokes of his neighbor, and he bought of him six cases of wine for spring, after the Prussians had gone.

As soon as supper was finished, as they were worn out with fatigue, they retired.

However, Loiseau, who had observed things, after getting his wife to bed, glued his eye and then his ear to a hole in the wall, to try and discover what are known as "the mysteries of the corridor."

At the end of about an hour, he heard a groping, and, looking quickly, he perceived Ball-of-Fat, who appeared still more plump in a blue cashmere negligée trimmed with white lace. She had a candle in her hand and was directing her steps toward the great door at the end of the corridor. But a door at the side opened, and when she returned at the end of some minutes Cornudet, in his suspenders, followed her. They spoke low, then they stopped. Ball-of-Fat seemed to be defending the entrance to her room with energy. Loiseau, unfortunately, could not hear all their words, but, finally, as they raised their voices, he was able to catch a few. Cornudet insisted with vivacity. He said:

"Come, now, you are a silly woman; what harm can be done?"

She had an indignant air in responding: "No, my dear, there are moments when such things are out of place. Here it would be a shame."

He doubtless did not comprehend and asked why. Then she cried out, raising her voice still more:

"Why? you do not see why? When there are Prussians in the house, in the very next room, perhaps?"

He was silent. This patriotic shame of the harlot, who would not suffer his caress so near the enemy, must have awakened the latent dignity in his heart, for after simply kissing her, he went back to his own door with a bound.

Loiseau, much excited, left the aperture, cut a caper in his room, put on his pajamas, turned back the clothes that covered the bony carcass of his companion, whom he awakened with a kiss, murmuring: "Do you love me, dearie?"

Then all the house was still. And immediately there arose somewhere, from an uncertain quarter, which might be the cellar but was quite as likely to be the garret, a powerful snoring, monotonous and regular, a heavy, prolonged sound, like a great kettle under pressure. Mr. Follenvie was asleep.

As they had decided that they would set out at eight o'clock the next morning, they all collected in the kitchen. But the carriage, the roof of which was covered with snow, stood undisturbed in the courtyard, without horses and without a conductor. They sought him in vain in the stables, in the hay, and in the coach-house. Then they resolved to scour the town, and started out. They found themselves in a square, with a church at one end and some low houses on either side, where they perceived some Prussian soldiers. The first one they saw was paring potatoes. The second, further off, was cleaning the hairdresser's shop. Another, bearded to the eyes, was tending a troublesome brat, cradling it and trying to appease it; and the great peasant women, whose husbands were "away in the army," indicated by signs to their obedient conquerors the work they wished to have done: cutting wood, cooking the soup, grinding the coffee, or what not. One of them

189

even washed the linen of his hostess, an impotent old grandmother.

The Count, astonished, asked questions of the beadle who came out of the rectory. The old man responded:

"Oh! those men are not wicked; they are not the Prussians we hear about. They are from far off, I know not where; and they have left wives and children in their country; it is not amusing to them, this war, I can tell you! I am sure they also weep for their homes, and that it makes as much sorrow among them as it does among us. Here, now, there is not so much unhappiness for the moment, because the soldiers do no harm and they work as if they were in their own homes. You see, sir, among poor people it is necessary that they aid one another. These are the great traits which war develops."

Cornudet, indignant at the cordial relations between the conquerors and the conquered, preferred to shut himself up in the inn. Loiseau had a joke for the occasion: "They will repeople the land."

Mr. Carré-Lamadon had a serious word: "They try to make amends."

But they did not find the driver. Finally, they discovered him in a *café* of the village, sitting at table fraternally with the officer of ordnance. The Count called out to him:

"Were you not ordered to be ready at eight o'clock?"

"Well, yes; but another order has been given me since."

"By whom?"

"Faith! the Prussian commander."

"What was it?"

"Not to harness at all."

"Why?"

"I know nothing about it. Go and ask him.
They tell me not to harness, and I don't harness.
That's all."

"Did he give you the order himself?"

"No, sir, the innkeeper gave the order for him."

"When was that?"

"Last evening, as I was going to bed."

The three men returned, much disturbed. They
asked for Mr. Follenvie, but the servant answered
that that gentleman, because of his asthma, never rose
before ten o'clock. And he had given strict orders
not to be wakened before that, except in case of fire.

They wished to see the officer, but that was absolutely impossible, since, while he lodged at the inn,
Mr. Follenvie alone was authorized to speak to him
upon civil affairs. So they waited. The women went
up to their rooms again and occupied themselves
with futile tasks.

Cornudet installed himself near the great chimney
in the kitchen, where there was a good fire burning.
He ordered one of the little tables to be brought from
the *café*, then a can of beer, he then drew out his
pipe, which plays among democrats a part almost
equal to his own, because in serving Cornudet it was
serving its country. It was a superb pipe, an admirably colored meerschaum, as black as the teeth of its
master, but perfumed, curved, glistening, easy to the
hand, completing his physiognomy. And he remained
motionless, his eyes as much fixed upon the flame of
the fire as upon his favorite tipple and its frothy

crown; and each time that he drank, he passed his long, thin fingers through his scanty, gray hair, with an air of satisfaction, after which he sucked in his mustache fringed with foam.

Loiseau, under the pretext of stretching his legs, went to place some wine among the retailers of the country. The Count and the manufacturer began to talk politics. They could foresee the future of France. One of them believed in an Orléans, the other in some unknown savior for the country, a hero who would reveal himself when all were in despair: a Guesclin, or a Joan of Arc, perhaps, or would it be another Napoleon First? Ah! if the Prince Imperial were not so young!

Cornudet listened to them and smiled like one who holds the word of destiny. His pipe perfumed the kitchen.

As ten o'clock struck, Mr. Follenvie appeared. They asked him hurried questions; but he could only repeat two or three times without variation, these words:

"The officer said to me: 'Mr. Follenvie, you see to it that the carriage is not harnessed for those travelers to-morrow. I do not wish them to leave without my order. That is sufficient.'"

Then they wished to see the officer. The Count sent him his card, on which Mr. Carré-Lamadon wrote his name and all his titles. The Prussian sent back word that he would meet the two gentlemen after he had breakfasted, that is to say, about one o'clock.

The ladies reappeared and ate a little something, despite their disquiet. Ball-of-Fat seemed ill and prodigiously troubled.

They were finishing their coffee when the word came that the officer was ready to meet the gentlemen. Loiseau joined them; but when they tried to enlist Cornudet, to give more solemnity to their proceedings, he declared proudly that he would have nothing to do with the Germans; and he betook himself to his chimney corner and ordered another liter of beer.

The three men mounted the staircase and were introduced to the best room of the inn, where the officer received them, stretched out in an armchair, his feet on the mantelpiece, smoking a long, porcelain pipe, and enveloped in a flamboyant dressing-gown, appropriated, without doubt, from some dwelling belonging to a common citizen of bad taste. He did not rise, nor greet them in any way, not even looking at them. It was a magnificent display of natural blackguardism transformed into the military victor.

At the expiration of some moments, he asked: "What is it you wish?"

The Count became spokesman: "We desire to go on our way, sir."

"No."

"May I ask the cause of this refusal?"

"Because I do not wish it."

"But, I would respectfully observe to you, sir, that your General-in-chief gave us permission to go to Dieppe; and I know of nothing we have done to merit your severity."

"I do not wish it—that is all; you can go."

All three having bowed, retired.

The afternoon was lamentable. They could not understand this caprice of the German; and the most singular ideas would come into their heads to trouble them. Everybody stayed in the kitchen and discussed the situation endlessly, imagining all sorts of unlikely things. Perhaps they would be retained as hostages —but to what end?—or taken prisoners—or rather a considerable ransom might be demanded. At this thought a panic prevailed. The richest were the most frightened, already seeing themselves constrained to pay for their lives with sacks of gold poured into the hands of this insolent soldier. They racked their brains to think of some acceptable falsehoods to conceal their riches and make them pass themselves off for poor people, very poor people. Loiseau took off the chain to his watch and hid it away in his pocket. The falling night increased their apprehensions. The lamp was lighted, and as there was still two hours before dinner, Madame Loiseau proposed a game of Thirty-one. It would be a diversion. They accepted. Cornudet himself, having smoked out his pipe, took part for politeness.

The Count shuffled the cards, dealt, and Ball-of-Fat had thirty-one at the outset; and immediately the interest was great enough to appease the fear that haunted their minds. Then Cornudet perceived that the house of Loiseau was given to tricks.

As they were going to the dinner table, Mr. Follenvie again appeared, and, in wheezing, rattling voice, announced:

"The Prussian officer orders me to ask Miss Elizabeth Rousset if she has yet changed her mind."

Ball-of-Fat remained standing and was pale; then suddenly becoming crimson, such a stifling anger took possession of her that she could not speak. But

194

finally she flashed out: "You may say to the dirty beast, that idiot, that carrion of a Prussian, that I shall never change it; you understand, never, never, never!"

The great innkeeper went out. Then Ball-of-Fat was immediately surrounded, questioned, and solicited by all to disclose the mystery of his visit. She resisted, at first, but soon becoming exasperated, she said: "What does he want? You really want to know what he wants? He wants to sleep with me."

Everybody was choked for words, and indignation was rife. Cornudet broke his glass, so violently did he bring his fist down upon the table. There was a clamor of censure against this ignoble soldier, a blast of anger, a union of all for resistance, as if a demand had been made on each one of the party for the sacrifice exacted of her. The Count declared with disgust that those people conducted themselves after the fashion of the ancient barbarians. The women, especially, showed to Ball-of-Fat a most energetic and tender commiseration. The good sisters who only showed themselves at mealtime, lowered their heads and said nothing.

They all dined, nevertheless, when the first *furore* had abated. But there was little conversation; they were thinking.

The ladies retired early, and the men, all smoking, organized a game at cards to which Mr. Follenvie was invited, as they intended to put a few casual questions to him on the subject of conquering the resistance of this officer. But he thought of nothing but the cards and, without listening or answering, would keep repeating: "To the game, sirs, to the game." His attention was so taken that he even forgot to expectorate, which must have put him some points to the good with the organ in his breast. His whistling lungs ran the whole asthmatic scale, from deep, profound tones to the sharp rustiness of a young cock essaying to crow.

He even refused to retire when his wife, who had fallen asleep previously, came to look for him. She went away alone, for she was an "early bird," always up with the sun, while her husband was a "night owl," always ready to pass the night with his friends. He cried out to her: "Leave my creamed chicken before the fire!" and then went on with his game. When they saw that they could get nothing from him, they declared that it was time to stop, and each sought his bed.

They all rose rather early the next day, with an undefined hope of getting away, which desire the terror of passing another day in that horrible inn greatly increased.

Alas! the horses remained in the stable and the driver was invisible. For want of better employment, they went out and walked around the carriage.

The breakfast was very doleful; and it became apparent that a coldness had arisen toward Ball-of-Fat, and that the night, which brings counsel, had slightly modified their judgments. They almost wished now that the Prussian had secretly found this girl, in order to give her companions a pleasant surprise in the morning. What could be more simple? Besides, who would know anything about it? She could save appearances by telling the officer that she took pity on their distress. To her, it would make so little difference!

No one had avowed these thoughts yet.

In the afternoon, as they were almost perishing from *ennui,* the Count proposed that they take a walk around the village. Each wrapped up warmly and the little party set out, with the exception of Cornudet, who preferred to remain near the fire, and the good sisters, who passed their time in the church or at the curate's.

The cold, growing more intense every day, cruelly pinched their noses and ears; their feet became so numb that each step was torture; and when they came to a field it seemed to them frightfully sad under this limitless white, so that everybody returned immediately, with hearts hard pressed and souls congealed.

The four women walked ahead, the three gentlemen followed just behind. Loiseau, who understood the situation, asked suddenly if they thought that girl there was going to keep them long in such a place as this. The Count, always courteous, said that they could not exact from a woman a sacrifice so hard, unless it should come of her own will. Mr. Carré-Lamadon remarked that if the French made their return through Dieppe, as they were likely to, a battle would surely take place at Tôtes. This reflection made the two others anxious.

"If we could only get away on foot," said Loiseau.

The Count shrugged his shoulders: "How can we think of it in this snow? and with our wives?" he said. "And then, we should be pursued and caught in ten minutes and led back prisoners at the mercy of these soldiers."

It was true, and they were silent.

The ladies talked of their clothes, but a certain constraint seemed to disunite them. Suddenly at the end of the street, the officer appeared. His tall, wasp-like figure in uniform was outlined upon the horizon formed by the snow, and he was marching with knees apart, a gait particularly military, which is affected that they may not spot their carefully blackened boots.

He bowed in passing near the ladies and looked disdainfully at the men, who preserved their dignity by not seeing him, except Loiseau, who made a motion toward raising his hat.

Ball-of-Fat reddened to the ears, and the three married women resented the great humiliation of being thus met by this soldier in the company of this girl whom he had treated so cavalierly.

But they spoke of him, of his figure and his face. Madame Carré-Lamadon, who had known many officers and considered herself a connoisseur of them, found this one not at all bad; she regretted even that he was not French, because he would make such a pretty hussar, one all the women would rave over.

Again in the house, no one knew what to do. Some sharp words, even, were said about things very insignificant. The dinner was silent, and almost immediately after it, each one went to his room to kill time in sleep.

They descended the next morning with weary faces and exasperated hearts. The women scarcely spoke to Ball-of-Fat.

A bell began to ring. It was for a baptism. The fat girl had a child being brought up among the peasants of Yvetot. She had not seen it for a year, or thought of it; but now the idea of a child being baptized threw into her heart a sudden and violent tenderness for her own, and she strongly wished to be present at the ceremony.

As soon as she was gone, everybody looked at each other, then pulled their chairs together, for they thought that finally something should be decided upon. Loiseau had an inspiration: it was to hold Ball-of-Fat alone and let the others go.

Mr. Follenvie was charged with the commission, but he returned almost immediately, for the German, who understood human nature, had put him out. He pretended that he would retain everybody so long as his desire was not satisfied.

Then the commonplace nature of Mrs. Loiseau burst out with:

"Well, we are not going to stay here to die of old age. Since it is the trade of this creature to accommodate herself to all kinds, I fail to see how she has the right to refuse one more than another. I can tell you she has received all she could find in Rouen, even the coachmen! Yes, Madame, the prefect's coachman! I know him very well, for he bought his wine at our house. And to think that to-day we should be drawn into this embarrassment by this affected woman, this minx! For my part, I find that this officer conducts himself very well. He has perhaps suffered privations for a long time; and doubtless he would have preferred us three; but no, he is contented with common property. He respects married women. And we must remember too that he is master. He has only to say 'I wish,' and he could take us by force with his soldiers."

The two women had a cold shiver. Pretty Mrs. Carré-Lamadon's eyes grew brilliant and she became a little pale, as if she saw herself already taken by force by the officer.

The men met and discussed the situation. Loiseau, furious, was for delivering "the wretch" bound hand and foot to the enemy. But the Count, descended through three generations of ambassadors, and endowed with the temperament of a diplomatist, was the advocate of ingenuity.

"It is best to decide upon something," said he. Then they conspired.

The women kept together, the tone of their voices was lowered, each gave advice and the discussion was general. Everything was very harmonious. The ladies especially found delicate shades and charming subtleties of expression for saying the most unusual things. A stranger would have understood nothing, so great was the precaution of language observed. But the light edge of modesty, with which every woman of the world is barbed, only covers the surface; they blossom out in a scandalous adventure of this kind, being deeply amused and feeling themselves in their element, mixing love with sensuality as a greedy cook prepares supper for his master.

Even gaiety returned, so funny did the whole story seem to them at last. The Count found some of the jokes a little off color, but they were so well told that he was forced to smile. In his turn, Loiseau came out with some still bolder tales, and yet nobody was wounded. The brutal thought, expressed by his wife, dominated all minds: "Since it is her trade, why should she refuse this one more than another?" The genteel Mrs. Carré-Lamadon seemed to think that in her place, she would refuse this one less than some others.

They prepared the blockade at length, as if they were about to surround a fortress. Each took some rôle to play, some arguments he would bring to bear, some maneuvers that he would endeavor to put into execution. They decided on the plan of attack, the ruse to employ, the surprise of assault, that should force this living citadel to receive the enemy in her room.

Cornudet remained apart from the rest, and was a stranger to the whole affair.

So entirely were their minds distracted that they did not hear Ball-of-Fat enter. The Count uttered a light "Ssh!" which turned all eyes in her direction. There she was. The abrupt silence and a certain embarrassment hindered them from speaking to her at first. The Countess, more accustomed to the duplicity of society than the others, finally inquired: "Was it very amusing, that baptism?"

The fat girl, filled with emotion, told them all about it, the faces, the attitudes, and even the appearance of the church. She added: "It is good to pray sometimes."

And up to the time for luncheon these ladies continued to be amiable toward her, in order to increase her docility and her confidence in their counsel. At the table they commenced the approach. This was in the shape of a vague conversation upon devotion.

They cited ancient examples: Judith and Holophernes, then, without reason, Lucrece and Sextus, and Cleopatra obliging all the generals of the enemy to pass by her couch and reducing them in servility to slaves. Then they brought out a fantastic story, hatched in the imagination of these ignorant millionaires, where the women of Rome went to Capua for the purpose of lulling Hannibal to sleep in their arms, and his lieutenants and phalanxes of mercenaries as well. They cited all the women who have been taken by conquering armies, making a battlefield of their bodies, making them also a weapon, and a means of success; and all those hideous and detestable beings who have conquered by their heroic caresses, and sacrificed their chastity to vengeance or a beloved cause. They even spoke in veiled terms of that great English family which allowed one of its women to be inoculated with a horrible and contagious disease in order to transmit it to Bonaparte, who was miraculously saved by a sudden illness at the hour of the fatal rendezvous.

And all this was related in an agreeable, temperate fashion, except as it was enlivened by the enthusiasm deemed proper to excite emulation.

One might finally have believed that the sole duty of woman here below was a sacrifice of her person, and a continual abandonment to soldierly caprices.

The two good sisters seemed not to hear, lost as they were in profound thought. Ball-of-Fat said nothing.

During the whole afternoon they let her reflect. But, in the place of calling her "Madame" as they had up to this time, they simply called her "Mademoiselle" without knowing exactly why, as if they had a desire to put her down a degree in their esteem, which she had taken by storm, and make her feel her shameful situation.

The moment supper was served, Mr. Follenvie appeared with his old phrase: "The Prussian officer orders me to ask if Miss Elizabeth Rousset has yet changed her mind."

Ball-of-Fat responded dryly: "No, sir."

But at dinner the coalition weakened. Loiseau made three unhappy remarks. Each one beat his wits for new examples but found nothing; when the Countess, without premeditation, perhaps feeling some vague need of rendering homage to religion, asked the elder of the good sisters to tell them some great deeds in the lives of the saints. It appeared that many of their acts would have been considered crimes in our eyes; but the Church gave absolution of them readily, since they were done for the glory of God, or for the good of all. It was a powerful argument; the Countess made the most of it.

Thus it may be by one of those tacit understandings, or the veiled complacency in which anyone who wears the ecclesiastical garb excels, it may be simply from the effect of a happy unintelligence, a helpful stupidity, but in fact the religious sister lent a formidable support to the conspiracy. They had thought her timid, but she showed herself courageous, verbose, even violent. She was not troubled by the chatter of the casuist; her doctrine seemed a bar of iron; her faith never hesitated; her conscience had no scruples. She found the sacrifice of Abraham perfectly simple, for she would immediately kill father or mother on an order from on high. And nothing, in her opinion, could displease the Lord, if the intention was laudable. The Countess put to use the authority of her unwitting accomplice, and added to it the edifying paraphrase and axiom of Jesuit morals: "The end justifies the means."

Then she asked her: "Then, my sister, do you think that God accepts intentions, and pardons the deed when the motive is pure?"

"Who could doubt it, Madame? An action blamable in itself often becomes meritorious by the thought it springs from."

And they continued thus, unraveling the will of God, foreseeing his decisions, making themselves interested in things that, in truth, they would never think of noticing. All this was guarded, skillful, discreet. But each word of the saintly sister in a cap helped to break down the resistance of the unworthy courtesan. Then the conversation changed a little, the woman of the chaplet speaking of the houses of her order, of her Superior, of herself, of her dainty neighbor, the dear sister Saint-Nicephore. They had been called to the hospitals of Havre to care for the hundreds of soldiers stricken with smallpox. They depicted these miserable creatures, giving details of the malady. And while they were stopped, *en route,* by the caprice of this Prussian officer, a great number of Frenchmen might die, whom perhaps they could have saved! It was a specialty with her, caring for soldiers. She had been in Crimea, in Italy, in Austria, and, in telling of her campaigns, she revealed herself as one of those religious aids to drums and trumpets, who seem made to follow camps, pick up the wounded in the thick of battle, and, better than an officer, subdue with a word great bands of undisciplined recruits. A true, good sister of the rataplan, whose ravaged face, marked with innumerable scars, appeared the image of the devastation of war.

No one could speak after her, so excellent seemed the effect of her words.

As soon as the repast was ended they quickly went up to their rooms, with the purpose of not coming down the next day until late in the morning.

The luncheon was quiet. They had given the grain of seed time to germinate and bear fruit. The Countess proposed that they take a walk in the afternoon. The Count, being agreeably inclined, gave an arm to Ball-of-Fat and walked behind the others with her. He talked to her in a familiar, paternal tone, a little disdainful, after the manner of men having girls in their employ, calling her "my dear child," from the height of his social position, of his undisputed honor. He reached the vital part of the question at once:

"Then you prefer to leave us here, exposed to the violences which follow a defeat, rather than consent to a favor which you have so often given in your life?"

Ball-of-Fat answered nothing.

Then he tried to reach her through gentleness, reason, and then the sentiments. He knew how to remain "The Count," even while showing himself gallant or complimentary, or very amiable if it became necessary. He exalted the service that she would render them, and spoke of their appreciation; then suddenly became gaily familiar, and said:

"And you know, my dear, it would be something for him to boast of that he had known a pretty girl; something it is difficult to find in his country."

Ball-of-Fat did not answer but joined the rest of the party. As soon as they entered the house she went to her room and did not appear again. The disquiet was extreme. What were they to do? If she continued to resist, what an embarrassment!

The dinner hour struck. They waited in vain. Mr. Follenvie finally entered and said that Miss Rousset was indisposed, and would not be at the table. Everybody pricked up his ears. The Count went to the innkeeper and said in a low voice:

"Is he in there?"

"Yes."

For convenience, he said nothing to his companions, but made a slight sign with his head. Immediately a great sigh of relief went up from every breast and a light appeared in their faces. Loiseau cried out:

"Holy Christopher! I pay for the champagne, if there is any to be found in the establishment." And Mrs. Loiseau was pained to see the proprietor return with four quart bottles in his hands.

Each one had suddenly become communicative and buoyant. A wanton joy filled their hearts. The Count suddenly perceived that Mrs. Carré-Lamadon was charming, the manufacturer paid compliments to the Countess. The conversation was lively, gay, full of touches.

Suddenly Loiseau, with anxious face and hand upraised, called out: "Silence!" Everybody was silent, surprised, already frightened. Then he listened intently and said: "S-s-sh!" his two eyes and his hands raised toward the ceiling, listening, and then continuing, in his natural voice: "All right! All goes well!"

They failed to comprehend at first, but soon all laughed. At the end of a quarter of an hour he began the same farce again, renewing it occasionally during the whole afternoon. And he pretended to call to some one in the story above, giving him advice in a double meaning, drawn from the fountainhead — the mind of a commercial traveler. For some moments he would assume a sad air, breathing in a whisper: "Poor girl!" Then he would murmur between his teeth, with an appearance of rage: "Ugh! That scamp of a Prussian." Sometimes, at a moment when no more was thought about it, he would say, in an affected voice, many times over: "Enough! enough!" and add, as if speaking to himself: "If we could only see her again, it isn't necessary that he should kill her, the wretch!"

Although these jokes were in deplorable taste, they amused all and wounded no one, for indignation, like other things, depends upon its surroundings, and the atmosphere which had been gradually created around them was charged with sensual thoughts.

At the dessert the women themselves made some delicate and discreet allusions. Their eyes glistened; they had drunk much. The Count, who preserved, even in his flights, his grand appearance of gravity, made a comparison, much relished, upon the subject of those wintering at the pole, and the joy of shipwrecked sailors who saw an opening toward the south.

Loiseau suddenly arose, a glass of champagne in his hand, and said: "I drink to our deliverance." Everybody was on his feet; they shouted in agreement. Even the two good sisters consented to touch their lips to the froth of the wine which they had never before tasted. They declared that it tasted like charged lemonade, only much nicer.

Loiseau resumed: "It is unfortunate that we have no piano, for we might make up a quadrille."

Cornudet had not said a word, nor made a gesture; he appeared plunged in very grave thoughts, and made sometimes a furious motion, so that his great beard seemed to wish to free itself. Finally, toward midnight, as they were separating, Loiseau, who was staggering, touched him suddenly on the stomach and said to him in a stammer: "You are not very funny, this evening; you have said nothing, citizen!" Then Cornudet raised his head brusquely and, casting a brilliant, terrible glance around the company, said: "I tell you all that you have been guilty of infamy!" He rose, went to the door, and again repeated: "Infamy, I say!" and disappeared.

This made a coldness at first. Loiseau, interlocutor, was stupefied; but he recovered immediately and laughed heartily as he said: "He is very green, my friends. He is very green." And then, as they did not comprehend, he told them about the "mysteries of the corridor." Then there was a return of gaiety. The women behaved like lunatics. The Count and Mr. Carré-Lamadon wept from the force of their laughter. They could not believe it.

"How is that? Are you sure?"

"I tell you I saw it."

"And she refused —"

"Yes, because the Prussian officer was in the next room."

"Impossible!"

"I swear it!"

The Count was stifled with laughter. The industrial gentleman held his sides with both hands. Loiseau continued:

"And now you understand why he saw nothing funny this evening! No, nothing at all!" And the three started out half ill, suffocated.

They separated. But Mrs. Loiseau, who was of a spiteful nature, remarked to her husband as they were getting into bed, that "that *grisette*" of a little Carré-Lamadon was yellow with envy all the evening. "You know," she continued, "how some women will take to a uniform, whether it be French or Prussian! It is all the same to them! Oh! what a pity!"

And all night, in the darkness of the corridor, there were to be heard light noises, like whisperings and walking in bare feet, and imperceptible creakings. They did not go to sleep until late, that is sure, for there were threads of light shining under the doors for a long time. The champagne had its effect; they say it troubles sleep.

The next day a clear winter's sun made the snow very brilliant. The diligence, already harnessed, waited before the door, while an army of white pigeons, in their thick plumage, with rose-colored eyes, with a black spot in the center, walked up and down gravely among the legs of the six horses, seeking their livelihood in the manure there scattered.

The driver, enveloped in his sheepskin, had a

lighted pipe under the seat, and all the travelers, radiant, were rapidly packing some provisions for the rest of the journey. They were only waiting for Ball-of-Fat. Finally she appeared.

She seemed a little troubled, ashamed. And she advanced timidly toward her companions, who all, with one motion, turned as if they had not seen her. The Count, with dignity, took the arm of his wife and removed her from this impure contact.

The fat girl stopped, half stupefied; then, plucking up courage, she approached the manufacturer's wife with "Good morning, Madame," humbly murmured. The lady made a slight bow of the head which she accompanied with a look of outraged virtue. Everybody seemed busy, and kept themselves as far from her as if she had had some infectious disease in her skirts. Then they hurried into the carriage, where she came last, alone, and where she took the place she had occupied during the first part of the journey.

They seemed not to see her or know her; although Madame Loiseau, looking at her from afar, said to her husband in a half-tone: "Happily, I don't have to sit beside her."

The heavy carriage began to move and the remainder of the journey commenced. No one spoke at first. Ball-of-Fat dared not raise her eyes. She felt indignant toward all her neighbors, and at the same time humiliated at having yielded to the foul kisses of this Prussian, into whose arms they had hypocritically thrown her.

Then the Countess, turning toward Mrs. Carré-Lamadon, broke the difficult silence:

"I believe you know Madame d'Etrelles?"

"Yes, she is one of my friends."

"What a charming woman!"

"Delightful! A very gentle nature, and well educated, besides; then she is an artist to the tips of her fingers, sings beautifully, and draws to perfection."

The manufacturer chatted with the Count, and in the midst of the rattling of the glass, an occasional word escaped such as "coupon — premium — limit — expiration."

Loiseau, who had pilfered the old pack of cards from the inn, greasy through five years of contact with tables badly cleaned, began a game of bezique with his wife.

The good sisters took from their belt the long rosary which hung there, made together the sign of the cross, and suddenly began to move their lips in a lively manner, hurrying more and more, hastening their vague murmur, as if they were going through the whole of the "Oremus." And from time to time they kissed a medal, made the sign anew, then recommenced their muttering, which was rapid and continued.

Cornudet sat motionless, thinking.

At the end of three hours on the way, Loiseau put up the cards and said: "I am hungry."

His wife drew out a package from whence she brought a piece of cold veal. She cut it evenly in thin pieces and they both began to eat.

"Suppose we do the same," said the Countess. They consented to it and she undid the provisions prepared for the two couples. It was in one of those dishes whose lid is decorated with a china hare, to

211

signify that a *pâté* of hare is inside, a succulent dish
of pork, where white rivers of lard cross the brown
flesh of the game, mixed with some other viands
hashed fine. A beautiful square of Gruyère cheese,
wrapped in a piece of newspaper, preserved the im-
print "divers things" upon the unctuous plate.

The two good sisters unrolled a big sausage which
smelled of garlic; and Cornudet plunged his two hands
into the vast pockets of his overcoat, at the same
time, and drew out four hard eggs and a piece o
bread. He removed the shells and threw them in the
straw under his feet; then he began to eat the eggs,
letting fall on his vast beard some bits of clear yellow, which looked like stars caught there.

Ball-of-Fat, in the haste and distraction of he
rising, had not thought of anything; and she looked
at them exasperated, suffocating with rage, at all o
them eating so placidly. A tumultuous anger swep
over her at first, and she opened her mouth to cry
out at them, to hurl at them a flood of injury which
mounted to her lips; but she could not speak, he
exasperation strangled her.

No one looked at her or thought of her. She fel
herself drowned in the scorn of these honest scoun
drels, who had first sacrificed her and then rejecte
her, like some improper or useless article. Sh
thought of her great basket full of good things which
they had greedily devoured, of her two chicken
shining with jelly, of her *pâtés*, her pears, and th
four bottles of Bordeaux; and her fury suddenly fall
ing, as a cord drawn too tightly breaks, she fel
ready to weep. She made terrible efforts to preven
it, making ugly faces, swallowing her sobs as chil

dren do, but the tears came and glistened in the corners of her eyes, and then two great drops, detaching themselves from the rest, rolled slowly down her cheeks. Others followed rapidly, running down like little streams of water that filter through rock, and, falling regularly, rebounded upon her breast. She sits erect, her eyes fixed, her face rigid and pale, hoping that no one will notice her.

But the Countess perceives her and tells her husband by a sign. He shrugs his shoulders, as much as to say:

"What would you have me do, it is not my fault."

Mrs. Loiseau indulged in a mute laugh of triumph and murmured:

"She weeps for shame."

The two good sisters began to pray again, after having wrapped in a paper the remainder of their sausage.

Then Cornudet, who was digesting his eggs, extended his legs to the seat opposite, crossed them, folded his arms, smiled like a man who is watching a good farce, and began to whistle the "Marseillaise."

All faces grew dark. The popular song assuredly did not please his neighbors. They became nervous and agitated, having an appearance of wishing to howl, like dogs, when they hear a barbarous organ. He perceived this but did not stop. Sometimes he would hum the words:

> "Sacred love of country
> Help, sustain th' avenging arm;
> Liberty, sweet Liberty
> Ever fight, with no alarm."

They traveled fast, the snow being harder. But as far as Dieppe, during the long, sad hours of the journey, across the jolts in the road, through the falling night, in the profound darkness of the carriage, he continued his vengeful, monotonous whistling with a ferocious obstinacy, constraining his neighbors to follow the song from one end to the other, and to recall the words that belonged to each measure.

And Ball-of-Fat wept continually; and sometimes a sob, which she was not able to restrain, echoed between the two rows of people in the shadows.

YVETTE

CHAPTER I.

THE INITIATION OF SAVAL

A S THEY were leaving the Café Riche, Jean de Servigny said to Léon Saval: "If you don't object, let us walk. The weather is too fine to take a cab."

His friend answered: "I would like nothing better."

Jean replied: "It is hardly eleven o'clock. We shall arrive much before midnight, so let us go slowly."

A restless crowd was moving along the boulevard, that throng peculiar to summer nights, drinking, chatting, and flowing like a river, filled with a sense of comfort and joy. Here and there a *café* threw a flood of light upon a knot of patrons drinking at little tables on the sidewalk, which were covered with bottles and glasses, hindering the passing of the hurrying multitude. On the pavement the cabs with their red, blue, or green lights dashed by, showing for a second, in the glimmer, the thin shadow of the horse, the raised profile of the coachman, and the dark box of the carriage. The cabs of the Urbaine Company made clear and rapid spots when their yellow panels were struck by the light.

The two friends walked with slow steps, cigars in their mouths, in evening dress and overcoats on their arms, with a flower in their buttonholes, and their hats a trifle on one side, as men will carelessly wear them sometimes, after they have dined well and the air is mild.

They had been linked together since their college days by a close, devoted, and firm affection. Jean de Servigny, small, slender, a trifle bald, rather frail, with elegance of mien, curled mustache, bright eyes, and fine lips, was a man who seemed born and bred upon the boulevard. He was tireless in spite of his languid air, strong in spite of his pallor, one of those slight Parisians to whom gymnastic exercise, fencing, cold shower and hot baths give a nervous, artificial strength. He was known by his marriage as well as by his wit, his fortune, his connections, and by that sociability, amiability, and fashionable gallantry peculiar to certain men.

A true Parisian, furthermore, light, sceptical, changeable, captivating, energetic, and irresolute, capable of everything and of nothing; selfish by principle and generous on occasion, he lived moderately upon his income, and amused himself with hygiene. Indifferent and passionate, he gave himself rein and drew back constantly, impelled by conflicting instincts, yielding to all, and then obeying, in

216

the end, his own shrewd man-about-town judgment, whose weather-vane logic consisted in following the wind and drawing profit from circumstances without taking the trouble to originate them.

His companion, Léon Saval, rich also, was one of those superb and colossal figures who make women turn around in the streets to look at them. He gave the idea of a statue turned into a man, a type of a race, like those sculptured forms which are sent to the Salons. Too handsome, too tall, too big, too strong, he sinned a little from the excess of everything, the excess of his qualities. He had on hand countless affairs of passion.

As they reached the Vaudeville theater, he asked: "Have you warned that lady that you are going to take me to her house to see her?"

Servigny began to laugh: "Forewarn the Marquise Obardi! Do you warn an omnibus driver that you shall enter his stage at the corner of the boulevard?"

Saval, a little perplexed, inquired: "What sort of person is this lady?"

His friend replied: "An upstart, a charming hussy, who came from no one knows where, who made her appearance one day, nobody knows how, among the adventuresses of Paris, knowing perfectly well how to take care of herself. Besides, what difference does it make to us? They say that her real name, her maiden name—for she still has every claim to the title of maiden except that of innocence—is Octavia Bardin, from which she constructs the name Obardi by prefixing the first letter of her first name and dropping the last letter of the last name.

"Moreover, she is a lovable woman, and you, from your physique, are inevitably bound to become her lover. Hercules is not introduced into Messalina's home without making some disturbance. Nevertheless I make bold to add that if there is free entrance to this house, just as there is in bazaars, you are not exactly compelled to buy what is for sale. Love and cards are on the programme, but nobody compels you to take up with either. And the exit is as free as the entrance.

"She settled down in the Etoile district, a suspicious neighborhood, three years ago, and opened her drawing-room to that froth of the continents which comes to Paris to practice its various formidable and criminal talents.

"I don't remember just how I went to her house. I went as we all go, because there is card playing, because the women are compliant, and the men dishonest. I love that social mob of buccaneers with decorations of all sorts of orders, all titled, and all entirely unknown at their embassies, except to the spies. They are always dragging in the subject of honor, quoting the list of their ancestors on the slightest provocation, and telling the story of their life at every opportunity, braggarts, liars, sharpers, dangerous as their cards, false as their names, brave because they have to be, like the assassins who can not pluck their victims except by exposing their own lives. In a word, it is the aristocracy of the bagnio.

"I like them. They are interesting to fathom and to know, amusing to listen to, often witty, never commonplace as the ordinary French guests. Their women are always pretty, with a little flavor of foreign knavery, with the mystery of their past existence, half of which, perhaps, spent in a House of Correction. They generally have fine eyes and glorious hair, the true physique of the profession, an intoxicating grace, a seductiveness which drives men to folly, an unwholesome, irresistible charm! They conquer like the highwaymen of old. They are rapacious creatures, true birds of prey. I like them, too.

"The Marquise Obardi is one of the type of these elegant good-for-nothings. Ripe and pretty, with a feline charm, you can see that she is vicious to the marrow. Everybody has a good time at her house, with cards, dancing, and suppers; in fact there is everything which goes to make up the pleasures of fashionable society life."

"Have you ever been or are you now her lover?" Léon Saval asked.

"I have not been her lover, I am not now, and I never shall be. I only go to the house to see her daughter."

"Ah! She has a daughter, then?"

"A daughter! A marvel, my dear man. She is the principal attraction of the den to-day. Tall, magnificent, just ripe, eighteen years old, as fair as her mother is dark, always merry, always ready for an entertainment, always laughing, and ready to dance like mad. Who will be the lucky man to capture her, or who has already done so? Nobody can tell that. She has ten of us in her train, all hoping.

"Such a daughter in the hands of a woman like the Marquise is a fortune. And they play the game together, the two charmers. No one knows just what they are planning. Perhaps they are waiting for a better bargain than I should prove. But I tell you that I shall close the bargain if I ever get a chance.

"That girl Yvette absolutely baffles me, moreover. She is a mystery. If she is not the most complete monster of astuteness and perversity that I have ever seen, she certainly is the most marvelous phenomenon of innocence that can be imagined. She lives in that atmosphere of infamy with a calm and triumphing ease which is either wonderfully profligate or entirely artless. Strange scion of an adventuress, cast upon the muck-heap of that set, like a magnificent plant nurtured upon corruption, or rather like the daughter of some noble race, of some great artist, or of some grand lord, of some prince or dethroned king, tossed some evening into her mother's arms, nobody can make out what she is nor what she thinks. But you are going to see her."

Saval began to laugh and said: "You are in love with her."

"No. I am on the list, which is not precisely the same thing. I will introduce you to my most serious rivals. But the chances are in my favor. I am in the lead, and some little distinction is shown to me."

"You are in love," Saval repeated.

"No. She disquiets me, seduces and disturbs me, attracts and frightens me away. I mistrust her as I would a trap, and I long for her as I long for a sherbet when I am thirsty. I yield to her charm, and I only approach her with the apprehension that I would feel concerning a man who was known to be a skillful thief. In her presence I have an irrational impulse toward belief in her possible purity and a very reasonable mistrust of her not less probable trickery. I feel myself in contact with an abnormal being, beyond the pale of natural laws, an exquisite or detestable creature — I don't know which."

For the third time Saval said: "I tell you that you are in love. You speak of her with the magniloquence of a poet and the feeling of a troubadour. Come, search your heart, and confess."

Servigny walked a few steps without answering. Then he replied:

"That is possible, after all. In any case, she fills my mind almost continually. Yes, perhaps I am in love. I dream about her too much. I think of her when I am asleep and when I awake — that is surely a grave indication. Her face follows me, accompanies me ceaselessly, ever before me, around me, with me. Is this love, this physical infatuation? Her features are so stamped upon my vision that I see her the moment I shut my eyes. My heart beats quickly every time I look at her, I don't deny it.

"So I am in love with her, but in a queer fashion. I have the strongest desire for her, and yet the idea of making her my wife would seem to me a folly, a piece of stupidity, a monstrous thing. And I have a little fear of her, as well, the fear which a bird feels over which a hawk is hovering.

"And again I am jealous of her, jealous of all of which I am ignorant in her incomprehensible heart. I am always wondering: 'Is she a charming youngster or a wretched jade?' She says things that would make an army shudder; but so does a parrot. She is at times so indiscreet and yet modest that I am forced to believe in her spotless purity, and again so incredibly artless that I must suspect that she has never been chaste. She allures me, excites me, like a woman of a certain category, and at the same time acts like an impeccable virgin. She seems to love me and yet makes fun of me; she deports herself in public as if she were my mistress and treats me in private as if I were her brother or footman.

"There are times when I fancy that she has as many lovers as her mother. And at other times I imagine that she suspects absolutely nothing of that sort of life, you understand. Furthermore, she is a great novel reader. I am at present, while awaiting something better, her book purveyor. She calls me her 'librarian.' Every week the New Book Store sends her, on my orders, everything new that has appeared, and I believe that she reads everything at random. It must make a strange sort of mixture in her head.

"That kind of literary hasty-pudding accounts perhaps for some of the girl's peculiar ways. When a young woman looks at existence through the medium of fifteen thousand novels, she must see it in a strange light, and construct queer ideas about matters and things in general. As for me, I am waiting. It is certain at any rate that I never have had for any other woman the devotion which I have had for her. And still it is quite certain that I shall never marry her. So if she has had numbers, I shall swell the number. And if she has not, I shall take the first ticket, just as I would do for a street car.

"The case is very simple. Of course, she will never marry. Who in the world would marry the

Marquise Obardi's daughter, the child of Octavia Bardin? Nobody, for a thousand reasons. Where would they ever find a husband for her? In society? Never. The mother's house is a sort of liberty-hall whose patronage is attracted by the daughter. Girls don't get married under those conditions.

"Would she find a husband among the tradespeople? Still less would that be possible. And besides the Marquise is not the woman to make a bad bargain; she will give Yvette only to a man of high position, and that man she will never discover.

"Then perhaps she will look among the common people. Still less likely. There is no solution of the problem, then. This young lady belongs neither to society, nor to the tradesmen's class, nor to the common people, and she can never enter any of these ranks by marriage.

"She belongs through her mother, her birth, her education, her inheritance, her manners, and her customs, to the vortex of the most rapid life of Paris. She can never escape it, save by becoming a nun, which is not at all probable with her manners and tastes. She has only one possible career, a life of pleasure. She will come to it sooner or later, if indeed she has not already begun to tread its primrose path. She cannot escape her fate. From being a young girl she will take the inevitable step, quite simply. And I would like to be the pivot of this transformation.

"I am waiting. There are many lovers. You will see among them a Frenchman, Monsieur de Belvigne; a Russian, called Prince Kravalow, and an Italian, Chevalier Valreali, who have all announced their candidacies and who are consequently maneuvering to the best of their ability. In addition to these there are several freebooters of less importance. The Marquise waits and watches. But I think that she has views about me. She knows that I am very rich, and she makes less of the others.

"Her drawing-room is, moreover, the most astounding that I know of, in such exhibitions. You even meet very decent men there, like ourselves. As for the women, she has culled the best there is from the basket of pickpockets. Nobody knows where she found them. It is a set apart from Bohemia, apart from everything. She has had one inspiration showing genius, and that is the knack of selecting especially those adventuresses who have children, generally girls. So that a fool might believe that in her house he was among respectable women!"

They had reached the avenue of the Champs-Elysées. A gentle breeze softly stirred the leaves and touched the faces of passers-by, like the breaths of a giant fan, waving somewhere in the sky. Silent shadows wandered beneath the trees; others, on benches, made a dark spot. And these shadows spoke very low, as if they were telling each other important or shameful secrets.

"You can't imagine what a collection of fictitious titles are met in this lair," said Servigny. "By the way, I shall present you by the name of Count Saval; plain Saval would not do at all."

"Oh, no, indeed!" cried his friend; "I would not have anyone think me capable of borrowing a title, even for an evening, even among those people. Ah, no!"

224

Servigny began to laugh.

"How stupid you are! Why, in that set they call me the Duke de Servigny. I don't know how nor why. But at any rate the Duke de Servigny I am and shall remain, without complaining or protesting. It does not worry me. I should have no footing there whatever without a title."

But Saval would not be convinced.

"Well, you are of rank, and so you may remain. But, as for me, no. I shall be the only common person in the drawing-room. So much the worse, or, so much the better. It will be my mark of distinction and superiority."

Servigny was obstinate.

"I tell you that it is not possible. Why, it would almost seem monstrous. You would have the effect of a ragman at a meeting of emperors. Let me do as I like. I shall introduce you as the Vice-Roi du 'Haut-Mississippi,' and no one will be at all astonished. When a man takes on greatness, he can't take too much."

"Once more, no, I do not wish it."

"Very well, have your way. But, in fact, I am very foolish to try to convince you. I defy you to get in without some one giving you a title, just as they give a bunch of violets to the ladies at the entrance to certain stores."

They turned to the right in the Rue de Barrie, mounted one flight of stairs in a fine modern house, and gave their overcoats and canes into the hands of four servants in knee-breeches. A warm odor, as of a festival assembly, filled the air, an odor of flowers, perfumes, and women; and a composed and continuous murmur came from the adjoining rooms, which were filled with people.

A kind of master of ceremonies, tall, erect, wide of girth, serious, his face framed in white whiskers, approached the newcomers, asking with a short and haughty bow: "Whom shall I announce?"

"Monsieur Saval," Servigny replied.

Then with a loud voice, the man opening the door cried out to the crowd of guests:

"Monsieur the Duke de Servigny.

"Monsieur the Baron Saval."

The first drawing-room was filled with women. The first thing which attracted attention was the display of bare shoulders, above a flood of brilliant gowns.

The mistress of the house who stood talking with three friends, turned and came forward with a majestic step, with grace in her mien and a smile on her lips. Her forehead was narrow and very low, and was covered with a mass of glossy black hair, encroaching a little upon the temples.

She was tall, a trifle too large, a little too stout, over ripe, but very pretty, with a heavy, warm, potent beauty. Beneath that mass of hair, full of dreams and smiles, rendering her mysteriously captivating, were enormous black eyes. Her nose was a little narrow, her mouth large and infinitely seductive, made to speak and to conquer.

Her greatest charm was in her voice. It came from that mouth as water from a spring, so natural, so light, so well modulated, so clear, that there was a physical pleasure in listening to it. It was a joy for the ear to hear the flexible words flow with the

grace of a babbling brook, and it was a joy for the
eyes to see those pretty lips, a trifle too red, open as
the words rippled forth.

She gave one hand to Servigny, who kissed it,
and dropping her fan on its little gold chain, she gave
the other to Saval, saying to him: "You are welcome, Baron, all the Duke's friends are at home
here."

Then she fixed her brilliant eyes upon the Colossus
who had just been introduced to her. She had just
the slightest down on her upper lip, a suspicion of a
mustache, which seemed darker when she spoke.
There was a pleasant odor about her, pervading, intoxicating, some perfume of America or of the Indies.
Other people came in, marquesses, counts or princes.
She said to Servigny, with the graciousness of a
mother: "You will find my daughter in the other
parlor. Have a good time, gentlemen, the house is
yours."

And she left them to go to those who had come
later, throwing at Saval that smiling and fleeting
glance which women use to show that they are
pleased. Servigny grasped his friend's arm.

"I will pilot you," said he. "In this parlor
where we now are, women, the temples of the
fleshly, fresh or otherwise. Bargains as good as
new, even better, for sale or on lease. At the right,
gaming, the temple of money. You understand all
about that. At the lower end, dancing, the temple
of innocence, the sanctuary, the market for young
girls. They are shown off there in every light.
Even legitimate marriages are tolerated. It is the
future, the hope, of our evenings. And the most

curious part of this museum of moral diseases are these young girls whose souls are out of joint, just like the limbs of the little clowns born of mountebanks. Come and look at them."

He bowed, right and left, courteously, a compliment on his lips, sweeping each low-gowned woman whom he knew with the look of an expert.

The musicians, at the end of the second parlor, were playing a waltz; and the two friends stopped at the door to look at them. A score of couples were whirling — the men with a serious expression, and the women with a fixed smile on their lips. They displayed a good deal of shoulder, like their mothers; and the bodices of some were only held in place by a slender ribbon, disclosing at times more than is generally shown.

Suddenly from the end of the room a tall girl darted forward, gliding through the crowd, brushing against the dancers, and holding her long train in her left hand. She ran with quick little steps as women do in crowds, and called out: "Ah! How is Muscade? How do you do, Muscade?"

Her features wore an expression of the bloom of life, the illumination of happiness. Her white flesh seemed to shine, the golden-white flesh which goes with red hair. The mass of her tresses, twisted on her head, fiery, flaming locks, nestled against her supple neck, which was still a little thin.

She seemed to move just as her mother was made to speak, so natural, noble, and simple were her gestures. A person felt a moral joy and physical pleasure in seeing her walk, stir about, bend her head, or lift her arm.

"Ah! Muscade, how do you do, Muscade?" she repeated.

Servigny shook her hand violently, as he would a man's, and said: "Mademoiselle Yvette, my friend, Baron Saval."

"Good evening, Monsieur. Are you always as tall as that?"

Servigny replied in that bantering tone which he always used with her, in order to conceal his mistrust and his uncertainty:

"No, Mam'zelle. He has put on his greatest dimensions to please your mother, who loves a colossus."

And the young girl remarked with a comic seriousness: "Very well! But when you come to see me you must diminish a little if you please. I prefer the medium height. Now Muscade has just the proportions which I like."

And she gave her hand to the newcomer. Then she asked: "Do you dance, Muscade? Come, let us waltz." Without replying, with a quick movement, passionately, Servigny clasped her waist and they disappeared with the fury of a whirlwind.

They danced more rapidly than any of the others, whirled and whirled, and turned madly, so close together that they seemed but one, and with the form erect, the legs almost motionless, as if some invisible mechanism, concealed beneath their feet, caused them to twirl. They appeared tireless. The other dancers stopped from time to time. They still danced on, alone. They seemed not to know where they were nor what they were doing, as if they had gone far away from the ball, in an ecstasy. The musicians

continued to play, with their looks fixed upon this
mad couple; all the guests gazed at them, and when
finally they did stop dancing, everyone applauded
them.

She was a little flushed, with strange eyes, ardent
and timid, less daring than a moment before, troubled
eyes, blue, yet with a pupil so black that they seemed
hardly natural. Servigny appeared giddy. He leaned
against a door to regain his composure.

"You have no head, my poor Muscade, I am
steadier than you," said Yvette to Servigny.

He smiled nervously, and devoured her with a
look. His animal feelings revealed themselves in his
eyes and in the curl of his lips. She stood beside
him looking down, and her bosom rose and fell in
short gasps as he looked at her.

Then she said softly: "Really, there are times
when you are like a tiger about to spring upon his
prey. Come, give me your arm, and let us find
your friend."

Silently he offered her his arm and they went
down the long drawing-room together.

Saval was not alone, for the Marquise Obardi had
rejoined him. She conversed with him on ordinary
and fashionable subjects with a seductiveness in her
tones which intoxicated him. And, looking at her
with his mental eye, it seemed to him that her lips
uttered words far different from those which they
formed. When she saw Servigny her face immediately lighted up, and turning toward him she said:

"You know, my dear Duke, that I have just
leased a villa at Bougival for two months, and I
count upon your coming to see me there, and upon

your friend also. Listen. We take possession next Monday, and shall expect both of you to dinner the following Saturday. We shall keep you over Sunday."

Perfectly serene and tranquil Yvette smiled, saying with a decision which swept away hesitation on his part:

"Of course Muscade will come to dinner on Saturday. We have only to ask him, for he and I intend to commit a lot of follies in the country."

He thought he divined the birth of a promise in her smile, and in her voice he heard what he thought was invitation.

Then the Marquise turned her big, black eyes upon Saval: "And you will, of course, come, Baron?"

With a smile that forbade doubt, he bent toward her, saying, "I shall be only too charmed, Madame."

Then Yvette murmured with malice that was either naïve or traitorous: "We will set all the world by the ears down there, won't we, Muscade, and make my regiment of admirers fairly mad." And with a look, she pointed out a group of men who were looking at them from a little distance.

Said Servigny to her: "As many follies as *you* may please, Mam'zelle."

In speaking to Yvette, Servigny never used the word "Mademoiselle," by reason of his close and long intimacy with her.

Then Saval asked: "Why does Mademoiselle always call my friend Servigny 'Muscade'?"

Yvette assumed a very frank air and said:

"I will tell you: It is because he always slips through my hands. Now I think I have him, and then I find I have not."

231

The Marquise, with her eyes upon Saval, and evidently preoccupied, said in a careless tone: "You children are very funny."

But Yvette bridled up: "I do not intend to be funny; I am simply frank. Muscade pleases me, and is always deserting me, and that is what annoys me."

Servigny bowed profoundly, saying: "I will never leave you any more, Mam'zelle, neither day nor night."

She made a gesture of horror:

"My goodness! no—what do you mean? You are all right during the day, but at night you might embarrass me."

With an air of impertinence he asked: "And why?"

Yvette responded calmly and audaciously, "Because you would not look well *en déshabillé.*"

The Marquise, without appearing at all disturbed, said: "What extraordinary subjects for conversation. One would think that you were not at all ignorant of such things."

And Servigny jokingly added: "That is also my opinion, Marquise."

Yvette turned her eyes upon him, and in a haughty, yet wounded, tone said: "You are becoming very vulgar—just as you have been several times lately." And turning quickly she appealed to an individual standing by:

"Chevalier, come and defend me from insult."

A thin, brown man, with an easy carriage, came forward.

"Who is the culprit?" said he, with a constrained smile.

Yvette pointed out Servigny with a nod of her head:

"There he is, but I like him better than I do you, because he is less of a bore."

The Chevalier Valreali bowed:

"I do what I can, Mademoiselle. I may have less ability, but not less devotion."

A gentleman came forward, tall and stout, with gray whiskers, saying in loud tones: "Mademoiselle Yvette, I am your most devoted slave."

Yvette cried: "Ah, Monsieur de Belvigne." Then turning toward Saval, she introduced him.

"My last adorer — big, fat, rich, and stupid. Those are the kind I like. A veritable drum-major — but of the *table d'hôte*. But see, you are still bigger than he. How shall I nickname you? Good! I have it. I shall call you 'M. Colossus of Rhodes, Junior,' from the Colossus who certainly was your father. But you two ought to have very interesting things to say to each other up there, above the heads of us all — so, by-bye."

And she left them quickly, going to the orchestra to make the musicians strike up a quadrille.

Madame Obardi seemed preoccupied. In a soft voice she said to Servigny:

"You are always teasing her. You will warp her character and bring out many bad traits."

Servigny replies: "Why, haven't you finished her education?"

She appeared not to understand, and continued talking in a friendly way. But she noticed a solemn looking man, wearing a perfect constellation of crosses and orders, standing near her, and she ran to him:

"Ah! Prince, Prince, what good fortune!"

Servigny took Saval's arm and drew him away:

"That is the latest serious suitor, Prince Krava-low. Isn't she superb?"

"To my mind they are both superb. The mother would suffice for me perfectly," answered Saval.

Servigny nodded and said: "At your disposal, my dear boy."

The dancers elbowed them aside, as they were forming for a quadrille.

"Now let us go and see the sharpers," said Servigny. And they entered the gambling-room.

Around each table stood a group of men, looking on. There was very little conversation. At times the clink of gold coins, tossed upon the green cloth or hastily seized, added its sound to the murmur of the players, just as if the money was putting in its word among the human voices.

All the men were decorated with various orders, and odd ribbons, and they all wore the same severe expression, with different countenances. The especially distinguishing feature was the beard.

The stiff American with his horseshoe, the haughty Englishman with his fan-beard open on his breast, the Spaniard with his black fleece reaching to the eyes, the Roman with that huge mustache which Italy copied from Victor Emmanuel, the Austrian with his whiskers and shaved chin, a Russian general whose lip seemed armed with two twisted lances, and a Frenchman with a dainty mustache, displayed the fancies of all the barbers in the world.

"You won't join the game?" asked Servigny.

"No, shall you?"

"Not now. If you are ready to go, we will come back some quieter day. There are too many people here to-day, and we can't do anything."

"Well, let us go."

And they disappeared behind a door-curtain into the hall. As soon as they were in the street Servigny asked: "Well, what do you think of it?"

"It certainly is interesting, but I fancy the women's side of it more than the men's."

"Indeed! Those women are the best of the tribe for us. Don't you find that you breathe the odor of love among them, just as you scent the perfumes at a hairdresser's?"

"Really such houses are the place for one to go. And what experts, my dear fellow! What artists! Have you ever eaten bakers' cakes? They look well, but they amount to nothing. The man who bakes them only knows how to make bread. Well! the love of a woman in ordinary society always reminds me of these bake-shop trifles, while the love you find at houses like the Marquise Obardi's, don't you see, is the real sweetmeat. Oh! they know how to make cakes, these charming pastry-cooks. Only you pay five sous, at their shops, for what costs two sous elsewhere."

"Who is the master of the house just now?" asked Saval.

Servigny shrugged his shoulders, signifying his ignorance.

"I don't know, the latest one known was an English peer, but he left three months ago. At present she must live off the common herd, or the gambling, perhaps, and on the gamblers, for she has her caprices. But tell me, it is understood that we dine with her on Saturday at Bougival, is it not? People are more free in the country, and I shall succeed in finding out what ideas Yvette has in her head!"

"I should like nothing better," replied Saval. "I have nothing to do that day."

Passing down through the Champs-Elysées, under the steps they disturbed a couple making love on one of the benches, and Servigny muttered: "What foolishness and what a serious matter at the same time! How commonplace and amusing love is, always the same and always different! And the beggar who gives his sweetheart twenty sous gets as much return as I would for ten thousand francs from some Obardi, no younger and no less stupid perhaps than this nondescript. What nonsense!"

He said nothing for a few minutes; then he began again: "All the same, it would be good to become Yvette's first lover. Oh! for that I would give—"

He did not add what he would give, and Saval said good night to him as they reached the corner of the Rue Royale.

CHAPTER II.

BOUGIVAL AND LOVE

THEY had set the table on the veranda which overlooked the river. The Printemps villa, leased by the Marquise Obardi, was halfway up this hill, just at the corner of the Seine, which turned before the garden wall, flowing toward Marly.

Opposite the residence, the island of Croissy formed a horizon of tall trees, a mass of verdure, and they could see a long stretch of the big river as far as the floating *café* of La Grenouillère hidden beneath the foliage.

The evening fell, one of those calm evenings at the waterside, full of color yet soft, one of those peaceful evenings which produces a sensation of pleasure. No breath of air stirred the branches, no shiver of wind ruffled the smooth clear surface of the Seine. It was not too warm, it was mild — good weather to live in. The grateful coolness of the banks of the Seine rose toward a serene sky.

The sun disappeared behind the trees to shine on

other lands, and one seemed to absorb the serenity of the already sleeping earth, to inhale, in the peace of space, the life of the infinite.

As they left the drawing-room to seat themselves at the table everyone was joyous. A softened gaiety filled their hearts, they felt that it would be so delightful to dine there in the country, with that great river and that twilight for a setting, breathing that pure and fragrant air.

The Marquise had taken Saval's arm, and Yvette, Servigny's. The four were alone by themselves. The two women seemed entirely different persons from what they were at Paris, especially Yvette. She talked but little, and seemed languid and grave.

Saval, hardly recognizing her in this frame of mind, asked her: "What is the matter, Mademoiselle? I find you changed since last week. You have become quite a serious person."

"It is the country that does that for me," she replied. "I am not the same, I feel queer; besides I am never two days alike. To-day I have the air of a mad woman, and to-morrow shall be as grave as an elegy. I change with the weather, I don't know why. You see, I am capable of anything, according to the moment. There are days when I would like to kill people,— not animals, I would never kill animals,— but people, yes, and other days when I weep at a mere thing. A lot of different ideas pass through my head. It depends, too, a good deal on how I get up. Every morning, on waking, I can tell just what I shall be in the evening. Perhaps it is our dreams that settle it for us, and it depends on the book I have just read."

She was clad in a white flannel suit which delicately enveloped her in the floating softness of the material. Her bodice, with full folds, suggested, without displaying and without restraining, her free chest, which was firm and already ripe. And her superb neck emerged from a froth of soft lace, bending with gentle movements, fairer than her gown, a pilaster of flesh, bearing the heavy mass of her golden hair.

Servigny looked at her for a long time: "You are adorable this evening, Mam'zelle," said he, "I wish I could always see you like this."

"Don't make a declaration, Muscade. I should take it seriously, and that might cost you dear."

The Marquise seemed happy, very happy. All in black, richly dressed in a plain gown which showed her strong, full lines, a bit of red at the bodice, a cincture of red carnations falling from her waist like a chain, and fastened at the hips, and a red rose in her dark hair, she carried in all her person something fervid,—in that simple costume, in those flowers which seemed to bleed, in her look, in her slow speech, in her peculiar gestures.

Saval, too, appeared serious and absorbed. From time to time he stroked his pointed beard, trimmed in the fashion of Henri III., and seemed to be meditating on the most profound subjects.

Nobody spoke for several minutes. Then as they were serving the trout, Servigny remarked:

"Silence is a good thing, at times. People are often nearer to each other when they are keeping still than when they are talking. Isn't that so, Marquise?"

She turned a little toward him and answered:

"It is quite true. It is so sweet to think together about agreeable things.

She raised her warm glance toward Saval, and they continued for some seconds looking into each other's eyes. A slight, almost inaudible movement took place beneath the table.

Servigny resumed: "Mam'zelle Yvette, you will make me believe that you are in love if you keep on being as good as that. Now, with whom could you be in love? Let us think together, if you will; I put aside the army of vulgar sighers. I'll only take the principal ones. Is it Prince Kravalow?"

At this name Yvette awoke: "My poor Muscade, can you think of such a thing? Why, the Prince has the air of a Russian in a wax-figure museum, who has won medals in a hairdressing competition."

"Good! We'll drop the Prince. But you have noticed the Viscount Pierre de Belvigne?"

This time she began to laugh, and asked: "Can you imagine me hanging to the neck of 'Raisiné'?" She nicknamed him according to the day, Raisiné, Malvoisie,* Argenteuil, for she gave everybody nicknames. And she would murmur to his face: "My dear little Pierre," or "My divine Pedro, darling Pierrot, give your bow-wow's head to your dear little girl, who wants to kiss it."

"Scratch out number two. There still remains the Chevalier Valreali whom the Marquise seems to favor," continued Servigny.

Yvette regained all her gaiety: "'Teardrop'?

---

* Preserved grapes and pears, malmsey, — a poor wine.

Why he weeps like a Magdalene. He goes to all the first-class funerals. I imagine myself dead every time he looks at me."

"That settles the third. So the lightning will strike Baron Saval, here."

"Monsieur the Colossus of Rhodes, Junior? No. He is too strong. It would seem to me as if I were in love with the triumphal arch of L'Etoile."

"Then Mam'zelle, it is beyond doubt that you are in love with me, for I am the only one of your adorers of whom we have not yet spoken. I left myself for the last through modesty and through discretion. It remains for me to thank you."

She replied with happy grace: "In love with you, Muscade? Ah! no. I like you, but I don't love you. Wait — I — I don't want to discourage you. I don't love you — yet. You have a chance — perhaps. Persevere, Muscade, be devoted, ardent, submissive, full of little attentions and considerations, docile to my slightest caprices, ready for anything to please me, and we shall see — later."

"But, Mam'zelle, I would rather furnish all you demand afterward than beforehand, if it be the same to you."

She asked with an artless air: "After what, Muscade?"

"After you have shown me that you love me, by Jove!"

"Well, act as if I loved you, and believe it, if you wish."

"But you —"

"Be quiet, Muscade; enough on the subject."

The sun had sunk behind the island, but the

241

whole sky still flamed like a fire, and the peaceful water of the river seemed changed to blood. The reflections from the horizon reddened houses, objects, and persons. The scarlet rose in the Marquise's hair had the appearance of a splash of purple fallen from the clouds upon her head.

As Yvette looked on from her end, the Marquise rested, as if by carelessness, her bare hand upon Saval's hand; but the young girl made a motion and the Marquise withdrew her hand with a quick gesture, pretending to readjust something in the folds of her corsage.

Servigny, who was looking at them, said:

"If you like, Mam'zelle, we will take a walk on the island after dinner."

"Oh, yes! That will be delightful. We will go all alone, won't we, Muscade?"

"Yes, all alone, Mam'zelle!"

The vast silence of the horizon, the sleepy tranquillity of the evening captured heart, body, and voice. There are peaceful, chosen hours when it becomes almost impossible to talk.

The servants waited on them noiselessly. The firmamental conflagration faded away, and the soft night spread its shadows over the earth.

"Are you going to stay long in this place?" asked Saval.

And the Marquise answered, dwelling on each word: "Yes, as long as I am happy."

As it was too dark to see, lamps were brought. They cast upon the table a strange, pale gleam beneath the great obscurity of space; and very soon a shower of gnats fell upon the tablecloth — the tiny

242

gnats which immolate themselves by passing over the glass chimneys, and, with wings and legs scorched, powder the table-linen, dishes, and cups with a kind of gray and hopping dust.

They swallowed them in the wine, they ate them in the sauces, they saw them moving on the bread, and had their faces and hands tickled by the countless swarm of these tiny insects. They were continually compelled to throw away the beverages, to cover the plates, and while eating to shield the food with infinite precautions.

It amused Yvette. Servigny took care to shelter what she bore to her mouth, to guard her glass, to hold his handkerchief stretched out over her head like a roof. But the Marquise, disgusted, became nervous, and the end of the dinner came quickly. Yvette, who had not forgotten Servigny's proposition, said to him:

"Now we'll go to the island."

Her mother cautioned her in a languid tone: "Don't be late, above all things. We will escort you to the ferry."

And they started in couples, the young girl and her admirer walking in front, on the road to the shore. They heard, behind them, the Marquise and Saval speaking very rapidly in low tones. All was dark, with a thick, inky darkness. But the sky swarmed with grains of fire, and seemed to sow them in the river, for the black water was flecked with stars.

The frogs were croaking monotonously upon the bank, and numerous nightingales were uttering their low, sweet song in the calm and peaceful air.

Yvette suddenly said: "Gracious! They are not walking behind us any more, where are they?" And she called out: "Mamma!" No voice replied. The young girl resumed: "At any rate, they can't be far away, for I heard them just now."

Servigny murmured: "They must have gone back. Your mother was cold, perhaps." And he drew her along.

Before them a light gleamed. It was the tavern of Martinet, restaurant-keeper and fisherman. At their call a man came out of the house, and they got into a large boat which was moored among the weeds of the shore.

The ferryman took his oars, and the unwieldy barge, as it advanced, disturbed the sleeping stars upon the water and set them into a mad dance, which gradually calmed down after they had passed. They touched the other shore and disembarked beneath the great trees. A cool freshness of damp earth permeated the air under the lofty and clustered branches, where there seemed to be as many nightingales as there were leaves. A distant piano began to play a popular waltz.

Servigny took Yvette's arm and very gently slipped his hand around her waist and gave her a slight hug.

"What are you thinking about?" he said.

"I? About nothing at all. I am very happy!"

"Then you don't love me?"

"Oh, yes, Muscade, I love you, I love you a great deal; only leave me alone. It is too beautiful here to listen to your nonsense."

He drew her toward him, although she tried, by

244

little pushes, to extricate herself, and through her soft
flannel gown he felt the warmth of her flesh. He
stammered:

"Yvette!"

"Well, what?"

"I do love you!"

"But you are not in earnest, Muscade."

"Oh, yes I am. I have loved you for a long
time."

She continually kept trying to separate herself from
him, trying to release the arm crushed between their
bodies. They walked with difficulty, trammeled by
this bond and by these movements, and went zigzagging along like drunken folk.

He knew not what to say to her, feeling that he
could not talk to a young girl as he would to a
woman. He was perplexed, thinking what he ought
to do, wondering if she consented or did not understand, and curbing his spirit to find just the right,
tender, and decisive words. He kept saying every
second:

"Yvette! Speak! Yvette!"

Then, suddenly, risking all, he kissed her on the
cheek. She gave a little start aside, and said with a
vexed air:

"Oh! you are absurd. Are you going to let me
alone?"

The tone of her voice did not at all reveal her
thoughts nor her wishes; and, not seeing her too
angry, he applied his lips to the beginning of her
neck, just beneath the golden hair, that charming
spot which he had so often coveted.

Then she made great efforts to free herself. But

he held her strongly, and placing his other hand on her shoulder, he compelled her to turn her head toward him and gave her a fond, passionate kiss, squarely on the mouth.

She slipped from his arms by a quick undulation of the body, and, free from his grasp, she disappeared into the darkness with a great swishing of skirts, like the whir of a bird as it flies away.

He stood motionless a moment, surprised by her suppleness and her disappearance, then hearing nothing, he called gently: "Yvette!"

She did not reply. He began to walk forward, peering through the shadows, looking in the underbrush for the white spot her dress should make. All was dark. He cried out more loudly:

"Mam'zelle Yvette! Mam'zelle Yvette!"

Nothing stirred. He stopped and listened. The whole island was still; there was scarcely a rustle of leaves over his head. The frogs alone continued their deep croakings on the shores. Then he wandered from thicket to thicket, going where the banks were steep and bushy and returning to places where they were flat and bare as a dead man's arm. He proceeded until he was opposite Bougival and reached the establishment of La Grenouillère, groping the clumps of trees, calling out continually:

"Mam'zelle Yvette, where are you? Answer. It is ridiculous! Come, answer! Don't keep me hunting like this."

A distant clock began to strike. He counted the hours: twelve. He had been searching through the island for two hours. Then he thought that perhaps she had gone home; and he went back very anxiously, this time by way of the bridge. A servant dozing on a chair was waiting in the hall.

Servigny awakened him and asked: "Is it long since Mademoiselle Yvette came home? I left her at the foot of the place because I had a call to make."

And the valet replied: "Oh! yes, Monsieur, Mademoiselle came in before ten o'clock."

He proceeded to his room and went to bed. But he could not close his eyes. That stolen kiss had stirred him to the soul. He kept wondering what she thought and what she knew. How pretty and attractive she was!

His desires, somewhat wearied by the life he led, by all his procession of sweethearts, by all his explorations in the kingdom of love, awoke before this singular child, so fresh, irritating, and inexplicable. He heard one o'clock strike, then two. He could not sleep at all. He was warm, he felt his heart beat and his temples throb, and he rose to open the window. A breath of fresh air came in, which he inhaled deeply. The thick darkness was silent, black, motionless. But suddenly he perceived before him, in the shadows of the garden, a shining point; it seemed a little red coal.

"Well, a cigar!" he said to himself. "It must be Saval," and he called softly: "Léon!"

"Is it you, Jean?"

"Yes. Wait. I'll come down." He dressed, went out, and rejoining his friend who was smoking astride an iron chair, inquired: "What are you doing here at this hour?"

"I am resting," Saval replied. And he began to laugh.

Servigny pressed his hand: "My compliments, my dear fellow. And as for me, I—am making a fool of myself."

"You mean—"

"I mean that—Yvette and her mother do not resemble each other."

"What has happened? Tell me."

Servigny recounted his attempts and their failure. Then he resumed:

"Decidedly, that little girl worries me. Fancy my not being able to sleep! What a queer thing a girl is! She appears to be as simple as anything, and yet you know nothing about her. A woman who has lived and loved, who knows life, can be quickly understood. But when it comes to a young virgin, on the contrary, no one can guess anything about her. At heart I begin to think that she is making sport of me."

Saval tilted his chair. He said, very slowly:

"Take care, my dear fellow, she will lead you to marriage. Remember those other illustrious examples. It was just by this same process that Mademoiselle de Montijo, who was at least of good family, became empress. Don't play Napoleon."

Servigny murmured: "As for that, fear nothing. I am neither a simpleton nor an emperor. A man must be either one or the other to make such a move as that. But tell me, are you sleepy?"

"Not a bit."

"Will you take a walk along the river?"

"Gladly."

They opened the iron gate and began to walk along the river bank toward Marly.

It was the quiet hour which precedes dawn, the hour of deep sleep, of complete rest, of profound peacefulness. Even the gentle sounds of the night were hushed. The nightingales sang no longer; the frogs had finished their hubbub; some kind of an animal only, probably a bird, was making somewhere a kind of sawing sound, feeble, monotonous, and regular as a machine. Servigny, who had moments of poetry and of philosophy too, suddenly remarked:

"Now this girl completely puzzles me. In arithmetic, one and one make two. In love one and one ought to make one but they make two just the same. Have you ever felt that? That need of absorbing a woman in yourself or disappearing in her? I am not speaking of the animal embrace, but of that moral and mental eagerness to be but one with a being, to open to her all one's heart and soul, and to fathom her thoughts to the depths.

"And yet you can never lay bare all the fluctuations of her wishes, desires, and opinions. You can never guess, even slightly, all the unknown currents, all the mystery of a soul that seems so near, a soul hidden behind two eyes that look at you, clear as water, transparent as if there were nothing beneath a soul which talks to you by a beloved mouth, which seems your very own, so greatly do you desire it; a soul which throws you by words its thoughts, one by one, and which, nevertheless, remains further away from you than those stars are from each other, and more impenetrable. Isn't it queer, all that?"

"I don't ask so much," Saval rejoined. "I don't look behind the eyes. I care little for the contents, but much for the vessel."

And Servigny replied: "What a singular person Yvette is! How will she receive me this morning?"

As they reached the works at Marly they perceived that the sky was brightening. The cocks began to crow in the poultry-yards. A bird twittered in a park at the left, ceaselessly reiterating a tender little theme.

"It is time to go back," said Saval.

They returned, and as Servigny entered his room, he saw the horizon all pink through his open windows.

Then he shut the blinds, drew the thick, heavy curtains, went back to bed and fell asleep. He dreamed of Yvette all through his slumber. An odd noise awoke him. He sat on the side of the bed and listened, but heard nothing further. Then suddenly there was a crackling against the blinds, like falling hail. He jumped from the bed, ran to the window, opened it, and saw Yvette standing in the path and throwing handfuls of gravel at his face. She was clad in pink, with a wide-brimmed straw hat ornamented with a mousquetaire plume, and was laughing mischievously.

"Well! Muscade, are you asleep? What could you have been doing all night to make you wake so late? Have you been seeking adventures, my poor Muscade?"

He was dazzled by the bright daylight striking him full in the eyes, still overwhelmed with fatigue, and surprised at the jesting tranquillity of the young girl.

"I'll be down in a second, Mam'zelle," he answered. "Just time to splash my face with water, and I will join you."

"Hurry," she cried, "it is ten o'clock, and besides I have a great plan to unfold to you, a plot we are going to concoct. You know that we breakfast at eleven."

He found her seated on a bench, with a book in her lap, some novel or other. She took his arm in a familiar and friendly way, with a frank and gay manner, as if nothing had happened the night before, and drew him toward the end of the garden.

"This is my plan," she said. "We will disobey mamma, and you shall take me presently to La Grenouillère restaurant. I want to see it. Mamma says that decent women cannot go to the place. Now it is all the same to me whether persons can go there or cannot. You'll take me, won't you, Muscade? And we will have a great time — with the boatmen."

She exhaled a delicious fragrance, although he could not exactly define just what light and vague odor enveloped her. It was not one of those heavy perfumes of her mother, but a discreet breath in which he fancied he could detect a suspicion of iris powder, and perhaps a suggestion of vervain.

Whence emanated that indiscernible perfume? From her dress, her hair, or her skin? He puzzled over this, and as he was speaking very close to her, he received full in the face her fresh breath, which seemed to him just as delicious to inhale.

Then he thought that this evasive perfume which he was trying to recognize was perhaps only evoked by her charming eyes, and was merely a sort of deceptive emanation of her young and alluring grace.

"That is agreed, isn't it, Muscade? As it will be very warm after breakfast, mamma will not go out.

She always feels the heat very much. We will leave her with your friend, and you shall take me. They will think that we have gone into the forest. If you knew how much it will amuse me to see La Grenouillère!

They reached the iron gate opposite the Seine. A flood of sunshine fell upon the slumberous, shining river. A slight heat-mist rose from it, a sort of haze of evaporated water, which spread over the surface of the stream a faint gleaming vapor.

From time to time, boats passed by, a quick yawl or a heavy passage boat, and short or long whistles could be heard, those of the trains which every Sunday poured the citizens of Paris into the suburbs, and those of the steamboats signaling their approach to pass the locks at Marly.

But a tiny bell sounded. Breakfast was announced, and they went back into the house. The repast was a silent one. A heavy July noon overwhelmed the earth, and oppressed humanity. The heat seemed thick, and paralyzed both mind and body. The sluggish words would not leave the lips, and all motion seemed laborious, as if the air had become a resisting medium, difficult to traverse. Only Yvette, although silent, seemed animated and nervous with impatience. As soon as they had finished the last course she said:

"If we were to go for a walk in the forest, it would be deliciously cool under the trees."

The Marquise murmured with a listless air: "Are you mad? Does anyone go out in such weather?"

And the young girl, delighted, rejoined: "Oh, well! We will leave the Baron to keep you company. Muscade and I will climb the hill and sit on the grass and read."

And turning toward Servigny she asked: "That is understood?"

"At your service, Mam'zelle," he replied.

Yvette ran to get her hat. The Marquise shrugged her shoulders with a sigh. "She certainly is mad." she said.

Then with an indolence in her amorous and lazy gestures, she gave her pretty white hand to the Baron, who kissed it softly. Yvette and Servigny started. They went along the river, crossed the bridge and went on to the island, and then seated themselves on the bank, beneath the willows, for it was too soon to go to La Grenouillére.

The young girl at once drew a book from her pocket and smilingly said: "Muscade, you are going to read to me." And she handed him the volume.

He made a motion as if of fright. "I, Mam'zelle? I don't know how to read!"

She replied with gravity: "Come, no excuses, no objections; you are a fine suitor, you! All for nothing, is that it? Is that your motto?"

He took the book, opened it, and was astonished. It was a treatise on entomology. A history of ants by an English author. And as he remained inert, believing that he was making sport of her, she said with impatience: "Well, read!"

"Is it a wager, or just a simple fad?" he asked.

"No, my dear. I saw that book in a shop. They told me that it was the best authority on ants and I thought that it would be interesting to learn about

WORKS OF GUY DE MAUPASSANT

the life of these little insects while you see them running over the grass; so read, if you please."

She stretched herself flat upon the grass, her elbows resting upon the ground, her head between her
hands, her eyes fixed upon the ground. He began to
read as follows:

"The anthropoid apes are undoubtedly the animals which approach nearest to man by their anatomical structure, but if we consider the habits of the ants, their organization into societies, their vast
communities, the houses and roads that they construct, their custom
of domesticating animals, and sometimes even of making slaves of
them, we are compelled to admit that they have the right to claim a
place near to man in the scale of intelligence."

He continued in a monotonous voice, stopping
from time to time to ask: "Isn't that enough?"

She shook her head, and having caught an ant on
the end of a severed blade of grass, she amused herself by making it go from one end to the other of
the sprig, which she tipped up whenever the insect
reached one of the ends. She listened with mute and
contented attention to all the wonderful details of the
life of these frail creatures: their subterranean homes;
the manner in which they seize, shut up, and feed
plant-lice to drink the sweet milk which they secrete,
as we keep cows in our barns; their custom of domesticating little blind insects which clean the ant-
hills, and of going to war to capture slaves who will
take care of their victors with such tender solicitude
that the latter even lose the habit of feeding themselves.

And little by little, as if a maternal tenderness had
sprung up in her heart for the poor insect which was

so tiny and so intelligent, Yvette made it climb on her
finger, looking at it with a moved expression, almost
wanting to embrace it.

And as Servigny read of the way in which they live
in communities, and play games of strength and skill
among themselves, the young girl grew enthusiastic
and sought to kiss the insect which escaped her and
began to crawl over her face. Then she uttered a
piercing cry, as if she had been threatened by a terrible danger, and with frantic gestures tried to brush
it off her face. With a loud laugh Servigny caught
it near her tresses and imprinted on the spot where
he had seized it a long kiss without Yvette withdraw-
ing her forehead.

Then she exclaimed as she rose: "That is better
than a novel. Now let us go to La Grenouillère."

They reached that part of the island which is set
out as a park and shaded with great trees. Couples
were strolling beneath the lofty foliage along the
Seine, where the boats were gliding by.

The boats were filled with young people, working-
girls and their sweethearts, the latter in their shirt-
sleeves, with coats on their arms, tall hats tipped
back, and a jaded look. There were tradesmen with
their families, the women dressed in their best and
the children flocking like little chicks about their
parents. A distant, continuous sound of voices, a
heavy, scolding clamor announced the proximity of
the establishment so dear to the boatmen.

Suddenly they saw it. It was a huge boat, roofed
over, moored to the bank. On board were many
men and women drinking at tables, or else standing
up, shouting, singing, bandying words, dancing, ca-

pering, to the sound of a piano which was groaning
—out of tune and rattling as an old kettle.

Two tall, russet-haired, half-tipsy girls, with red
lips, were talking coarsely. Others were dancing
madly with young fellows half clad, dressed like jock-
eys, in linen trousers and colored caps. The odors
of a crowd and of rice-powder were noticeable.

The drinkers around the tables were swallowing
white, red, yellow, and green liquids, and vociferat-
ing at the top of their lungs, feeling as it were, the
necessity of making a noise, a brutal need of having
their ears and brains filled with uproar. Now and
then a swimmer, standing on the roof, dived into the
water, splashing the nearest guests, who yelled like
savages.

On the stream passed the flotillas of light craft,
long, slender wherries, swiftly rowed by bare-armed
oarsmen, whose muscles played beneath their bronzed
skin. The women in the boats, in blue or red flannel skirts, with umbrellas, red or blue, opened over
their heads and gleaming under the burning sun,
leaned back in their chairs at the stern of the boats,
and seemed almost to float upon the water, in motionless and slumberous pose.

The heavier boats proceeded slowly, crowded with
people. A collegian, wanting to show off, rowed
like a windmill against all the other boats, bringing
the curses of their oarsmen down upon his head, and
disappearing in dismay after almost drowning two
swimmers, followed by the shouts of the crowd
thronging in the great floating *café*.

Yvette, radiantly happy, taking Servigny's arm,
went into the midst of this noisy mob. She seemed

to enjoy the crowding, and stared at the girls with a calm and gracious glance.

"Look at that one, Muscade," she said. "What pretty hair she has! They seem to be having such fun!"

As the pianist, a boatman dressed in red with a huge straw hat, began a waltz, Yvette grasped her companion and they danced so long and madly that everybody looked at them. The guests, standing on the tables, kept time with their feet; others threw glasses, and the musician, seeming to go mad, struck the ivory keys with great bangs, swaying his whole body and swinging his head covered with that immense hat. Suddenly he stopped and, slipping to the deck, lay flat, beneath his head-gear, as if dead with fatigue. A loud laugh arose and everybody applauded.

Four friends rushed forward, as they do in cases of accident, and lifting up their comrade, they carried him by his four limbs, after carefully placing his great hat on his stomach. A joker following them intoned the "De Profundis," and a procession formed and threaded the paths of the island, guests and strollers and everyone they met falling into line.

Yvette darted forward, delighted, laughing with her whole heart, chatting with everybody, stirred by the movement and the noise. The young men gazed at her, crowded against her, seeming to devour her with their glances; and Servigny began to fear lest the adventure should terminate badly.

The procession still kept on its way, hastening its step; for the four bearers had taken a quick pace, followed by the yelling crowd. But suddenly, they turned toward the shore, stopped short as they reached the bank, swung their comrade for a moment, and then, all four acting together, flung him into the river.

A great shout of joy rang out from all mouths, while the poor pianist, bewildered, paddled, swore, coughed, and spluttered, and though sticking in the mud managed to get to the shore. His hat which floated down the stream was picked up by a boat.

Yvette danced with joy, clapping and repeating: "Oh! Muscade, what fun! what fun!"

Servigny looked on, having become serious, a little disturbed, a little chilled to see her so much at her ease in this common place. A sort of instinct revolted in him, that instinct of the proper, which a well-born man always preserves even when he casts himself loose, that instinct which avoids too common familiarities and too degrading contacts. Astonished, he muttered to himself:

"Egad! Then *you* are at home here, are you?" And he wanted to speak familiarly to her, as a man does to certain women the first time he meets them. He no longer distinguished her from the russet-haired, hoarse-voiced creatures who brushed against them. The language of the crowd was not at all choice, but nobody seemed shocked or surprised. Yvette did not even appear to notice it.

"Muscade, I want to go in bathing," she said. "We'll go into the river together."

"At your service," said he.

They went to the bath-office to get bathing-suits. She was ready the first, and stood on the bank waiting for him, smiling on everyone who looked at her. Then side by side they went into the luke--warm water.

She swam with pleasure, with intoxication, caressed by the wave, throbbing with a sensual delight, raising herself at each stroke as if she were going to spring from the water. He followed her with difficulty, breathless, and vexed to feel himself mediocre at the sport.

But she slackened her pace, and then, turning over suddenly, she floated, with her arms folded and her eyes wide open to the blue sky. He observed, thus stretched out on the surface of the river, the undulating lines of her form, her firm neck and shoulders, her slightly submerged hips, and bare ankles, gleaming in the water, and the tiny foot that emerged.

He saw her thus exhibiting herself, as if she were doing it on purpose, to lure him on, or again to make sport of him. And he began to long for her with a passionate ardor and an exasperating impatience. Suddenly she turned, looked at him, and burst into laughter.

"You have a fine head," she said.

He was annoyed at this bantering, possessed with the anger of a baffled lover. Then yielding brusquely to a half felt desire for retaliation, a desire to avenge himself, to wound her, he said:

"Well, does this sort of life suit you?"

She asked with an artless air: "What do you mean?"

"Oh, come, don't make game of me. You know well enough what I mean!"

"No, I don't, on my word of honor."

"Oh, let us stop this comedy! Will you or will you not?"

"I do not understand you."

"You are not as stupid as all that; besides I told you last night."

"Told me what? I have forgotten!"

"That I love you."

"You?"

"Yes."

"What nonsense!"

"I swear it."

"Then prove it."

"That is all I ask."

"What is?"

"To prove it."

"Well, do so."

"But you did not say so last night."

"You did not ask anything."

"What absurdity!"

"And besides it is not to me to whom you should make your proposition."

"To whom, then?"

"Why, to mamma, of course."

He burst into laughter. "To your mother. No, that is too much!"

She had suddenly become very grave, and looking him straight in the eyes, said:

"Listen, Muscade, if you really love me enough to marry me, speak to mamma first, and I will answer you afterward."

He thought she was still making sport of him, and angrily replied: "Mam'zelle, you must be taking me for somebody else."

She kept looking at him with her soft, clear eyes. She hesitated and then said:

"I don't understand you at all."

Then he answered quickly with somewhat of ill nature in his voice:

"Come now, Yvette, let us cease this absurd comedy, which has already lasted too long. You are playing the part of a simple little girl, and the rôle does not fit you at all, believe me. You know perfectly well that there can be no question of marriage between us, but merely of love. I have told you that I love you. It is the truth. I repeat, I love you. Don't pretend any longer not to understand me, and don't treat me as if I were a fool."

They were face to face, treading water, merely moving their hands a little, to steady themselves. She was still for a moment, as if she could not make out the meaning of his words, then she suddenly blushed up to the roots of her hair. Her whole face grew purple from her neck to her ears, which became almost violet, and without answering a word she fled toward the shore, swimming with all her strength with hasty strokes. He could not keep up with her and panted with fatigue as he followed. He saw her leave the water, pick up her cloak, and go to her dressing-room without looking back.

It took him a long time to dress, very much perplexed as to what he ought to do, puzzled over what he should say to her, and wondering whether he ought to excuse himself or persevere. When he was ready, she had gone away all alone. He went back slowly, anxious and disturbed.

The Marquise was strolling, on Saval's arm, in the circular path around the lawn. As she observed Servigny, she said, with that careless air which she had maintained since the night before:

"I told you not to go out in such hot weather. And now Yvette has come back almost with a sun stroke. She has gone to lie down. She was as red as a poppy, the poor child, and she has a frightful headache. You must have been walking in the full sunlight, or you must have done something foolish. You are as unreasonable as she."

The young girl did not come down to dinner. When they wanted to send her up something to eat she called through the door that she was not hungry, for she had shut herself in, and she begged that they would leave her undisturbed. The two young men left by the ten o'clock train, promising to return the following Thursday, and the Marquise seated herself at the open window to dream, hearing in the distance the orchestra of the boatmen's ball, with its sprightly music, in the deep and solemn silence of the night.

Swayed by love as a person is moved by a fondness for horses or boating, she was subject to sudden tendernesses which crept over her like a disease. These passions took possession of her suddenly, penetrated her entire being, maddened her, enervated or overwhelmed her, in measure as they were of an exalted, violent, dramatic, or sentimental character.

She was one of those women who are created to love and to be loved. Starting from a very low station in life, she had risen in her adventurous career, acting instinctively, with inborn cleverness, accept ing money and kisses, naturally, without distinguishing between them, employing her extraordinary ability in an unthinking and simple fashion. From all her experiences she had never known either a genuine tenderness or a great repulsion.

She had had various friends, for she had to live, as in traveling a person eats at many tables. But occasionally her heart took fire, and she really fell in love, which state lasted for some weeks or months, according to conditions. These were the delicious moments of her life, for she loved with all her soul. She cast herself upon love as a person throws himself into the river to drown himself, and let herself be carried away, ready to die, if need be, intoxicated, maddened, infinitely happy. She imagined each time that she never had experienced anything like such an attachment, and she would have been greatly astonished if some one had told her of how many men she had dreamed whole nights through, looking at the stars.

Saval had captivated her, body and soul. She dreamed of him, lulled by his face and his memory, in the calm exaltation of consummated love, of present and certain happiness.

A sound behind her made her turn around. Yvette had just entered, still in her daytime dress, but pale, with eyes glittering, as sometimes is the case after some great fatigue. She leaned on the sill of the open window, facing her mother.

"I want to speak to you," she said.

The Marquise looked at her in astonishment. She loved her like an egotistical mother, proud of her beauty, as a person is proud of a fortune, too pretty

263

still herself to become jealous, too indifferent to plan the schemes with which they charged her, too clever, nevertheless, not to have full consciousness of her daughter's value.

"I am listening, my child," she said; "what is it?"

Yvette gave her a piercing look, as if to read the depths of her soul and to seize all the sensations which her words might awake.

"It is this. Something strange has just happened."

"What can it be?"

"Monsieur de Servigny has told me that he loves me."

The Marquise, disturbed, waited a moment, and, as Yvette said nothing more, she asked:

"How did he tell you that? Explain yourself!"

Then the young girl, sitting at her mother's feet, in a coaxing attitude common with her, and clasping her hands, added:

"He asked me to marry him."

Madame Obardi made a sudden gesture of stupefaction and cried:

"Servigny! Why! you are crazy!"

Yvette had not taken her eyes off her mother's face, watching her thoughts and her surprise. She asked with a serious voice:

"Why am I crazy? Why should not Monsieur de Servigny marry me?"

The Marquise, embarrassed, stammered:

"You are mistaken, it is not possible. You either did not hear or did not understand. Monsieur de Servigny is too rich for you, and too much of a Parisian to marry."

Yvette rose softly. She added: "But if he loves me as he says he does, mamma?"

Her mother replied, with some impatience: "I thought you big enough and wise enough not to have such ideas. Servigny is a man-about-town and an egotist. He will never marry anyone but a woman of his set and his fortune. If he asked you in marriage, it is only that he wants—"

The Marquise, incapable of expressing her meaning, was silent for a moment, then continued: "Come now, leave me alone and go to bed."

And the young girl, as if she had learned what she sought to find out, answered in a docile voice: "Yes, mamma!"

She kissed her mother on the forehead and withdrew with a calm step. As she reached the door, the Marquise called out: "And your sunstroke?" she said.

"I did not have one at all. It was that which caused everything."

The Marquise added: "We will not speak of it again. Only don't stay alone with him for some time from now, and be very sure that he will never marry you, do you understand, and that he merely means to—compromise you."

She could not find better words to express her thought. Yvette went to her room. Madame Obardi began to dream. Living for years in an opulent and loving repose, she had carefully put aside all reflections which might annoy or sadden her. Never had she been willing to ask herself the question—What would become of Yvette? It would be soon enough to think about the difficulties when they arrived. She well knew, from her experience, that her daughter could not marry a man who was rich and of good society, excepting by a totally improbable chance, by one of those surprises of love which place adventuresses on thrones.

She had not considered it, furthermore, being too much occupied with herself to make any plans which did not directly concern herself.

Yvette would do as her mother, undoubtedly. She would lead a gay life. Why not? But the Marquise had never dared ask when, or how. That would all come about in time.

And now her daughter, all of a sudden, without warning, had asked one of those questions which could not be answered, forcing her to take an attitude in an affair, so delicate, so dangerous in every respect, and so disturbing to the conscience which a woman is expected to show in matters concerning her daughter.

Sometimes nodding but never asleep, she had too much natural astuteness to be deceived a minute about Servigny's intentions, for she knew men by experience, and especially men of that set. So at the first words uttered by Yvette, she had cried almost in spite of herself: "Servigny, marry you? You are crazy!"

How had he come to employ that old method, he, that sharp man of the world? What would he do now? And she, the young girl, how should she warn her more clearly and even forbid her, for she might make great mistakes. Would anyone have believed that this big girl had remained so artless, so ill informed, so guileless?

And the Marquise, greatly perplexed and already wearied with her reflections, endeavored to make up her mind what to do without finding a solution of the problem, for the situation seemed to her very embarrassing. Worn out with this worry, she thought:

"I will watch them more clearly, I will act according to circumstances. If necessary, I will speak to Servigny, who is sharp and will take a hint."

She did not think out what she should say to him, nor what he would answer, nor what sort of an understanding could be established between them, but happy at being relieved of this care without having had to make a decision, she resumed her dreams of the handsome Saval, and turning toward that misty light which hovers over Paris, she threw kisses with both hands toward the great city, rapid kisses which she tossed into the darkness, one after the other, without counting; and, very low, as if she were talking to Saval still, she murmured:

"I love you, I love you!"

CHAPTER III.

ENLIGHTENMENT

YVETTE, also, could not sleep. Like her mother, she leaned upon the sill of the open window, and tears, her first bitter tears, filled her eyes. Up to this time she had lived, had grown up, in the heedless and serene confidence of happy youth. Why should she have dreamed, reflected, puzzled? Why should she not have been a young girl, like all other young girls? Why should a doubt, a fear, or painful suspicion have come to her?

She seemed posted on all topics because she had a way of talking on all subjects, because she had taken the tone, demeanor, and words of the people who lived around her. But she really knew no more than a little girl raised in a convent; her audacities of speech came from her memory, from that unconscious faculty of imitation and assimilation which women possess, and not from a mind instructed and emboldened.

She spoke of love as the son of a painter or a musician would, at the age of ten or twelve years,

speak of painting or music. She knew or rather
suspected very well what sort of mystery this word
concealed, — too many jokes had been whispered before her, for her innocence not to be a trifle enlight-
ened, — but how could she have drawn the conclusion
from all this, that all families did not resemble hers?

They kissed her mother's hand with the sem-
blance of respect; all their friends had titles; they all
were rich or seemed to be so; they all spoke familiarly of the princes of the royal line. Two sons of
kings had even come often, in the evening, to the
Marquise's house. How should she have known?

And, then, she was naturally artless. She did not
estimate or sum up people as her mother did. She
lived tranquilly, too joyous in her life to worry herself about what might appear suspicious to creatures
more calm, thoughtful, reserved, less cordial, and
sunny.

But now, all at once, Servigny, by a few words,
the brutality of which she felt without understanding
them, awakened in her a sudden disquietude, unreasoning at first, but which grew into a tormenting
apprehension. She had fled home, had escaped like a
wounded animal, wounded in fact most deeply by
those words which she ceaselessly repeated to get all
their sense and bearing: "You know very well that
there can be no question of marriage between us—
but only of love."

What did he mean? And why this insult? Was
she then in ignorance of something, some secret,
some shame? She was the only one ignorant of it,
no doubt. But what could she do? She was frightened, startled, as a person is when he discovers some

hidden infamy, some treason of a beloved friend, one of those heart-disasters which crush.

She dreamed, reflected, puzzled, wept, consumed by fears and suspicions. Then her joyous young soul reassuring itself, she began to plan an adventure, to imagine an abnormal and dramatic situation, founded on the recollections of all the poetical romances she had read. She recalled all the moving catastrophes, or sad and touching stories; she jumbled them together, and concocted a story of her own with which she interpreted the half-understood mystery which enveloped her life.

She was no longer cast down. She dreamed, she lifted veils, she imagined unlikely complications, a thousand singular, terrible things, seductive, nevertheless, by their very strangeness. Could she be, by chance, the natural daughter of a prince? Had her poor mother, betrayed and deserted, made Marquise by some king, perhaps King Victor Emmanuel, been obliged to take flight before the anger of the family? Was she not rather a child abandoned by its relations, who were noble and illustrious, the fruit of a clandestine love, taken in by the Marquise, who had adopted and brought her up?

Still other suppositions passed through her mind. She accepted or rejected them according to the dictates of her fancy. She was moved to pity over her own case, happy at the bottom of her heart, and sad also, taking a sort of satisfaction in becoming a sort of a heroine of a book who must assume a noble attitude, worthy of herself.

She laid out the part she must play, according to events at which she guessed. She vaguely outlined this rôle, like one of Scribe's or of George Sand's. It should be endued with devotion, self-abnegation, greatness of soul, tenderness, and fine words. Her pliant nature almost rejoiced in this new attitude. She pondered almost till evening what she should do, wondering how she should manage to wrest the truth from the Marquise.

And when night came, favorable to tragic situations, she had thought out a simple and subtle trick to obtain what she wanted: it was, brusquely, to say that Servigny had asked for her hand in marriage.

At this news, Madame Obardi, taken by surprise, would certainly let a word escape her lips, a cry which would throw light into the mind of her daughter. And Yvette had accomplished her plan.

She expected an explosion of astonishment, an expansion of love, a confidence full of gestures and tears. But, instead of this, her mother, without appearing stupefied or grieved, had only seemed bored; and from the constrained, discontented, and worried tone in which she had replied, the young girl, in whom there suddenly awaked all the astuteness, keenness, and sharpness of a woman, understanding that she must not insist, that the mystery was of another nature, that it would be painful to her to learn it, and that she must puzzle it out all alone, had gone back to her room, her heart oppressed, her soul in distress, possessed now with the apprehensions of a real misfortune, without knowing exactly either whence or why this emotion came to her. So she wept, leaning at the window.

She wept long, not dreaming of anything now, not seeking to discover anything more, and little by

little, weariness overcoming her, she closed her eyes.
She dozed for a few minutes, with that deep sleep of
people who are tired out and have not the energy to
undress and go to bed, that heavy sleep, broken by
dreams, when the head nods upon the breast.

She did not go to bed until the first break of day,
when the cold of the morning, chilling her, compelled
her to leave the window.

The next day and the day after, she maintained a
reserved and melancholy attitude. Her thoughts were
busy; she was learning to spy out, to guess at con-
clusions, to reason. A light, still vague, seemed to
illumine men and things around her in a new manner;
she began to entertain suspicions against all, against
everything that she had believed, against her mother.
She imagined all sorts of things during these two
days. She considered all the possibilities, taking the
most extreme resolutions with the suddenness of her
changeable and unrestrained nature. Wednesday she
hit upon a plan, an entire schedule of conduct and a
system of spying. She rose Thursday morning with
the resolve to be very sharp and armed against everybody.

She determined even to take for her motto these
two words: "Myself alone," and she pondered for more
than an hour how she should arrange them to produce a good effect engraved about her crest, on her
writing paper.

Saval and Servigny arrived at ten o'clock. The
young girl gave her hand with reserve, without embarrassment, and in a tone, familiar though grave,
she said:

"Good morning, Muscade, are you well?"

272

"Good morning, Mam'zelle, fairly, thanks, and you?" He was watching her. "What comedy will she play me," he said to himself.

The Marquise having taken Saval's arm, he took Yvette's, and they began to stroll about the lawn, appearing and disappearing every minute, behind the clumps of trees.

Yvette walked with a thoughtful air, looking at the gravel of the pathway, appearing hardly to hear what her companion said and scarcely answering him.

Suddenly she asked: "Are you truly my friend, Muscade?"

"Why, of course, Mam'zelle."

"But truly, truly, now?"

"Absolutely your friend, Mam'zelle, body and soul."

"Even enough of a friend not to lie to me once, just once?"

"Even twice, if necessary."

"Even enough to tell me the absolute, exact truth?"

"Yes, Mam'zelle."

"Well, what do you think, way down in your heart, of the Prince of Kravalow?"

"Ah, the devil!"

"You see that you are already preparing to lie."

"Not at all, but I am seeking the words, the proper words. Great Heavens, Prince Kravalow is a Russian, who speaks Russian, who was born in Russia, who has perhaps had a passport to come to France, and about whom there is nothing false but his name and title."

273

She looked him in the eyes: "You mean that he is — ?"

"An adventurer, Mam'zelle."

"Thank you, and Chevalier Valreali is no better?"

"You have hit it."

"And Monsieur de Belvigne?"

"With him it is a different thing. He is of provincial society, honorable up to a certain point, but only a little scorched from having lived too rapidly."

"And you?"

"I am what they call a butterfly, a man of good family, who had intelligence and who has squandered it in making phrases, who had good health and who has injured it by dissipation, who had some worth perhaps and who has scattered it by doing nothing. There is left to me a certain knowledge of life, a complete absence of prejudice, a large contempt for mankind, including women, a very deep sentiment of the uselessness of my acts and a vast tolerance for the mob.

"Nevertheless, at times, I can be frank, and I am even capable of affection, as you could see, if you would. With these defects and qualities I place myself at your orders, Mam'zelle, morally and physically, to do what you please with me."

She did not laugh; she listened, weighing his words and his intentions; then she resumed:

"What do you think of the Countess de Lammy?"

He replied, vivaciously: "You will permit me not to give my opinion about the women."

"About none of them?"

"About none of them."

"Then you must have a bad opinion of them all. Come, think; won't you make a single exception?"

He sneered with that insolent air which he generally wore; and with that brutal audacity which he used as a weapon, he said: "Present company is always excepted."

She blushed a little, but calmly asked: "Well, what do you think of me?"

"You want me to tell. Well, so be it. I think you are a young person of good sense, and practicalness, or if you prefer, of good practical sense, who knows very well how to arrange her pastime, to amuse people, to hide her views, to lay her snares, and who, without hurrying, awaits events."

"Is that all?" she asked.

"That's all."

Then she said with a serious earnestness: "I shall make you change that opinion, Muscade."

Then she joined her mother, who was proceeding with short steps, her head down, with that manner assumed in talking very low, while walking, of very intimate and very sweet things. As she advanced she drew shapes in the sand, letters perhaps, with the point of her sunshade, and she spoke, without looking at Saval, long, softly, leaning on his arm, pressed against him.

Yvette suddenly fixed her eyes upon her, and a suspicion, rather a feeling than a doubt, passed through her mind as a shadow of a cloud driven by the wind passes over the ground.

The bell rang for breakfast. It was silent and almost gloomy. There was a storm in the air. Great solid clouds rested upon the horizon, mute and heavy, but charged with a tempest. As soon as they had taken their coffee on the terrace, the Marquise asked:

"Well, darling, are you going to take a walk to-day with your friend Servigny? It is a good time to enjoy the coolness under the trees."

Yvette gave her a quick glance.

"No, mamma, I am not going out to-day."

The Marquise appeared annoyed, and insisted. "Oh, go and take a stroll, my child, it is excellent for you."

Then Yvette distinctly said: "No, mamma, I shall stay in the house to-day, and you know very well why, because I told you the other evening."

Madame Obardi gave it no further thought, pre-occupied with the thought of remaining alone with Saval. She blushed and was annoyed, disturbed on her own account, not knowing how she could find a free hour or two. She stammered:

"It is true. I was not thinking of it. I don't know where my head is."

And Yvette taking up some embroidery, which she called "the public safety," and at which she worked five or six times a year, on dull days, seated herself on a low chair near her mother, while the two young men, astride folding-chairs, smoked their cigars.

The hours passed in a languid conversation. The Marquise fidgety, cast longing glances at Saval, seeking some pretext, some means, of getting rid of her daughter. She finally realized that she would not succeed, and not knowing what ruse to employ, she said to Servigny:

276

"You know, my dear Duke, that I am going to keep you both this evening. To-morrow we shall breakfast at the Fournaise restaurant, at Chaton."

He understood, smiled, and bowed : "I am at your orders, Marquise."

The day wore on slowly and painfully under the threatenings of the storm. The hour for dinner gradually approached. The heavy sky was filled with slow and heavy clouds. There was not a breath of air stirring. The evening meal was silent, too. An oppression, an embarrassment, a sort of vague fear, seemed to make the two men and the two women mute.

When the covers were removed, they sat long upon the terrace ; only speaking at long intervals. Night fell, a sultry night. Suddenly the horizon was torn by an immense flash of lightning, which illumined with a dazzling and wan light the four faces shrouded in darkness. Then a far-off sound, heavy and feeble, like the rumbling of a carriage upon a bridge, passed over the earth; and it seemed that the heat of the atmosphere increased, that the air suddenly became more oppressive, and the silence of the evening deeper.

Yvette rose. "I am going to bed," she said, "the storm makes me ill."

And she offered her brow to the Marquise, gave her hand to the two young men, and withdrew.

As her room was just above the terrace, the leaves of a great chestnut-tree growing before the door soon gleamed with a green hue, and Servigny kept his eyes fixed on this pale light in the foliage, in which at times he thought he saw a shadow pass. But suddenly the light went out. Madame Obardi gave a great sigh.

"My daughter has gone to bed," she said.

Servigny rose, saying: "I am going to do as much, Marquise, if you will permit me." He kissed the hand she held out to him and disappeared in turn.

She was left alone with Saval, in the night. In a moment she was clasped in his arms. Then, although he tried to prevent her, she kneeled before him murmuring: "I want to see you by the lightning flashes."

But Yvette, her candle snuffed out, had returned to her balcony, barefoot, gliding like a shadow, and she listened, consumed by an unhappy and confused suspicion. She could not see, as she was above them, on the roof of the terrace.

She heard nothing but a murmur of voices, and her heart beat so fast that she could actually hear its throbbing. A window closed on the floor above her. Servigny, then, must have just gone up to his room. Her mother was alone with the other man.

A second flash of lightning, clearing the sky, lighted up for a second all the landscape she knew so well, with a startling and sinister gleam, and she saw the great river, with the color of melted lead, as a river appears in dreams in fantastic scenes.

Just then a voice below her uttered the words: "I love you!" And she heard nothing more. A strange shudder passed over her body, and her soul shivered in frightful distress. A heavy, infinite silence, which seemed eternal, hung over the world. She could no longer breathe, her breast oppressed by something unknown and horrible. Another flash of lightning illumined space, lighting up the horizon for an instant, then another almost immediately came, followed by still others. And the voice, which she had already heard, repeated more loudly: "Oh! how I love you! how I love you!" And Yvette recognized the voice; it was her mother's.

A large drop of warm rain fell upon her brow, and a slight and almost imperceptible motion ran through the leaves, the quivering of the rain which was now beginning. Then a noise came from afar, a confused sound, like that of the wind in the branches: it was the deluge descending in sheets on earth and river and trees. In a few minutes the water poured about her, covering her, drenching her like a shower-bath. She did not move, thinking only of what was happening on the terrace.

She heard them get up and go to their rooms. Doors were closed within the house; and the young girl, yielding to an irresistible desire to learn what was going on, a desire which maddened and tortured her, glided downstairs, softly opened the outer door, and, crossing the lawn under the furious downpour, ran and hid in a clump of trees, to look at the windows.

Only one window was lighted, her mother's. And suddenly two shadows appeared in the luminous square, two shadows, side by side. Then distracted, without reflection, without knowing what she was doing, she screamed with all her might, in a shrill voice: "Mamma!" as a person would cry out to warn people in danger of death.

Her desperate cry was lost in the noise of the rain, but the couple separated, disturbed. And one of the shadows disappeared, while the other tried to discover something, peering through the darkness of the garden.

Fearing to be surprised, or to meet her mother at that moment, Yvette rushed back to the house, ran upstairs, dripping wet, and shut herself in her room, resolved to open her door to no one.

Without taking off her streaming dress, which clung to her form, she fell on her knees, with clasped hands, in her distress imploring some superhuman protection, the mysterious aid of Heaven, the unknown support which a person seeks in hours of tears and despair.

The great lightning flashes threw for an instant their livid reflections into her room, and she saw herself in the mirror of her wardrobe, with her wet and disheveled hair, looking so strange that she did not recognize herself. She remained there so long that the storm abated without her perceiving it. The rain ceased, a light filled the sky, still obscured with clouds, and a mild, balmy, delicious freshness, a freshness of grass and wet leaves, came in through the open window.

Yvette rose, took off her wet, cold garments, without thinking what she was doing, and went to bed. She stared with fixed eyes at the dawning day. Then she wept again, and then she began to think.

Her mother! A lover! What a shame! She had read so many books in which women, even mothers, had overstepped the bounds of propriety, to regain their honor at the pages of the climax, that she was not astonished beyond measure at finding herself enveloped in a drama similar to all those of her reading. The violence of her first grief, the cruel shock of surprise, had already worn off a little, in the confused remembrance of analogous situations. Her mind had rambled among such tragic adventures, painted by the novel-writers, that the horrible discovery seemed, little by little, like the natural continuation of some serial story, begun the evening before.

She said to herself: "I will save my mother." And almost reassured by this heroic resolution, she felt herself strengthened, ready at once for the devotion and the struggle. She reflected on the means which must be employed. A single one seemed good, which was quite in keeping with her romantic nature. And she rehearsed the interview which she should have with the Marquise, as an actor rehearses the scene which he is going to play.

The sun had risen. The servants were stirring about the house. The chambermaid came with the chocolate. Yvette put the tray on the table and said:

"You will say to my mother that I am not well, that I am going to stay in bed until those gentlemen leave, that I could not sleep last night, and that I do not want to be disturbed because I am going to try to rest."

The servant, surprised, looked at the wet dress, which had fallen like a rag on the carpet.

"So Mademoiselle has been out?" she said.

"Yes, I went out for a walk in the rain to refresh myself."

The maid picked up the skirts, stockings, and wet shoes; then she went away carrying on her arm, with fastidious precautions, these garments, soaked

as the clothes of a drowned person. And Yvette
waited, well knowing that her mother would come
to her.

The Marquise entered, having jumped from her
bed at the first words of the chambermaid, for a
suspicion had possessed her heart since that cry:
"Mamma!" heard in the dark.

"What is the matter?" she said.

Yvette looked at her and stammered: "I—I—"
Then overpowered by a sudden and terrible emotion,
she began to choke.

The Marquise, astonished, again asked: "What
in the world is the matter with you?"

Then, forgetting all her plans and prepared phrases,
the young girl hid her face in both hands and stammered:

"Oh! mamma! Oh! mamma!"

Madame Obardi stood by the bed, too much affected thoroughly to understand, but guessing almost
everything, with that subtle instinct whence she de-
rived her strength. As Yvette could not speak, choked
with tears, her mother, worn out finally and feeling
some fearful explanation coming, brusquely asked:

"Come, will you tell me what the matter is?"

Yvette could hardly utter the words: "Oh! last
night—I saw—your window."

The Marquise, very pale, said: "Well? what
of it?"

Her daughter repeated, still sobbing: "Oh! mamma!
Oh! mamma!"

Madame Obardi, whose fear and embarrassment
turned to anger, shrugged her shoulders and turned
to go.

"I really believe that you are crazy. When this ends, you will let me know."

But the young girl, suddenly took her hands from her face, which was streaming with tears.

"No, listen, I must speak to you, listen. You must promise me — we must both go away, very far off, into the country, and we must live like the country people; and no one must know what has become of us. Say you will, mamma; I beg you, I implore you; will you?"

The Marquise, confused, stood in the middle of the room. She had in her veins the irascible blood of the common people. Then a sense of shame, a mother's modesty, mingled with a vague sentiment of fear and the exasperation of a passionate woman whose love is threatened, and she shuddered, ready to ask for pardon, or to yield to some violence.

"I don't understand you," she said.

Yvette replied:

"I saw you, mamma, last night. You cannot — if you knew — we will both go away. I will love you so much that you will forget —"

Madame Obardi said in a trembling voice: "Listen, my daughter, there are some things which you do not yet understand. Well, don't forget — don't forget — that I forbid you ever to speak to me about those things."

But the young girl, brusquely taking the rôle of savior which she had imposed upon herself, rejoined:

"No, mamma, I am no longer a child, and I have the right to know. I know that we receive persons of bad repute, adventurers, and I know that, on that account, people do not respect us. I know more. Well, it must not be, any longer, do you hear? I do not wish it. We will go away: you will sell your jewels; we will work, if need be, and we will live as honest women, somewhere very far away. And if I can marry, so much the better."

She answered: "You are crazy. You will do me the favor to rise and come down to breakfast with all the rest."

"No, mamma. There is some one whom I shall never see again, you understand me. I want him to leave, or I shall leave. You shall choose between him and me."

She was sitting up in bed, and she raised her voice, speaking as they do on the stage, playing, finally, the drama which she had dreamed, almost forgetting her grief in the effort to fulfill her mission.

The Marquise, stupefied, again repeated: "You are crazy —" not finding anything else to say.

Yvette replied with a theatrical energy: "No, mamma, that man shall leave the house, or I shall go myself, for I will not weaken."

"And where will you go? What will you do?"

"I do not know, it matters little — I want you to be an honest woman."

These words which recurred, aroused in the Marquise a perfect fury, and she cried:

"Be silent. I do not permit you to talk to me like that. I am as good as anybody else, do you understand? I lead a certain sort of life, it is true, and I am proud of it; the 'honest women' are not as good as I am."

284

Yvette, astonished, looked at her, and stammered: "Oh! mamma!"

But the Marquise, carried away with excitement, continued:

"Yes, I lead a certain life — what of it? Otherwise you would be a cook, as I was once, and earn thirty sous a day. You would be washing dishes, and your mistress would send you to market — do you understand — and she would turn you out if you loitered, just as you loiter now because I am — because I lead this life. Listen. When a person is only a nursemaid, a poor girl, with fifty francs saved up, she must know how to manage, if she does not want to starve to death; and there are not two ways for us, there are not two ways, do you understand, when we are servants. We cannot make our fortune with official positions, nor with stockjobbing tricks. We have only one way — only one way."

She struck her breast as a penitent at the confessional, and flushed and excited, coming toward the bed, she continued: "So much the worse. A pretty girl must live or suffer — she has no choice!" Then returning to her former idea: "Much they deny themselves, your 'honest women.' They are worse, because nothing compels them. They have money to live on and amuse themselves, and they choose vicious lives of their own accord. They are the bad ones in reality."

She was standing near the bed of the distracted Yvette, who wanted to cry out "Help," to escape. Yvette wept aloud, like children who are whipped. The Marquise was silent and looked at her daughter, and, seeing her overwhelmed with despair, felt, herself, the pangs of grief, remorse, tenderness, and pity, and throwing herself upon the bed with open arms, she also began to sob and stammered:

"My poor little girl, my poor little girl, if you knew how you were hurting me." And they wept together, a long while.

Then the Marquise, in whom grief could not long endure, softly rose, and gently said:

"Come, darling, it is unavoidable; what would you have? Nothing can be changed now. We must take life as it comes to us."

Yvette continued to weep. The blow had been too harsh and too unexpected to permit her to reflect and to recover at once.

Her mother resumed: "Now, get up and come down to breakfast, so that no one will notice anything."

The young girl shook her head as if to say, "No," without being able to speak. Then she said, with a slow voice full of sobs:

"No, mamma, you know what I said, I won't alter my determination. I shall not leave my room till they have gone. I never want to see one of those people again, never, never. If they come back, you will see no more of me."

The Marquise had dried her eyes, and wearied with emotion, she murmured:

"Come, reflect, be reasonable."

Then, after a moment's silence:

"Yes, you had better rest this morning. I will come up to see you this afternoon." And having kissed her daughter on the forehead, she went to dress herself, already calmed.

Yvette, as soon as her mother had disappeared, rose, and ran to bolt the door, to be alone, all alone; then she began to think. The chambermaid knocked about eleven o'clock, and asked through the door:

"Madame the Marquise wants to know if Mademoiselle wishes anything, and what she will take for her breakfast."

Yvette answered: "I am not hungry, I only ask not to be disturbed."

And she remained in bed, just as if she had been ill. Toward three o'clock, some one knocked again. She asked:

"Who is there?"

It was her mother's voice which replied: "It is I, darling, I have come to see how you are."

She hesitated what she should do. She opened the door, and then went back to bed. The Marquise approached, and, speaking in low tones, as people do to a convalescent, said:

"Well, are you better? Won't you eat an egg?"

"No, thanks, nothing at all."

Madame Obardi sat down near the bed. They remained without saying anything, then, finally, as her daughter stayed quiet, with her hands inert upon the bedclothes, she asked:

"Don't you intend to get up?"

Yvette answered: "Yes, pretty soon."

Then in a grave and slow tone she said: "I have thought a great deal, mamma, and this — this is my resolution. The past is the past, let us speak no more of it. But the future shall be different or I know what is left for me to do. Now, let us say no more about it."

WORKS OF GUY DE MAUPASSANT

The Marquise, who thought the explanation finished, felt her impatience gaining a little. It was too
much. This big goose of a girl ought to have known
about things long ago. But she did not say anything in reply, only repeating:

"You are going to get up?"

"Yes, I am ready."

Then her mother became maid for her, bringing
her stockings, her corset, and her skirts. Then she
kissed her.

"Will you take a walk before dinner?"

"Yes, mamma."

And they took a stroll along the water, speaking
only of commonplace things.

CHAPTER IV.

From Emotion to Philosophy

The following day, early in the morning, Yvette went out alone to the place where Servigny had read her the history of the ants. She said to herself:

"I am not going away from this spot without having formed a resolution."

Before her, at her feet, the water flowed rapidly, filled with large bubbles which passed in silent flight with deep whirlings. She already had summed up the points of the situation and the means of extricating herself from it. What should she do if her mother would not accept the conditions which she had imposed, would not renounce her present way of living, her set of visitors — everything and go and hide with her in a distant land?

She might go alone, take flight, but where, and how? What would she live on? By working? At what? To whom should she apply to find work? And, then, the dull and humble life of working-women, daughters of the people, seemed a little disgraceful, unworthy of her. She thought of becoming a governess, like young girls in novels, and of becoming loved by the son of the house, and then marrying him. But to accomplish that she must have been of good birth, so that, when the exasperated father should approach her with having stolen his son's love, she might say in a proud voice:

"My name is Yvette Obardi."

She could not do this. And then, even that would have been a trite and threadbare method.

The convent was not worth much more. Besides, she felt no vocation for a religious life, having only an intermittent and fleeting piety. No one would save her by marrying her, being what she was! No aid was acceptable from a man, no possible issue, no definite resource.

And then she wished to do something energetic and really great and strong, which should serve as an example: so she resolved upon death.

She decided upon this step suddenly, but tranquilly, as if it were a journey, without reflecting, without looking at death, without understanding that it is the end without recommencement, the departure without return, the eternal farewell to earth and to this life.

She immediately settled on this extreme measure, with the lightness of young and excited souls, and she thought of the means which she would employ. But they all seemed to her painful and hazardous, and, furthermore, required a violence of action which repelled her.

She quickly abandoned the poniard and revolver, which might wound only, blind her or disfigure her,

and which demanded a practiced and steady hand.
She decided against the rope; it was so common,
the poor man's way of suicide, ridiculous and ugly;
and against water because she knew how to swim.
So poison remained — but which kind ? Almost all of
them cause suffering and incite vomitings. She did
not want either of these things.

Then she thought of chloroform, having read in a
newspaper how a young woman had managed to
asphyxiate herself by this process. And she felt at
once a sort of joy in her resolution, an inner pride,
a sensation of bravery. People should see what
she was, and what she was worth.

She returned to Bougival and went to a druggist,
from whom she asked a little chloroform for a tooth
which was aching. The man, who knew her, gave
her a tiny bottle of the narcotic.

Then she set out on foot for Croissy, where she
procured a second phial of poison. She obtained a
third at Chaton, a fourth at Ruril, and got home late
for breakfast.

As she was very hungry after this long walk, she
ate heartily with the pleasurable appetite of people
who have taken exercise.

Her mother, happy to see her so hungry, and now
feeling tranquil herself, said to her as they left the
table:

"All our friends are coming to spend Sunday with
us. I have invited the Prince, the Chevalier, and
Monsieur de Belvigne."

Yvette turned a little pale, but did not reply. She
went out almost immediately, reached the railway
station, and took a ticket for Paris. And during all

the afternoon, she went from druggist to druggist, buying from each one a few drops of chloroform. She came back in the evening with her pockets full of little bottles.

She began the same system on the following day, and by chance found a chemist who gave her, at one stroke, a quarter of a liter. She did not go out on Saturday; it was a lowering and sultry day; she passed it entirely on the terrace, stretched on a long wicker-chair.

She thought of almost nothing, very resolute and very calm. She put on the next morning, a blue costume which was very becoming to her, wishing to look well. Then looking at herself in the glass, she suddenly said:

"To-morrow, I shall be dead." And a peculiar shudder passed over her body. "Dead! I shall speak no more, think no more, no one will see me more, and I shall never see anything again."

And she gazed attentively at her countenance, as if she had never observed it, examining especially her eyes, discovering a thousand things in herself, a secret character in her physiognomy which she had not known before, astonished to see herself, as if she had opposite her a strange person, a new friend.

She said to herself: "It is I, in the mirror, there. How queer it is to look at oneself. But without the mirror we would never know ourselves. Everybody else would know how we look, and we ourselves would know nothing."

She placed the heavy braids of her thick hair over her breast, following with her glance all her gestures, all her poses, and all her movements.

"How pretty I am!" she thought. "To-morrow I shall be dead, there, upon my bed." She looked at her bed, and seemed to see herself stretched out, white as the sheets.

Dead! In a week she would be nothing but dust, to dust returned! A horrible anguish oppressed her heart. The bright sunlight fell in floods upon the fields, and the soft morning air came in at the window.

She sat down thinking of it. Death! It was as if the world was going to disappear from her; but no, since nothing would be changed in the world, not even her bedroom. Yes, her room would remain just the same, with the same bed, the same chairs, the same toilette articles, but she would be forever gone, and no one would be sorry, except her mother, perhaps.

People would say: "How pretty she was! that little Yvette," and nothing more. And as she looked at her arm leaning on the arm of her chair, she thought again, ashes to ashes, dust to dust. And again a great shudder of horror ran over her whole body, and she did not know how she could disappear without the whole earth being blotted out, so much it seemed to her that she was a part of everything, of the fields, of the air, of the sunshine, of life itself.

There were bursts of laughter in the garden, a great noise of voices and of calls, the bustling gaiety of country house parties, and she recognized the sonorous tones of M. de Belvigne, singing:

> "I am underneath thy window,
> Oh, deign to show thy face."

She rose, without reflecting, and looked out. They all applauded. They were all five there, with two gentlemen whom she did not know.

She brusquely withdrew, annoyed by the thought that these men had come to amuse themselves at her mother's house, as at a public place.

The bell sounded for breakfast. "I will show them how to die," she said.

She went downstairs with a firm step, with something of the resolution of the Christian martyrs going into the circus, where the lions awaited them.

She pressed their hands, smiling in an affable but rather haughty manner. Servigny asked her:

"Are you less cross to-day, Mam'zelle?"

She answered in a severe and peculiar tone: "To-day, I am going to commit follies. I am in my Paris mood, look out!"

Then turning toward Monsieur de Belvigne, she said:

"You shall be my escort, my little Malmsey. I will take you all after breakfast to the *fête* at Marly."

There was, in fact, a *fête* at Marly. They introduced the two newcomers to her, the Comte de Tamine and the Marquis de Briquetot.

During the meal, she said nothing further, strengthening herself to be gay in the afternoon, so that no one should guess anything,—so that they should be all the more astonished, and should say: "Who would have thought it? She seemed so happy, so contented! What does take place in those heads?"

She forced herself not to think of the evening, the chosen hour, when they should all be upon the terrace.

She drank as much wine as she could stand, to
nerve herself, and two little glasses of brandy, and
she was flushed as she left the table, a little bewildered, heated in body and mind. It seemed to her
that she was strengthened now, and resolved for
everything.

"Let us start!" she cried. She took Monsieur de
Belvigne's arm and set the pace for the others.
"Come, you shall form my battalion, Servigny. I
choose you as sergeant; you will keep outside the
ranks, on the right. You will make the foreign
guard march in front — the two exotics, the Prince,
and the Chevalier — and in the rear the two recruits
who have enlisted to-day. Come!"

They started. And Servigny began to imitate the
trumpet, while the two newcomers made believe to
beat the drum. Monsieur de Belvigne, a little confused, said in a low tone:

"Mademoiselle Yvette, be reasonable, you will
compromise yourself."

She answered: "It is you whom I am compro-
mising, Raisiné. As for me, I don't care much about
it. To-morrow it will not occur. So much the
worse for you: you ought not to go out with girls
like me."

They went through Bougival to the amazement of
the passers-by. All turned to look at them; the citizens came to their doors; the travelers on the little
railway which runs from Ruril to Marly jeered at
them. The men on the platforms cried:

"To the water with them!"

Yvette marched with a military step, holding Belvigne by the arm, as a prisoner is led. She did not

laugh; upon her features sat a pale seriousness, a sort of sinister calm. Servigny interrupted his trumpet blasts only to shout orders. The Prince and the Chevalier were greatly amused, finding all this very funny and in good taste. The two recruits drummed away continually.

When they arrived at the *fête*, they made a sensation. Girls applauded; young men jeered, and a stout gentleman with his wife on his arm said enviously: "There are some people who are full of fun."

Yvette saw the wooden horses and compelled Belvigne to mount at her right, while her squad scrambled upon the whirling beasts behind. When the time was up she refused to dismount, constraining her escort to take several more rides on the back of these children's animals, to the great delight of the public, who shouted jokes at them. Monsieur de Belvigne was livid and dizzy when he got off.

Then she began to wander among the booths. She forced all her men to get weighed among a crowd of spectators. She made them buy ridiculous toys which they had to carry in their hands. The Prince and the Chevalier began to think the joke was being carried too far. Servigny and the drummers, alone, did not seem to be discouraged.

They finally came to the end of the place. Then she gazed at her followers in a peculiar manner, with a shy and mischievous glance, and a strange fancy came to her mind. She drew them up on the bank of the river.

"Let the one who loves me the most jump into the water," she said.

Nobody leaped. A mob gathered behind them.

296

Women in white aprons looked on in stupor. Two troopers, in red breeches, laughed loudly.

She repeated: "Then there is not one of you capable of jumping into the water at my desire?"

Servigny murmured: "Oh, yes, there is," and leaped feet foremost into the river. His plunge cast a splash over as far as Yvette's feet. A murmur of astonishment and gaiety arose in the crowd.

Then the young girl picked up from the ground a little piece of wood, and throwing it into the stream: "Fetch it," she cried.

The young man began to swim, and seizing the floating stick in his mouth, like a dog, he brought it ashore, and then climbing the bank he kneeled on one knee to present it.

Yvette took it. "You are handsome," said she, and with a friendly stroke, she caressed his hair.

A stout woman indignantly exclaimed: "Are such things possible!"

Another woman said: "Can people amuse themselves like that!"

A man remarked: "I would not take a plunge for that sort of a girl."

She again took Belvigne's arm, exclaiming in his face: "You are a goose, my friend; you don't know what you missed."

They now returned. She cast vexed looks on the passers-by. "How stupid all these people seem," she said. Then raising her eyes to the countenance of her companion, she added: "You, too, like all the rest."

M. de Belvigne bowed. Turning around she saw that the Prince and the Chevalier had disappeared.

Servigny, dejected and dripping, ceased playing on the trumpet, and walked with a gloomy air at the side of the two wearied young men, who also had stopped the drum playing. She began to laugh dryly, saying:

"You seem to have had enough; nevertheless, that is what you call having a good time, isn't it? You came for that; I have given you your money's worth."

Then she walked on, saying nothing further; and suddenly Belvigne perceived that she was weeping. Astounded, he inquired:

"What is the matter?"

She murmured: "Let me alone, it does not concern you."

But he insisted, like a fool: "Oh, Mademoiselle, come, what is the matter, has anyone annoyed you?"

She repeated impatiently: "Will you keep still?"

Then suddenly, no longer able to resist the despairing sorrow which drowned her heart, she began to sob so violently, that she could no longer walk. She covered her face with her hands, panting for breath, choked by the violence of her despair.

Belvigne stood still at her side, quite bewildered, repeating: "I don't understand this at all."

But Servigny brusquely came forward: "Let us go home, Mam'zelle, so that people may not see you weeping in the street. Why do you perpetrate follies like that when they only make you sad?"

And taking her arm he drew her forward. But as soon as they reached the iron gate of the villa she began to run, crossed the garden, and went upstairs, and shut herself in her room.

She did not appear again until the dinner hour, very pale and serious. Servigny had bought from a country storekeeper a workingman's costume, with velvet pantaloons, a flowered waistcoat and a blouse, and he adopted the local dialect. Yvette was in a hurry for them to finish, feeling her courage ebbing. As soon as the coffee was served she went to her room again.

She heard the merry voices beneath her window. The Chevalier was making equivocal jokes, foreign witticisms, vulgar and clumsy. She listened, in despair. Servigny, just a bit tipsy, was imitating the common workingman, calling the Marquise "the Missus." And all of a sudden he said to Saval: "Well, Boss?" That caused a general laugh.

Then Yvette decided. She first took a sheet of paper and wrote:

"Bougival, Sunday, nine o'clock in the evening.
"I die so that I may not become a kept woman.
"Yvette."

Then in a postscript:

"Adieu, my dear mother, pardon."

She sealed the envelope, and addressed it to the Marquise Obardi.

Then she rolled her long chair near the window, drew a little table within reach of her hand, and placed upon it the big bottle of chloroform beside a handful of wadding.

A great rose-tree covered with flowers, climbing as high as her window, exhaled in the night a soft and gentle perfume, in light breaths; and she stood for a moment enjoying it. The moon, in its first quarter, was floating in the dark sky, a little ragged at the left, and veiled at times by slight mists.

Yvette thought: "I am going to die!" And her heart, swollen with sobs, nearly bursting, almost suffocated her. She felt in her a need of asking mercy from some one, of being saved, of being loved.

The voice of Servigny aroused her. He was telling an improper story, which was constantly interrupted by bursts of laughter. The Marquise herself laughed louder than the others.

"There is nobody like him for telling that sort of thing," she said, laughing.

Yvette took the bottle, uncorked it, and poured a little of the liquid on the cotton. A strong, sweet, strange odor arose; and as she brought the piece of cotton to her lips, the fumes entered her throat and made her cough.

Then shutting her mouth, she began to inhale it. She took in long breaths of this deadly vapor, closing her eyes, and forcing herself to stifle in her mind all thoughts, so that she might not reflect, that she might know nothing more.

It seemed to her at first that her chest was growing larger, was expanding, and that her soul, recently heavy and burdened with grief, was becoming light, light, as if the weight which overwhelmed her was lifted, wafted away. Something lively and agreeable penetrated even to the extremities of her limbs, even to the tips of her toes and fingers and entered her flesh, a sort of dreamy intoxication, of soft fever.

She saw that the cotton was dry, and she was astonished that she was not already dead. Her senses seemed more acute, more subtle, more alert. She heard the lowest whisper on the terrace. Prince Kravalow was telling how he had killed an Austrian general in a duel.

Then, further off, in the fields, she heard the noise of the night, the occasional barkings of a dog, the short cry of the frogs, the almost imperceptible rustling of the leaves.

She took the bottle again, and saturated once more the little piece of wadding; then she began to breathe in the fumes again. For a few moments she felt nothing; then that soft and soothing feeling of comfort which she had experienced before enveloped her.

Twice she poured more chloroform upon the cotton, eager now for that physical and mental sensation, that dreamy torpor, which bewildered her soul.

It seemed to her that she had no more bones, flesh, legs, or arms. The drug had gently taken all these away from her, without her perceiving it. The chloroform had drawn away her body, leaving her only her mind, more awakened, more active, larger, and more free than she had ever felt it.

She recalled a thousand forgotten things, little details of her childhood, trifles which had given her pleasure. Endowed suddenly with an awakened agility, her mind leaped to the most diverse ideas, ran through a thousand adventures, wandered in the past, and lost itself in the hoped-for events of the future. And her lively and careless thoughts had a sensuous charm: she experienced a divine pleasure in dreaming thus.

She still heard the voices, but she could no longer distinguish the words, which to her seemed to have a different meaning. She was in a kind of strange and changing fairyland.

She was on a great boat which floated through a beautiful country, all covered with flowers. She saw people on the shore, and these people spoke very loudly; then she was again on land, without asking how, and Servigny, clad as a prince, came to seek her, to take her to a bull-fight.

The streets were filled with passers-by, who were talking, and she heard conversations which did not astonish her, as if she had known the people, for through her dreamy intoxication, she still heard her mother's friends laughing and talking on the terrace.

Then everything became vague. Then she awakened, deliciously benumbed, and she could hardly remember what had happened.

So, she was not yet dead. But she felt so calm, in such a state of physical comfort, that she was not in haste to finish with it — she wanted to make this exquisite drowsiness last forever.

She breathed slowly and looked at the moon, opposite her, above the trees. Something had changed in her spirit. She no longer thought as she had done just now. The chloroform quieting her body and her soul had calmed her grief and lulled her desire to die.

Why should she not live? Why should she not be loved? Why should she not lead a happy life?

Everything appeared possible to her now, and easy and certain. Everything in life was sweet, everything was charming. But as she wished to dream on still, she poured more of the dream-water on the cotton and began to breathe it in again, stopping at times, so as not to absorb too much of it and die.

She looked at the moon and saw in it a face, a woman's face. She began to scorn the country in the fanciful intoxication of the drug. That face swung in the sky; then it sang, it sang with a well-known voice the alleluia of love.

It was the Marquise, who had come in and seated herself at the piano.

Yvette had wings now. She was flying through a clear night, above the wood and streams. She was flying with delight, opening and closing her wings, borne by the wind as by a caress. She moved in the air, which kissed her skin, and she went so fast, so fast, that she had no time to see anything beneath her, and she found herself seated on the bank of a pond with a line in her hand; she was fishing.

Something pulled on the cord, and when she drew it out of the water, it bore a magnificent pearl necklace, which she had longed for some time ago. She was not at all astonished at this deed, and she looked at Servigny, who had come to her side — she knew not how. He was fishing also, and drew out of the river a wooden horse.

Then she had anew the feeling of awaking, and she heard some one calling down stairs. Her mother had said:

"Put out the candle."

Then Servigny's voice rose, clear and jesting:
"Put out your candle, Mam'zelle Yvette."

And all took up the chorus: "Mam'zelle Yvette,
put out your candle."

She again poured chloroform on the cotton, but,
as she did not want to die, she placed it far enough
from her face to breathe the fresh air, while nevertheless her room was filled with the asphyxiating
odor of the narcotic, for she knew that some one
was coming, and taking a suitable posture, a pose of
the dead, she waited.

The Marquise said: "I am a little uneasy! That
foolish child has gone to sleep leaving the light on
her table. I will send Clemence to put it out, and to
shut the balcony window, which is wide open."

And soon the maid rapped on the door calling:
"Mademoiselle, Mademoiselle!" After a moment's
silence, she repeated: "Mademoiselle, Madame the
Marquise begs you to put out your candle and shut
the window."

Clemence waited a little, then knocked louder, and
cried:
"Mademoiselle, Mademoiselle!"

As Yvette did not reply, the servant went away
and reported to the Marquise:

"Mademoiselle must have gone to sleep, her door
is bolted, and I could not awaken her."

Madame Obardi murmured:

"But she must not stay like that."

Then, at the suggestion of Servigny, they all gathered under the window, shouting in chorus:

"Hip! hip! hurrah! Mam'zelle Yvette."

Their clamor rose in the calm night, through the

transparent air beneath the moon, over the sleeping country; and they heard it die away in the distance like the sound of a disappearing train.

As Yvette did not answer the Marquise said: "I only hope that nothing has happened. I am beginning to be afraid."

Then Servigny, plucking red roses from a big rose-bush trained along the wall and buds not yet opened, began to throw them into the room through the window.

At the first rose that fell at her side, Yvette started and almost cried out. Others fell upon her dress, others upon her hair, while others going over her head fell upon the bed, covering it with a rain of flowers.

The Marquise, in a choking voice, cried: "Come, Yvette, answer."

Then Servigny declared: "Truly this is not natural; I am going to climb up by the balcony."

But the Chevalier grew indignant.

"Now, let me do it," he said. "It is a great favor I ask; it is too good a means, and too good a time to obtain a rendezvous."

All the rest, who thought the young girl was joking, cried: "We protest! He shall not climb up."

But the Marquise, disturbed, repeated: "And yet some one must go and see."

The Prince exclaimed with a dramatic gesture:

"She favors the Duke, we are betrayed."

"Let us toss a coin to see who shall go up," said the Chevalier. He took a five-franc piece from his pocket, and began with the Prince.

"Tail," said he. It was head.

The Prince tossed the coin in his turn saying to Saval: "Call, Monsieur."

Saval called "Head." It was tail.

The Prince then gave all the others a chance, and they all lost.

Servigny, who was standing opposite him, exclaimed in his insolent way: "*Parbleu!* he is cheating!"

The Russian put his hand on his heart and held out the gold piece to his rival, saying: "Toss it yourself, my dear Duke."

Servigny took it and spinning it up, said: "Head." It was tail.

He bowed and pointing to the pillar of the balcony said: "Climb up, Prince." But the Prince looked about him with a disturbed air.

"What are you looking for?" asked the Chevalier.

"Well,—I—would—like—a ladder." A general laugh followed.

Saval, advancing, said: "We will help you."

He lifted him in his arms, as strong as those of Hercules, telling him:

"Now climb to that balcony."

The Prince immediately clung to it, and Saval letting him go, he swung there, suspended in the air, moving his legs in empty space.

Then Servigny, seeing his struggling legs which sought a resting place, pulled them downward with all his strength; the hands lost their grip and the Prince fell in a heap on Monsieur de Belvigne, who was coming to aid him.

"Whose turn next?" asked Servigny. No one claimed the privilege.

"Come, Belvigne, courage!"

"Thank you, my dear boy, I am thinking of my bones."

"Come, Chevalier, you must be used to scaling walls."

"I give my place to you, my dear Duke."

"Ha, ha, that is just what I expected."

Servigny, with a keen eye, turned to the pillar. Then with a leap, clinging to the balcony, he drew himself up like a gymnast and climbed over the balustrade.

All the spectators, gazing at him, applauded. But he immediately reappeared, calling:

"Come, quick! Come, quick! Yvette is unconscious." The Marquise uttered a loud cry, and rushed for the stairs.

The young girl, her eyes closed, pretended to be dead. Her mother entered distracted, and threw herself upon her.

"Tell me what is the matter with her, what is the matter with her?"

Servigny picked up the bottle of chloroform which had fallen upon the floor.

"She has drugged herself," said he.

He placed his ear to her heart; then he added:

"But she is not dead; we can resuscitate her. Have you any ammonia?"

The maid, bewildered, repeated: "Any what, Monsieur?"

"Any smelling-salts."

"Yes, Monsieur."

"Bring them at once, and leave the door open to make a draft of air."

The Marquise, on her knees, was sobbing: "Yvette! Yvette, my daughter, my daughter, listen, answer me, Yvette, my child. Oh, my God! my God! what has she done?"

The men, frightened, moved about without speaking, bringing water, towels, glasses, and vinegar. Some one said: "She ought to be undressed." And the Marquise, who had lost her head, tried to undress her daughter; but did not know what she was doing. Her hands trembled and faltered, and she groaned:

"I cannot,—I cannot—"

The maid had come back bringing a druggist's bottle which Servigny opened and from which he poured out half upon a handkerchief. Then he applied it to Yvette's nose, causing her to choke.

"Good, she breathes," said he. "It will be nothing."

And he bathed her temples, cheeks, and neck with the pungent liquid.

Then he made a sign to the maid to unlace the girl, and when she had nothing more on than a skirt over her chemise, he raised her in his arms and carried her to the bed, quivering, moved by the odor and contact of her flesh. Then she was placed in bed. He arose very pale.

"She will come to herself," he said, "it is nothing." For he had heard her breathe in a continuous and regular way. But seeing all the men with their eyes fixed on Yvette in bed, he was seized with a jealous irritation, and advanced toward them.

"Gentlemen," he said, "there are too many of us in this room; be kind enough to leave us alone,— Monsieur Saval and me—with the Marquise."

He spoke in a tone which was dry and full of authority.

Madame Obardi had grasped her lover, and with her head uplifted toward him she cried to him:

"Save her, oh, save her!"

But Servigny turning around saw a letter on the table. He seized it with a rapid movement, and read the address. He understood and thought: "Perhaps it would be better if the Marquise should not know of this," and tearing open the envelope, he devoured at a glance the two lines it contained:

"I die so that I may not become a kept woman.

"YVETTE.

"Adieu, my dear mother, pardon."

"The devil!" he thought, "this calls for reflection." And he hid the letter in his pocket.

Then he approached the bed, and immediately the thought came to him that the young girl had regained consciousness but that she dared not show it, from shame, from humiliation, and from fear of questioning. The Marquise had fallen on her knees now, and was weeping, her head on the foot of the bed. Suddenly she exclaimed:

"A doctor, we must have a doctor!"

But Servigny, who had just said something in a low tone to Saval, replied to her: "No, it is all over. Come, go out a minute, just a minute, and I promise you that she will kiss you when you come back."

And the Baron, taking Madame Obardi by the arm, led her from the room.

Then Servigny, sitting by the bed, took Yvette's hand and said: "Mam'zelle, listen to me."

She did not answer. She felt so well, so soft and warm in bed, that she would have liked never to move, never to speak, and to live like that forever. An infinite comfort had encompassed her, a comfort the like of which she had never experienced.

The mild night air coming in by velvety breaths touched her temples in an exquisite almost imperceptible way. It was a caress like a kiss of the wind, like the soft and refreshing breath of a fan made of all the leaves of the trees and of all the shadows of the night, of the mist of rivers, and of all the flowers too, for the roses tossed up from below into her room and upon her bed, and the roses climbing at her balcony, mingled their heavy perfume with the healthful savor of the evening breeze.

She drank in this air which was so good, her eyes closed, her heart reposing in the yet pervading intoxication of the drug, and she had no longer at all the desire to die, but a strong, imperious wish to live, to be happy—no matter how—to be loved, yes, to be loved.

Servigny repeated: "Mam'zelle Yvette, listen to me."

And she decided to open her eyes.

He continued, as he saw her reviving: "Come! Come! what does this nonsense mean?"

She murmured: "My poor Muscade, I was so unhappy."

He squeezed her hand: "And that led you into a pretty scrape! Come, you must promise me not to try it again."

She did not reply, but nodded her head slightly with an almost imperceptible smile. He drew from his pocket the letter which he had found on the table:

"Had I better show this to your mother?"

She shook her head, no. He knew not what more to say for the situation seemed to him without an outlet. So he murmured:

"My dear child, everyone has hard things to bear. I understand your sorrow and I promise you—"

She stammered: "You are good."

They were silent. He looked at her. She had in her glance something of tenderness, of weakness; and suddenly she raised both her arms, as if she would draw him to her; he bent over her, feeling that she called him, and their lips met.

For a long time they remained thus, their eyes closed.

But, knowing that he would lose his head, he drew away. She smiled at him now, most tenderly; and, with both her hands clinging to his shoulders, she held him.

"I am going to call your mother," he said.

She murmured: "Just a second more. I am so happy."

Then after a silence, she said in a tone so low that it could scarcely be heard: "Will you love me very much? Tell me!"

He kneeled beside her bed, and kissing the hand she had given him, said: "I adore you."

But some one was walking near the door. He arose with a bound, and called in his ordinary voice, which seemed nevertheless a little ironical: "You may come in. It is all right now."

The Marquise threw herself on her daughter, with both arms open, and clasped her frantically, covering her countenance with tears, while Servigny with radiant soul and quivering body went out upon the balcony to breathe the fresh air of the night, humming to himself the old couplet:

> "A woman changeth oft her mind:
> Yet fools still trust in womankind."

MADAME TELLIER'S
EXCURSION

MEN went there every evening at about eleven o'clock, just as they went to the *café*. Six or eight of them used to meet there ; always the same set, not fast men, but respectable tradesmen, and young men in government or some other employ; and they used to drink their Chartreuse, and tease the girls, or else they would talk seriously with Madame, whom everybody respected, and then would go home at twelve o'clock ! The younger men would sometimes stay the night.

It was a small, comfortable house, at the corner of a street behind Saint Etienne's church. From the windows one could see the docks, full of ships which were being unloaded, and on the hill the old, gray chapel, dedicated to the Virgin.

Madame, who came of a respectable family of peasant proprietors in the department of the Eure, had taken up her profession, just as she would have become a milliner or dressmaker. The prejudice against prostitution, which is so violent and deeply rooted in large towns, does not exist in the country places in Normandy. The peasant simply says: "It is a paying business," and sends his daughter to keep a harem of fast girls, just as he would send her to keep a girls' school.

She had inherited the house from an old uncle, to whom it had belonged. Monsieur and Madame, who had formerly been innkeepers near Yvetot, had immediately sold their house, as they thought that the business at Fécamp was more profitable. They arrived one fine morning to assume the direction of the enterprise, which was declining on account of the absence of a head. They were good people enough in their way, and soon made themselves liked by their staff and their neighbors.

Monsieur died of apoplexy two years later, for as his new profession kept him in idleness and without exercise, he had grown excessively stout, and his health had suffered. Since Madame had been a widow, all the frequenters of the establishment had wanted her; but people said that personally she was quite virtuous, and even the girls in the house could not discover anything against her. She was tall, stout, and affable, and her complexion, which had become pale in the dimness of her house, the shutters of which were scarcely ever opened, shone as if it had been varnished. She had a fringe of curly, false hair, which gave her a juvenile look, which in turn contrasted strongly with her matronly figure. She was always smiling and cheerful, and was fond of a joke, but there was a shade of reserve about her which her new occupation had not quite made her lose. Coarse words always shocked her, and when any young fellow who had been badly brought up called her establishment by its right name, she was angry and disgusted.

In a word, she had a refined mind, and although she treated her women as friends, yet she very frequently used to say that she and they were not made of the same stuff.

Sometimes during the week she would hire a carriage and take some of her girls into the country, where they used to enjoy themselves on the grass by the side of the little river. They behaved like a lot of girls let out from a school, and used to run races, and play childish games. They would have a cold dinner on the grass, and drink cider, and go home at night with a delicious feeling of fatigue, and in the carriage kiss Madame as a kind mother who was full of goodness and complaisance.

The house had two entrances. At the corner there was a sort of low *café*, which sailors and the lower orders frequented at night, and she had two girls whose special duty it was to attend to that part of the business. With the assistance of the waiter, whose name was Frederic, and who was a short, light-haired, beardless fellow, as strong as a horse, they set the half bottles of wine and the jugs of beer on the shaky marble tables and then, sitting astride on the customers' knees, would urge them to drink.

The three other girls (there were only five in all), formed a kind of aristocracy, and were reserved for the company on the first floor, unless they were wanted downstairs, and there was nobody on the first floor. The salon of Jupiter, where the

315

tradesmen used to meet, was papered in blue, and embellished with a large drawing representing Leda stretched out under the swan. That room was reached by a winding staircase, which ended at a narrow door opening on to the street, and above it, all night long a little lamp burned, behind wire bars, such as one still sees in some towns, at the foot of the shrine of some saint.

The house, which was old and damp, rather smelled of mildew. At times there was an odor of eau de Cologne in the passages, or a half open door downstairs allowed the noise of the common men sitting and drinking downstairs to reach the first floor, much to the disgust of the gentlemen who were there. Madame, who was quite familiar with those of her customers with whom she was on friendly terms, did not leave the salon. She took much interest in what was going on in the town, and they regularly told her all the news. Her serious conversation was a change from the ceaseless chatter of the three women; it was a rest from the doubtful jokes of those stout individuals who every evening indulged in the common-place amusement of drinking a glass of liquor in company with girls of easy virtue.

The names of the girls on the first floor were Fernande, Raphaelle, and Rosa "the Jade." As the staff was limited, Madame had endeavored that each member of it should be a pattern, an epitome of each feminine type, so that every customer might find as nearly as possible, the realization of his ideal. Fernande represented the handsome blonde; she was very tall, rather fat, and lazy; a country girl, who could not get rid of her freckles, and whose short.

light, almost colorless, tow-like hair, which was like combed-out flax, barely covered her head.

Raphaelle, who came from Marseilles, played the indispensable part of the handsome Jewess. She was thin, with high cheek-bones covered with rouge, and her black hair, which was always covered with pomatum, curled on to her forehead. Her eyes would have been handsome, if the right one had not had a speck in it. Her Roman nose came down over a square jaw, where two false upper teeth contrasted strangely with the bad color of the rest.

Rosa the Jade was a little roll of fat, nearly all stomach, with very short legs. From morning till night she sang songs, which were alternately indecent or sentimental, in a harsh voice, told silly, interminable tales, and only stopped talking in order to eat, or left off eating in order to talk. She was never still, was as active as a squirrel, in spite of her fat and her short legs; and her laugh, which was a torrent of shrill cries, resounded here and there, ceaselessly, in a bedroom, in the loft, in the *café*, everywhere, and always about nothing.

The two women on the ground floor were Louise, who was nicknamed "la Cocotte,"* and Flora, whom they called "Balançière,"† because she limped a little. The former always dressed as Liberty, with a tricolored sash, and the other as a Spanish woman, with a string of copper coins which jingled at every step she took, in her carroty hair. Both looked like cooks dressed up for the carnival, and were like all other women of the lower orders, neither uglier nor

* Slang for a lady of easy virtue.
† Swing, or seesaw.

better looking than they usually are. In fact they
looked just like servants at an inn, and were generally called "the Two Pumps."

A jealous peace, very rarely disturbed, reigned
among these five women, thanks to Madame's concil-
iatory wisdom and to her constant good humor; and
the establishment, which was the only one of the
kind in the little town, was very much frequented.
Madame had succeeded in giving it such a respectable appearance; she was so amiable and obliging to
everybody, her good heart was so well known, that
she was treated with a certain amount of consideration. The regular customers spent money on her,
and were delighted when she was especially friendly
toward them. When they met during the day, they
would say: "This evening, you know where," just
as men say: "At the *café*, after dinner." In a
word Madame Tellier's house was somewhere to go
to, and her customers very rarely missed their daily
meetings there.

One evening, toward the end of May, the first
arrival, Monsieur Poulin, who was a timber merchant,
and had been mayor, found the door shut. The little
lantern behind the grating was not alight; there was
not a sound in the house; everything seemed dead.
He knocked, gently at first, and then more loudly,
but nobody answered the door. Then he went slowly
up the street, and when he got to the market place,
he met Monsieur Duvert, the gun-maker, who was
going to the same place, so they went back together;
but did not meet with any better success. But suddenly they heard a loud noise close to them, and
on going round the corner of the house, they saw a

number of English and French sailors, who were hammering at the closed shutters of the *café* with their fists.

The two tradesmen immediately made their escape, for fear of being compromised, but a low *Pst* stopped them; it was Monsieur Tournevau, the fish-curer, who had recognized them, and was trying to attract their attention. They told him what had happened, and he was all the more vexed at it, as he, a married man, and father of a family, only went there on Saturdays — *securitatis causa*, as he said, alluding to a measure of sanitary policy, which his friend Doctor Borde had advised him to observe. That was his regular evening, and now he would be deprived of it for the whole week.

The three men went as far as the quay together, and on the way they met young Monsieur Philippe, the banker's son, who frequented the place regularly, and Monsieur Pinipesse, the collector. They all returned to the Rue aux Juifs together, to make a last attempt. But the exasperated sailors were besieging the house, throwing stones at the shutters, and shouting, and the five first-floor customers went away as quickly as possible, and walked aimlessly about the streets.

Presently they met Monsieur Dupuis, the insurance agent, and then Monsieur Vassi, the Judge of the Tribunal of Commerce, and they all took a long walk, going to the pier first of all. There they sat down in a row on the granite parapet, and watched the rising tide, and when the promenaders had sat there for some time, Monsieur Tournevau said: "This is not very amusing!"

"Decidedly not," Monsieur Pinipesse replied, and they started off to walk again.

After going through the street on the top of the hill, they returned over the wooden bridge which crosses the Retenue, passed close to the railway, and came out again on to the market place, when suddenly a quarrel arose between Monsieur Pinipesse and Monsieur Tournevau, about an edible fungus which one of them declared he had found in the neighborhood.

As they were out of temper already from annoyance, they would very probably have come to blows, if the others had not interfered. Monsieur Pinipesse went off furious, and soon another altercation arose between the ex-mayor, Monsieur Poulin, and Monsieur Dupuis, the insurance agent, on the subject of the tax-collector's salary, and the profits which he might make. Insulting remarks were freely passing between them, when a torrent of formidable cries were heard, and the body of sailors, who were tired of waiting so long outside a closed house, came into the square. They were walking arm-in-arm, two and two, and formed a long procession, and were shouting furiously. The landsmen went and hid themselves under a gateway, and the yelling crew disappeared in the direction of the abbey. For a long time they still heard the noise, which diminished like a storm in the distance, and then silence was restored. Monsieur Poulin and Monsieur Dupuis, who were enraged with each other, went in different directions, without wishing each other good-bye.

The other four set off again, and instinctively went in the direction of Madame Tellier's establishment, which was still closed, silent, impenetrable.

A quiet, but obstinate, drunken man was knocking at the door of the *café;* then he stopped and called Frederic, the waiter, in a low voice, but finding that he got no answer, he sat down on the doorstep, and awaited the course of events.

The others were just going to retire, when the noisy band of sailors reappeared at the end of the street. The French sailors were shouting the "Marseillaise," and the Englishmen, "Rule Britannia." There was a general lurching against the wall, and then the drunken brutes went on their way toward the quay, where a fight broke out between the two nations, in the course of which an Englishman had his arm broken, and a Frenchman his nose split.

The drunken man, who had stopped outside the door, was crying by this time, as drunken men and children cry when they are vexed, and the others went away. By degrees, calm was restored in the noisy town; here and there, at moments, the distant sound of voices could be heard, only to die away in the distance.

One man was still wandering about, Monsieur Tournevau, the fish-curer, who was vexed at having to wait until the next Saturday. He hoped for something to turn up, he did not know what; but he was exasperated at the police for thus allowing an establishment of such public utility, which they had under their control, to be thus closed.

He went back to it, examined the walls, and tried to find out the reason. On the shutter he saw a notice stuck up, so he struck a wax vesta, and read the following, in a large, uneven hand: "Closed on account of the Confirmation."

Then he went away, as he saw it was useless to remain, and left the drunken man lying on the pavement fast asleep, outside the inhospitable door.

The next day, all the regular customers, one after the other, found some reason for going through the Rue aux Juifs with a bundle of papers under their arm, to keep them in countenance, and with a furtive glance they all read that mysterious notice:

"CLOSED ON ACCOUNT OF THE CONFIRMATION."

II.

Madame had a brother, who was a carpenter in their native place, Virville, in the department of Eure. When Madame had still kept the inn at Yvetot, she had stood godmother to that brother's daughter, who had received the name of Constance, Constance Rivet; she herself being a Rivet on her father's side. The carpenter, who knew that his sister was in a good position, did not lose sight of her, although they did not meet often, as they were both kept at home by their occupations, and lived a long way from each other. But when the girl was twelve years old, and about to be confirmed, he seized the opportunity to write to his sister, and ask her to come and be present at the ceremony. Their old parents were dead, and as Madame could not well refuse, she accepted the invitation. Her brother, whose name was Joseph, hoped that by dint of showing his sister attentions,

322

she might be induced to make her will in the girl's favor, as she had no children of her own.

His sister's occupation did not trouble his scruples in the least, and, besides, nobody knew anything about it at Virville. When they spoke of her, they only said: "Madame Tellier is living at Fécamp," which might mean that she was living on her own private income. It was quite twenty leagues from Fécamp to Virville, and for a peasant, twenty leagues on land are more than is crossing the ocean to an educated person. The people at Virville had never been further than Rouen, and nothing attracted the people from Fécamp to a village of five hundred houses, in the middle of a plain, and situated in another department. At any rate, nothing was known about her business.

But the Confirmation was coming on, and Madame was in great embarrassment. She had no under-mistress, and did not at all care to leave her house, even for a day. She feared the rivalries between the girls upstairs and those downstairs would certainly break out; that Frederic would get drunk, for when he was in that state, he would knock anybody down for a mere word. At last, however, she made up her mind to take them all with her, with the exception of the man, to whom she gave a holiday, until the next day but one.

When she asked her brother, he made no objection, but undertook to put them all up for a night. So on Saturday morning the eight o'clock express carried off Madame and her companions in a second-class carriage. As far as Beuzeille they were alone, and chattered like magpies, but at that station a couple got in. The man, an aged peasant dressed in a blue blouse with a folding collar, wide sleeves tight at the wrist, and ornamented with white embroidery, wore an old high hat with long nap. He held an enormous green umbrella in one hand, and a large basket in the other, from which the heads of three frightened ducks protruded. The woman, who sat stiffly in her rustic finery, had a face like a fowl, and with a nose that was as pointed as a bill. She sat down opposite her husband and did not stir, as she was startled at finding herself in such smart company.

There was certainly an array of striking colors in the carriage. Madame was dressed in blue silk from head to foot, and had over her dress a dazzling red shawl of imitation French cashmere. Fernande was panting in a Scottish plaid dress, whose bodice, which her companions had laced as tight as they could, had forced up her falling bosom into a double dome, that was continually heaving up and down, and which seemed liquid beneath the material. Raphaelle, with a bonnet covered with feathers, so that it looked like a nest full of birds, had on a lilac dress with gold spots on it; there was something Oriental about it that suited her Jewish face. Rosa the Jade had on a pink petticoat with large flounces, and looked like a very fat child, an obese dwarf; while the Two Pumps looked as if they had cut their dresses out of old, flowered curtains, dating from the Restoration.

Perceiving that they were no longer alone in the compartment, the ladies put on staid looks, and began to talk of subjects which might give the others a high opinion of them. But at Bolbec a gentleman with light whiskers, with a gold chain, and wearing two or three rings, got in, and put several parcels wrapped in oil cloth into the net over his head. He looked inclined for a joke, and a good-natured fellow.

"Are you ladies changing your quarters?" he asked. The question embarrassed them all considerably. Madame, however, quickly recovered her composure, and said sharply, to avenge the honor of her corps:

"I think you might try and be polite!"

He excused himself, and said: "I beg your pardon, I ought to have said your nunnery."

As Madame could not think of a retort, or perhaps as she thought herself justified sufficiently, she gave him a dignified bow, and pinched in her lips.

Then the gentleman, who was sitting between Rosa the Jade and the old peasant, began to wink knowingly at the ducks, whose heads were sticking out of the basket. When he felt that he had fixed the attention of his public, he began to tickle them under their bills, and spoke funnily to them, to make the company smile.

"We have left our little pond, qu-ack! qu-ack! to make the acquaintance of the little spit, qu-ack! qu-ack!"

The unfortunate creatures turned their necks away to avoid his caresses, and made desperate efforts to get out of their wicker prison, and then, suddenly, all at once, uttered the most lamentable quacks of distress. The women exploded with laughter. They leaned forward and pushed each other, so as to see better; they were very much interested in the ducks, and the gentleman redoubled his airs, his wit, and his teasing.

Rosa joined in, and leaning over her neighbor's legs, she kissed the three animals on the head. Immediately all the girls wanted to kiss them in turn, and the gentleman took them on to his knees, made them jump up and down and pinched them. The two peasants, who were even in greater consternation than their poultry, rolled their eyes as if they were possessed, without venturing to move, and their old wrinkled faces had not a smile nor a movement.

Then the gentleman, who was a commercial traveler, offered the ladies braces by way of a joke, and taking up one of his packages, he opened it. It was a trick, for the parcel contained garters. There were blue silk, pink silk, red silk, violet silk, mauve silk garters, and the buckles were made of two gilt metal Cupids, embracing each other. The girls uttered exclamations of delight, and looked at them with that gravity which is natural to a woman when she is hankering after a bargain. They consulted one another by their looks or in a whisper, and replied in the same manner, and Madame was longingly handling a pair of orange garters that were broader and more imposing than the rest; really fit for the mistress of such an establishment.

The gentleman waited, for he was nourishing an idea.

"Come, my kittens," he said, "you must try them on."

There was a torrent of exclamations, and they squeezed their petticoats between their legs, as if they thought he was going to ravish them, but he quietly waited his time, and said: "Well, if you will not, I shall pack them up again."

326

And he added cunningly: "I offer any pair they like, to those who will try them on."

But they would not, and sat up very straight, and looked dignified.

But the Two Pumps looked so distressed that he renewed the offer to them. Flora especially hesitated, and he pressed her:

"Come, my dear, a little courage! Just look at that lilac pair; it will suit your dress admirably."

That decided her, and pulling up her dress she showed a thick leg fit for a milk-maid, in a badly-fitting, coarse stocking. The commercial traveler stooped down and fastened the garter below the knee first of all and then above it; and he tickled the girl gently, which made her scream and jump. When he had done, he gave her the lilac pair, and asked: "Who next?"

"I! I!" they all shouted at once, and he began on Rosa the Jade, who uncovered a shapeless, round thing without any ankle, a regular "sausage of a leg," as Raphaelle used to say.

The commercial traveler complimented Fernande, and grew quite enthusiastic over her powerful columns.

The thin tibias of the handsome Jewess met with less flattery, and Louise Cocotte, by way of a joke, put her petticoats over the man's head, so that Madame was obliged to interfere to check such unseemly behavior.

Lastly, Madame herself put out her leg, a handsome, muscular, Norman leg, and in his surprise and pleasure the commercial traveler gallantly took off his hat to salute that master calf, like a true French cavalier.

The two peasants, who were speechless from surprise, looked askance, out of the corners of their eyes. They looked so exactly like fowls, that the man with the light whiskers, when he sat up, said "Co — co — ri — co," under their very noses, and that gave rise to another storm of amusement.

The old people got out at Motteville, with their basket, their ducks, and their umbrella, and they heard the woman say to her husband, as they went away:

"They are sluts, who are off to that cursed place, Paris."

The funny commercial traveler himself got out at Rouen, after behaving so coarsely that Madame was obliged sharply to put him into his right place. She added, as a moral: "This will teach us not to talk to the first comer."

At Oissel they changed trains, and at a little station further on Monsieur Joseph Rivet was waiting for them with a large cart and a number of chairs in it, which was drawn by a white horse.

The carpenter politely kissed all the ladies, and then helped them into his conveyance.

Three of them sat on three chairs at the back, Raphaelle, Madame, and her brother on the three chairs in front, and Rosa, who had no seat, settled herself as comfortably as she could on tall Fernande's knees, and then they set off.

But the horse's jerky trot shook the cart so terribly, that the chairs began to dance, throwing the travelers into the air, to the right and to the left, as if they had been dancing puppets. This made them make horrible grimaces and screams, which, however, were cut short by another jolt of the cart.

They clung to the sides of the vehicle, their bonnets fell on to their backs, their noses on their shoulders, and the white horse trotted on, stretching out his head and holding out his tail quite straight, a little hairless rat's tail, with which he whisked his buttocks from time to time.

Joseph Rivet, with one leg on the shafts and the other bent under him, held the reins with elbows high and kept uttering a kind of chuckling sound, which made the horse prick up its ears and go faster.

The green country extended on either side of the road, and here and there the colza in flower presented a waving expanse of yellow, from which there arose a strong, wholesome, sweet and penetrating smell, which the wind carried to some distance.

The cornflowers showed their little blue heads among the rye, and the women wanted to pick them, but Monsieur Rivet refused to stop.

Then sometimes a whole field appeared to be covered with blood, so thickly were the poppies growing, and the cart, which looked as if it were filled with flowers of more brilliant hue, drove on through the fields colored with wild flowers, to disappear behind the trees of a farm, then to reappear and go on again through the yellow or green standing crops studded with red or blue.

One o'clock struck as they drove up to the carpenter's door. They were tired out, and very hungry, as they had eaten nothing since they left home. Madame Rivet ran out, and made them alight, one after another, kissing them as soon as they were on the ground. She seemed as if she would never tire of kissing her sister-in-law, whom she apparently wanted to monopolize. They had lunch in the work-shop, which had been cleared out for the next day's dinner.

A capital omelette, followed by boiled chitterlings, and washed down by good, sharp cider, made them all feel comfortable.

Rivet had taken a glass so that he might hob-nob with them, and his wife cooked, waited on them, brought in the dishes, took them out, and asked all of them in a whisper whether they had everything they wanted. A number of boards standing against the walls, and heaps of shavings that had been swept into the corners, gave out the smell of planed wood, of carpentering, that resinous odor which penetrates the lungs.

They wanted to see the little girl, but she had gone to church, and would not be back until evening, so they all went out for a stroll in the country.

It was a small village, through which the high road passed. Ten or a dozen houses on either side of the single street had for tenants the butcher, the grocer, the carpenter, the innkeeper, the shoemaker, and the baker, and others.

The church was at the end of the street. It was surrounded by a small churchyard, and four enormous lime-trees, which stood just outside the porch, shaded it completely. It was built of flint, in no particular style, and had a slated steeple. When you got past it, you were in the open country again, which was broken here and there by clumps of trees which hid some homestead.

Rivet had given his arm to his sister, out of politeness, although he was in his working clothes, and was walking with her majestically. His wife, who was overwhelmed by Raphaelle's gold-striped dress, was walking between her and Fernande, and rotund Rosa was trotting behind with Louise Cocotte and Flora, the see-saw, who was limping along, quite tired out.

The inhabitants came to their doors, the children left off playing, and a window curtain would be raised, so as to show a muslin cap, while an old woman with a crutch, who was almost blind, crossed herself as if it were a religious procession. They all looked for a long time after those handsome ladies from the town, who had come so far to be present at the confirmation of Joseph Rivet's little girl, and the carpenter rose very much in the public estimation.

As they passed the church, they heard some children singing; little shrill voices were singing a hymn, but Madame would not let them go in, for fear of disturbing the little cherubs.

After a walk, during which Joseph Rivet enumerated the principal landed proprietors, spoke about the yield of the land, and the productiveness of the cows and sheep, he took his flock of women home and installed them in his house, and as it was very small, he had put them into the rooms, two and two.

Just for once, Rivet would sleep in the workshop on the shavings; his wife was going to share her bed with her sister-in-law, and Fernande and Raphaelle were to sleep together in the next room. Louise and Flora were put into the kitchen, where they had a mattress on the floor, and Rosa had a

little dark cupboard at the top of the stairs to herself, close to the loft, where the candidate for confirmation was to sleep.

When the girl came in, she was overwhelmed
with kisses; all the women wished to caress her,
with that need of tender expansion, that habit of
professional wheedling, which had made them kiss
the ducks in the railway carriage.

They took her on to their laps, stroked her soft,
light hair, and pressed her in their arms with vehement and spontaneous outbursts of affection, and the
child, who was very good-natured and docile, bore
it all patiently.

As the day had been a fatiguing one for everybody, they all went to bed soon after dinner.
The whole village was wrapped in that perfect stillness of the country, which is almost like a religious
silence, and the girls, who were accustomed to the
noisy evenings of their establishment, felt rather
impressed by the perfect repose of the sleeping
village. They shivered, not with cold, but with those
little shivers of solitude which come over uneasy and
troubled hearts.

As soon as they were in bed, two and two
together, they clasped each other in their arms, as if
to protect themselves against this feeling of the calm
and profound slumber of the earth. But Rosa the
Jade, who was alone in her little dark cupboard, felt
a vague and painful emotion come over her.

She was tossing about in bed, unable to get to
sleep, when she heard the faint sobs of a crying child
close to her head, through the partition. She was
frightened, and called out, and was answered by a

weak voice, broken by sobs. It was the little girl who, being used to sleeping in her mother's room, was frightened in her small attic.

Rosa was delighted, got up softly so as not to awaken anyone, and went and fetched the child. She took her into her warm bed, kissed her and pressed her to her bosom, caressed her, lavished exaggerated manifestations of tenderness on her, and at last grew calmer herself and went to sleep. And till morning, the candidate for confirmation slept with her head on Rosa's naked bosom.

At five o'clock, the little church bell ringing the "Angelus" woke these women up, who as a rule slept the whole morning long.

The peasants were up already, and the women went busily from house to house, carefully bringing short, starched, muslin dresses in bandboxes, or very long wax tapers, with a bow of silk fringed with gold in the middle, and with dents in the wax for the fingers.

The sun was already high in the blue sky, which still had a rosy tint toward the horizon, like a faint trace of dawn, remaining. Families of fowls were walking about the henhouses, and here and there a black cock, with a glistening breast, raised his head, crowned by his red comb, flapped his wings, and uttered his shrill crow, which the other cocks repeated.

Vehicles of all sorts came from neighboring parishes, and discharged tall, Norman women, in dark dresses, with neck-handkerchiefs crossed over the bosom, and fastened with silver brooches, a hundred years old.

The men had put on blouses over their new frock coats, or over their old dress coats of green cloth, the tails of which hung down below their blouses. When the horses were in the stable, there was a double line of rustic conveyances along the road; carts, cabriolets, tilburies, char-à-bancs, traps of every shape and age, resting on their shafts, or pointing them in the air.

The carpenter's house was as busy as a beehive. The ladies, in dressing jackets and petticoats, with their long, thin, light hair, which looked as if it were faded and worn by dyeing, were busy dressing the child, who was standing motionless on a table, while Madame Tellier was directing the movements of her battalion. They washed her, did her hair, dressed her, and with the help of a number of pins, they arranged the folds of her dress, and took in the waist, which was too large.

Then, when she was ready, she was told to sit down and not to move, and the women hurried off to get ready themselves.

The church bell began to ring again, and its tinkle was lost in the air, like a feeble voice which is soon drowned in space. The candidates came out of the houses, and went toward the parochial building which contained the school and the mansion house. This stood quite at one end of the village, while the church was situated at the other.

The parents, in their very best clothes, followed their children with awkward looks, and with the clumsy movements of bodies that are always bent at work.

The little girls disappeared in a cloud of muslin

which looked like whipped cream, while the lads, who looked like embryo waiters in a *café*, and whose heads shone with pomatum, walked with their legs apart, so as not to get any dust or dirt on to their black trousers.

It was something for the family to be proud of; a large number of relatives from distant parts surrounded the child, and, consequently, the carpenter's triumph was complete.

Madame Tellier's regiment, with its mistress at its head, followed Constance; her father gave his arm to his sister, her mother walked by the side of Raphaelle, Fernande with Rosa, and the Two Pumps together. Thus they walked majestically through the village, like a general's staff in full uniform, while the effect on the village was startling.

At the school, the girls arranged themselves under the Sister of Mercy, and the boys under the schoolmaster, and they started off, singing a hymn as they went. The boys led the way, in two files, between the two rows of vehicles, from which the horses had been taken out, and the girls followed in the same order. As all the people in the village had given the town ladies the precedence out of politeness, they came immediately behind the girls, and lengthened the double line of the procession still more, three on the right and three on the left, while their dresses were as striking as a bouquet of fireworks.

When they went into the church, the congregation grew quite excited. They pressed against each other, they turned round, they jostled one another in order to see. Some of the devout ones almost spoke aloud, so astonished were they at the sight of these ladies, whose dresses were trimmed more elaborately than the priest's chasuble.

The Mayor offered them his pew, the first one on the right, close to the choir, and Madame Tellier sat there with her sister-in-law; Fernande and Raphaelle, Rosa the Jade, and the Two Pumps occupied the second seat, in company with the carpenter.

The choir was full of kneeling children, the girls on one side, and the boys on the other, and the long wax tapers which they held, looked like lances, pointing in all directions. Three men were standing in front of the lectern, singing as loud as they could.

They prolonged the syllables of the sonorous Latin indefinitely, holding on to the Amens with interminable *a—a's*, which the serpent of the organ kept up in the monotonous, long-drawn-out notes, emitted by the deep-throated pipes.

A child's shrill voice took up the reply, and from time to time a priest sitting in a stall and wearing a biretta, got up, muttered something, and sat down again. The three singers continued, with their eyes fixed on the big book of plain-song lying open before them on the outstretched wings of an eagle, mounted on a pivot.

Then silence ensued. The service went on, and toward the end of it, Rosa, with her head in both her hands, suddenly thought of her mother, and her village church on a similar occasion. She almost fancied that that day had returned, when she was so small, and almost hidden in her white dress, and she began to cry.

First of all she wept silently, the tears dropped slowly from her eyes, but her emotion increased with her recollections, and she began to sob. She took out her pocket-handkerchief, wiped her eyes, and held it to her mouth, so as not to scream, but it was useless.

A sort of rattle escaped her throat, and she was answered by two other profound, heart-breaking sobs; for her two neighbors, Louise and Flora, who were kneeling near her, overcome by similar recollections, were sobbing by her side. There was a flood of tears, and as weeping is contagious, Madame soon found that her eyes were wet, and on turning to her sister-in-law, she saw that all the occupants of the pew were crying.

Soon, throughout the church, here and there, a wife, a mother, a sister, seized by the strange sympathy of poignant emotion, and agitated by the grief of those handsome ladies on their knees, who were shaken by their sobs, was moistening her cambric pocket-handkerchief, and pressing her beating heart with her left hand.

Just as the sparks from an engine will set fire to dry grass, so the tears of Rosa and of her companions infected the whole congregation in a moment. Men, women, old men, and lads in new blouses were soon sobbing; something superhuman seemed to be hovering over their heads—a spirit, the powerful breath of an invisible and all-powerful being.

Suddenly a species of madness seemed to pervade the church, the noise of a crowd in a state of frenzy, a tempest of sobs and of stifled cries. It passed over the people like gusts of wind which bow the trees in a forest, and the priest, overcome by emotion, stammered out incoherent prayers, those inarticulate prayers of the soul, when it soars toward heaven.

The people behind him gradually grew calmer.
The cantors, in all the dignity of their white sur-
plices, went on in somewhat uncertain voices, and
the organ itself seemed hoarse, as if the instrument
had been weeping. The priest, however, raised his
hand, as a sign for them to be still, and went to the
chancel steps. All were silent, immediately.

After a few remarks on what had just taken place,
which he attributed to a miracle, he continued, turning to the seats where the carpenter's guests were
sitting:

"I especially thank you, my dear sisters, who have
come from such a distance, and whose presence
among us, whose evident faith and ardent piety have
set such a salutary example to all. You have edified
my parish; your emotion has warmed all hearts;
without you, this day would not, perhaps, have had
this really divine character. It is sufficient, at times,
that there should be one chosen to keep in the flock,
to make the whole flock blessed."

His voice failed him again, from emotion, and he
said no more, but concluded the service.

They all left the church as quickly as possible;
the children themselves were restless, tired with such
a prolonged tension of the mind. Besides, the elders
were hungry, and one after another left the churchyard, to see about dinner.

There was a crowd outside, a noisy crowd, a
babel of loud voices, in which the shrill Norman
accent was discernible. The villagers formed two
ranks, and when the children appeared, each family
seized their own.

The whole houseful of women caught hold of

Constance, surrounded her and kissed her, and Rosa
was especially demonstrative. At last she took hold
of one hand, while Madame Tellier held the other,
and Raphaelle and Fernande held up her long muslin
petticoat, so that it might not drag in the dust.
Louise and Flora brought up the rear with Madame
Rivet, and the child, who was very silent and thoughtful, set off home, in the midst of this guard of honor.

The dinner was served in the workshop, on long
boards supported by trestles, and through the open
door they could see all the enjoyment that was going
on. Everywhere people were feasting; through every
window could be seen tables surrounded by people
in their Sunday clothes. There was merriment in
every house — men sitting in their shirt sleeves, drinking cider, glass after glass.

In the carpenter's house the gaiety took on somewhat of an air of reserve, the consequence of the
emotion of the girls in the morning. Rivet was the
only one who was in good cue, and he was drinking
to excess. Madame Tellier was looking at the clock
every moment, for, in order not to lose two days following, they ought to take the 3.55 train, which
would bring them to Fécamp by dark.

The carpenter tried very hard to distract her attention, so as to keep his guests until the next day.
But he did not succeed, for she never joked when
there was business to be done, and as soon as they
had had their coffee she ordered her girls to make
haste and get ready. Then, turning to her brother,
she said:

"You must have the horse put in immediately,"
and she herself went to complete her preparations.

When she came down again, her sister-in-law was waiting to speak to her about the child, and a long conversation took place, in which, however, nothing was settled. The carpenter's wife finessed, and pretended to be very much moved, and Madame Tellier, who was holding the girl on her knees, would not pledge herself to anything definite, but merely gave vague promises: she would not forget her, there was plenty of time, and then, they were sure to meet again.

But the conveyance did not come to the door, and the women did not come downstairs. Upstairs, they even heard loud laughter, falls, little screams, and much clapping of hands, and so, while the carpenter's wife went to the stable to see whether the cart was ready, Madame went upstairs.

Rivet, who was very drunk and half undressed, was vainly trying to kiss Rosa, who was choking with laughter. The Two Pumps were holding him by the arms and trying to calm him, as they were shocked at such a scene after that morning's ceremony; but Raphaelle and Fernande were urging him on, writhing and holding their sides with laughter, and they uttered shrill cries at every useless attempt that the drunken fellow made.

The man was furious, his face was red, his dress disordered, and he was trying to shake off the two women who were clinging to him, while he was pulling Rosa's bodice, with all his might, and ejaculating: "Won't you, you slut?"

But Madame, who was very indignant, went up to her brother, seized him by the shoulders, and threw him out of the room with such violence that he fell against a wall in the passage, and a minute afterward, they heard him pumping water on to his head in the yard. When he came back with the cart, he was already quite calmed down.

They seated themselves in the same way as they had done the day before, and the little white horse started off with his quick, dancing trot. Under the hot sun, their fun, which had been checked during dinner, broke out again. The girls now were amused at the jolts which the wagon gave, pushed their neighbors' chairs, and burst out laughing every moment, for they were in the vein for it, after Rivet's vain attempt.

There was a haze over the country, the roads were glaring, and dazzled their eyes. The wheels raised up two trails of dust, which followed the cart for a long time along the highroad, and presently Fernande, who was fond of music, asked Rosa to sing something. She boldly struck up the "Gros Curé de Meudon," but Madame made her stop immediately, as she thought it a song which was very unsuitable for such a day, and added:

"Sing us something of Béranger's."

After a moment's hesitation, Rosa began Béranger's song, "The Grandmother," in her worn-out voice, and all the girls, and even Madame herself, joined in the chorus:

> "How I regret
> My dimpled arms,
> My well-made legs,
> And my vanished charms."

"That is first-rate," Rivet declared, carried away by the rhythm. They shouted the refrain to every verse, while Rivet beat time on the shafts with his foot, and on the horse's back with the reins. The animal, himself, carried away by the rhythm, broke into a wild gallop, and threw all the women in a heap, one on the top of the other, in the bottom of the conveyance.

They got up, laughing as if they were crazy, and the song went on, shouted at the top of their voices, beneath the burning sky and among the ripening grain, to the rapid gallop of the little horse, who set off every time the refrain was sung, and galloped a hundred yards, to their great delight. Occasionally a stone breaker by the roadside sat up, and looked at the wild and shouting female load, through his wire spectacles.

When they got out at the station, the carpenter said:

"I am sorry you are going; we might have had some fun together."

But Madame replied very sensibly: "Everything has its right time, and we cannot always be enjoying ourselves."

And then he had a sudden inspiration: "Look here, I will come and see you at Fécamp next month." And he gave a knowing look, with his bright and roguish eyes.

"Come," Madame said, "you must be sensible; you may come if you like, but you are not to be up to any of your tricks."

He did not reply, and as they heard the whistle of the train he immediately began to kiss them all. When it came to Rosa's turn, he tried to get to her mouth, which she, however, smiling with her lips closed, turned away from him each time by a rapid movement of her head to one side. He held her in his arms, but he could not attain his object, as his large whip, which he was holding in his hand and waving behind the girl's back in desperation, interfered with his efforts.

"Passengers for Rouen, take your seats, please!" a guard cried, and they got in. There was a slight whistle followed by a loud one from the engine, which noisily puffed out its first jet of steam, while the wheels began to turn a little, with visible effort. Rivet left the station and went to the gate by the side of the line to get another look at Rosa, and as the carriage full of human merchandise passed him, he began to crack his whip and to jump, singing at the top of his voice:

> "How I regret
>   My dimpled arms,
>   My well-made legs,
>   And my vanished charms!"

And then he watched a white pocket-handkerchief, which somebody was waving, as it disappeared in the distance.

III.

They slept the peaceful sleep of quiet consciences, until they got to Rouen. When they returned to the house, refreshed and rested, Madame could not help saying:

"It was all very well, but I was already longing to get home."

They hurried over their supper, and then, when they had put on their usual light evening costumes, waited for their usual customers. The little colored lamp outside the door told the passers-by that the flock had returned to the fold, and in a moment the news spread, nobody knew how, or by whom.

Monsieur Philippe, the banker's son, even carried his audacity so far as to send a special messenger to Monsieur Tournevau, who was in the bosom of his family.

The fish-curer used every Sunday to have several cousins to dinner, and they were having coffee, when a man came in with a letter in his hand. Monsieur Tournevau was much excited; he opened the envelope and grew pale; it only contained these words in pencil:

"The cargo of fish has been found; the ship has come into port; good business for you. Come immediately."

He felt in his pockets, gave the messenger twopence, and suddenly blushing to his ears, he said: "I must go out." He handed his wife the laconic and mysterious note, rang the bell, and when the servant came in, he asked her to bring him his hat and overcoat immediately. As soon as he was in the street, he began to run, and the way seemed to him to be twice as long as usual, in consequence of his impatience.

Madame Tellier's establishment had put on quite a holiday look. On the ground floor, a number of sailors were making a deafening noise, and Louise and Flora drank with one and the other, so as to merit their name of the Two Pumps more than ever.

They were being called for everywhere at once; already they were not quite sober enough for their business, and the night bid fair to be a very jolly one.

The upstairs room was full by nine o'clock. Monsieur Vassi, the Judge of the Tribunal of Commerce, Madame's usual Platonic wooer, was talking to her in a corner, in a low voice, and they were both smiling, as if they were about to come to an understanding.

Monsieur Poulin, the ex-mayor, was holding Rosa on his knees; and she, with her nose close to his, was running her hands through the old gentleman's white whiskers.

Tall Fernande, who was lying on the sofa, had both her feet on Monsieur Pinipesse the tax-collector's stomach, and her back on young Monsieur Philippe's waistcoat; her right arm was round his neck, and she held a cigarette in her left.

Raphaelle appeared to be discussing matters with Monsieur Dupuis, the insurance agent, and she finished by saying: "Yes, my dear, I will."

Just then, the door opened suddenly, and Monsieur Tournevau came in. He was greeted with enthusiastic cries of: "Long live Tournevau!" and Raphaelle, who was twirling round, went and threw herself into his arms. He seized her in a vigorous embrace, and without saying a word, lifting her up as if she had been a feather, he carried her through the room.

Rosa was chatting to the ex-mayor, kissing him every moment, and pulling both his whiskers at the same time in order to keep his head straight.

345

Fernande and Madame remained with the four men, and Monsieur Philippe exclaimed: "I will pay for some champagne; get three bottles, Madame Tellier." And Fernande gave him a hug, and whispered to him: "Play us a waltz, will you?" So he rose and sat down at the old piano in the corner, and managed to get a hoarse waltz out of the entrails of the instrument.

The tall girl put her arms round the tax-collector, Madame asked Monsieur Vassi to take her in his arms, and the two couples turned round, kissing as they danced. Monsieur Vassi, who had formerly danced in good society, waltzed with such elegance that Madame was quite captivated.

Frederic brought the champagne; the first cork popped, and Monsieur Philippe played the introduction to a quadrille, through which the four dancers walked in society fashion, decorously, with propriety of deportment, with bows, and curtsies, and then they began to drink.

Monsieur Philippe next struck up a lively polka, and Monsieur Tournevau started off with the handsome Jewess, whom he held up in the air, without letting her feet touch the ground. Monsieur Pinipesse and Monsieur Vassi had started off with renewed vigor and from time to time one or other couple would stop to toss off a long glass of sparkling wine. The dance was threatening to become never-ending, when Rosa opened the door.

"I want to dance," she exclaimed. And she caught hold of Monsieur Dupuis, who was sitting idle on the couch, and the dance began again.

346

But the bottles were empty. "I will pay for one," Monsieur Tournevau said.

"So will I," Monsieur Vassi declared.

"And I will do the same," Monsieur Dupuis remarked.

They all began to clap their hands, and it soon became a regular ball. From time to time, Louise and Flora ran upstairs quickly, had a few turns while their customers downstairs grew impatient, and then they returned regretfully to the *café*. At midnight they were still dancing.

Madame shut her eyes to what was going on, and she had long private talks in corners with Monsieur Vassi, as if to settle the last details of something that had already been agreed upon.

At last, at one o'clock, the two married men, Monsieur Tournevau and Monsieur Pinipesse, declared that they were going home, and wanted to pay. Nothing was charged for except the champagne, and that only cost six francs a bottle, instead of ten, which was the usual price, and when they expressed their surprise at such generosity, Madame, who was beaming, said to them:

"We don't have a holiday every day."

THE OLIVE GROVE

WHEN the 'longshoremen of Garandou, a little port of Provence, situated in the bay of Pisca, between Marseilles and Toulon, perceived the boat of the Abbé Vilbois entering the harbor, they went down to the beach to help him pull her ashore.

The priest was alone in the boat. In spite of his fifty-eight years, he rowed with all the energy of a real sailor. He had placed his hat on the bench beside him, his sleeves were rolled up, disclosing his powerful arms, his cassock was open at the neck and turned over his knees, and he wore a round hat of heavy, white canvas. His whole appearance bespoke an odd and strenuous priest of southern climes, better fitted for adventures than for clerical duties.

He rowed with strong and measured strokes, as if to show the southern sailors how the men of the north handle the oars, and from time to time he turned around to look at the landing point.

The skiff struck the beach and slid far up, the bow plowing through the sand; then it stopped abruptly. The five men watching for the abbé drew near, jovial and smiling.

"Well!" said one, with the strong accent of Provence, "have you been successful, Monsieur le Curé?"

The abbé drew in the oars, removed his canvas head-covering, put on his hat, pulled down his sleeves, and buttoned his coat. Then having assumed the usual appearance of a village priest, he replied proudly: "Yes, I have caught three red-snappers, two eels, and five sunfish."

The fishermen gathered around the boat to examine, with the air of experts, the dead fish, the fat red-snappers, the flat-headed eels, those hideous sea-serpents, and the violet sunfish, streaked with bright orange-colored stripes.

Said one: "I'll carry them up to your house, Monsieur le Curé."

"Thank you, my friend."

Having shaken hands all around, the priest started homeward, followed by the man with the fish; the others took charge of the boat.

The Abbé Vilbois walked along slowly with an air of dignity. The exertion of rowing had brought beads of perspiration to his brow and he uncovered his head each time that he passed through the shade of an olive grove. The warm evening air, freshened by a slight breeze from the sea, cooled his high forehead covered with short, white hair, a forehead far more suggestive of an officer than of a priest.

The village appeared, built on a hill rising from a large valley which descended toward the sea.

It was a summer evening. The dazzling sun, traveling toward the ragged crests of the distant hills, outlined on the white, dusty road the figure of the priest, the shadow of whose three-cornered hat bobbed merrily over the fields, sometimes apparently climbing the trunks of the olive-trees, only to fall immediately to the ground and creep among them.

With every step he took, he raised a cloud of fine, white dust, the invisible powder which, in summer, covers the roads of Provence; it clung to the edge of his cassock turning it grayish white. Completely refreshed, his hands deep in his pockets, he strode along slowly and ponderously, like a mountaineer. His eyes were fixed on the distant village where he had lived twenty years, and where he hoped to die. Its church — his church — rose above the houses clustered around it; the square turrets of gray stone, of unequal proportions and quaint design, stood outlined against the beautiful southern valley; and their architecture suggested the fortifications of some old château rather than the steeples of a place of worship.

The abbé was happy; for he had caught three red-snappers, two eels, and five sunfish. It would enable him to triumph again over his flock, which respected him, no doubt, because he was one of the most powerful men of the place, despite his years. These little innocent vanities were his greatest pleasures. He was a fine marksman; sometimes he practiced with his neighbor, a retired army provost who kept a tobacco shop; he could also swim better than anyone along the coast.

In his day he had been a well-known society man, the Baron de Vilbois, but had entered the priesthood after an unfortunate love-affair. Being the scion of an old family of Picardy, devout and royal-istic, whose sons for centuries had entered the army, the magistracy, or the Church, his first thought was to follow his mother's advice and become a priest. But he yielded to his father's suggestion that he should study law in Paris and seek some high office.

While he was completing his studies his father was carried off by pneumonia; his mother, who was greatly affected by the loss, died soon afterward. He came into a fortune, and consequently gave up the idea of following a profession to live a life of idle-ness. He was handsome and intelligent, but some-what prejudiced by the traditions and principles which he had inherited, along with his muscular frame, from a long line of ancestors.

Society gladly welcomed him and he enjoyed him-self after the fashion of a well-to-do and seriously in-clined young man. But it happened that a friend introduced him to a young actress, a pupil of the Conservatoire, who was appearing with great success at the Odéon. It was a case of love at first sight.

His sentiment had all the violence, the passion of a man born to believe in absolute ideas. He saw her act the romantic rôle in which she had achieved a triumph the first night of her appearance. She was pretty, and, though naturally perverse, possessed the face of an angel.

She conquered him completely; she transformed him into a delirious fool, into one of those ecstatic idiots whom a woman's look will forever chain to the pyre of fatal passions. She became his mistress and left the stage. They lived together four years, his love for her increasing during the time. He would have married her in spite of his proud name and family traditions, had he not discovered that for a long time she had been unfaithful to him with the friend who had introduced them.

The awakening was terrible, for she was about to become a mother, and he was awaiting the birth of the child to make her his wife.

When he held the proof of her transgressions,— some letters found in a drawer,— he confronted her with his knowledge and reproached her with all the savageness of his uncouth nature for her unfaithfulness and deceit. But she, a child of the people, being as sure of this man as of the other, braved and insulted him with the inherited daring of those women, who, in times of war, mounted with the men on the barricades.

He would have struck her to the ground — but she showed him her form. As white as death, he checked himself, remembering that a child of his would soon be born to this vile, polluted creature. He rushed at her to crush them both, to obliterate this double shame. Reeling under his blows, and seeing that he was about to stamp out the life of her unborn babe, she realized that she was lost. Throwing out her hands to parry the blows, she cried:

"Do not kill me! It is his, not yours!"

He fell back, so stunned with surprise that for a moment his rage subsided. He stammered:

"What? What did you say?"

Crazed with fright, having read her doom in his eyes and gestures, she repeated: "It's not yours, it's his."

Through his clenched teeth he stammered:
"The child?"
"Yes."
"You lie!"
And again he lifted his foot as if to crush her, while she struggled to her knees in a vain attempt to rise. "I tell you it's his. If it was yours, wouldn't it have come much sooner?"

He was struck by the truth of this argument. In a moment of strange lucidity, his mind evolved precise, conclusive, irresistible reasons to disclaim the child of this miserable woman, and he felt so appeased, so happy at the thought, that he decided to let her live.

He then spoke in a calmer voice: "Get up and leave, and never let me see you again."

Quite cowed, she obeyed him and went. He never saw her again.

Then he left Paris and came south. He stopped in a village situated in a valley, near the coast of the Mediterranean. Selecting for his abode an inn facing the sea, he lived there eighteen months in complete seclusion, nursing his sorrow and despair. The memory of the unfaithful one tortured him; her grace, her charm, her perversity haunted him, and withal came the regret of her caresses.

He wandered aimlessly in those beautiful vales of Provence, baring his head, filled with the thoughts of that woman, to the sun that filtered through the grayish-green leaves of the olive-trees.

His former ideas of religion, the abated ardor of his faith, returned to him during his sorrowful retreat. Religion had formerly seemed a refuge from

353

WORKS OF GUY DE MAUPASSANT

the unknown temptations of life, now it appeared as a refuge from its snares and tortures. He had never given up the habit of prayer. In his sorrow, he turned anew to its consolations, and often at dusk he would wander into the little village church, where in the darkness gleamed the light of the lamp hung above the altar, to guard the sanctuary and symbolize the Divine Presence.

He confided his sorrow to his God, told Him of his misery, asking advice, pity, help, and consolation. Each day, his fervid prayers disclosed stronger faith.

The bleeding heart of this man, crushed by love for a woman, still longed for affection; and soon his prayers, his seclusion, his constant communion with the Savior who consoles and cheers the weary, wrought a change in him, and the mystic love of God entered his soul, casting out the love of the flesh.

He then decided to take up his former plans and to devote his life to the Church.

He became a priest. Through family connections he succeeded in obtaining a call to the parish of this village which he had come across by chance. Devoting a large part of his fortune to the maintenance of charitable institutions, and keeping only enough to enable him to help the poor as long as he lived, he sought refuge in a quiet life filled with prayer and acts of kindness toward his fellow-men.

Narrow-minded but kind-hearted, a priest with a soldier's temperament, he guided his blind, erring flock forcibly through the mazes of this life in which every taste, instinct, and desire is a pitfall. But the old man in him never disappeared entirely. He continued to love out-of-door exercise and noble sports, but he hated every woman, having an almost childish fear of their dangerous fascination.

II.

The sailor who followed the priest, being a southerner, found it difficult to refrain from talking. But he did not dare start a conversation, for the abbé exerted a great prestige over his flock. At last he ventured a remark: "So you like your lodge, do you, Monsieur le Curé?"

This lodge was one of the tiny constructions that are inhabited during the summer by the villagers and the town people alike. It was situated in a field not far from the parish-house, and the abbé had hired it because the latter was very small and built in the heart of the village next to the church.

During the summer time, he did not live altogether at the lodge, but would remain a few days at a time to practice pistol-shooting and be close to nature.

"Yes, my friend," said the priest, "I like it very well."

The low structure could now be seen; it was painted pink, and the walls were almost hidden under the leaves and branches of the olive-trees that grew in the open field. A tall woman was passing in and out of the door, setting a small table at which she placed, at each trip, a knife and fork, a glass, a plate, a napkin, and a piece of bread. She wore the small cap of the women of Arles, a pointed cone of silk or black velvet, decorated with a white rosette.

When the abbé was near enough to make himself heard, he shouted:

"Eh! Marguerite!"

She stopped to ascertain whence the voice came, and recognizing her master: "Oh! it's you, Monsieur le Curé!"

"Yes. I have caught some fine fish, and want you to broil this sunfish immediately, do you hear?"

The servant examined, with a critical and approving glance, the fish that the sailor carried.

"Yes, but we are going to have a chicken for dinner," she said.

"Well, it cannot be helped. To-morrow the fish will not be as fresh as it is now. I mean to enjoy a little feast — it does not happen often — and the sin is not great."

The woman picked out a sunfish and prepared to go into the house. "Ah!" she said, "a man came to see you three times while you were out, Monsieur le Curé."

Indifferently he inquired: "A man! What kind of man?"

"Why, a man whose appearance was not in his favor."

"What! a beggar?"

"Perhaps — I don't know. But I think he is more of a 'maoufatan.'"

The abbé smiled at this word, which, in the language of Provence means a highwayman, a tramp, for he was well aware of Marguerite's timidity, and

356

knew that every day and especially every night she fancied they would be murdered.

He handed a few sous to the sailor, who departed. And just as he was saying: "I am going to wash my hands,"—for his past dainty habits still clung to him,—Marguerite called to him from the kitchen where she was scraping the fish with a knife, thereby detaching its blood-stained, silvery scales:

"There he comes!"

The abbé looked down the road and saw a man coming slowly toward the house; he seemed poorly dressed, indeed, so far as he could distinguish. He could not help smiling at his servant's anxiety, and thought, while he waited for the stranger: "I think, after all, she is right; he does look like a 'maou-fatan.'"

The man walked slowly, with his eyes on the priest and his hands buried deep in his pockets. He was young and wore a full, blond beard; strands of curly hair escaped from his soft felt hat, which was so dirty and battered that it was impossible to imagine its former color and appearance. He was clothed in a long, dark overcoat, from which emerged the frayed edge of his trousers; on his feet were bathing shoes that deadened his steps, giving him the stealthy walk of a sneak thief.

When he had come within a few steps of the priest, he doffed, with a sweeping motion, the ragged hat that shaded his brow. He was not bad looking, though his face showed signs of dissipation and the top of his head was bald, an indication of premature fatigue and debauch, for he certainly was not over twenty-five years old.

The priest responded at once to his bow, feeling that this fellow was not an ordinary tramp, a mechanic out of work, or a jail-bird, hardly able to speak any other tongue but the mysterious language of prisons.

"How do you do, Monsieur le Curé?" said the man. The priest answered simply, "I salute you," unwilling to address this ragged stranger as "Monsieur." They considered each other attentively; the abbé felt uncomfortable under the gaze of the tramp, invaded by a feeling of unrest unknown to him.

At last the vagabond continued: "Well, do you recognize me?"

Greatly surprised, the priest answered: "Why, no, you are a stranger to me."

"Ah! you do not know me? Look at me well."

"I have never seen you before."

"Well, that may be true," replied the man sarcastically, "but let me show you some one whom you will know better."

He put on his hat and unbuttoned his coat, revealing his bare chest. A red sash wound around his spare frame held his trousers in place. He drew an envelope from his coat pocket, one of those soiled wrappers destined to protect the sundry papers of the tramp, whether they be stolen or legitimate property, those papers which he guards jealously and uses to protect himself against the too zealous gendarmes. He pulled out a photograph about the size of a folded letter, one of those pictures which were popular long ago; it was yellow and dim with age, for he had carried it around with him everywhere and the heat of his body had faded it.

Pushing it under the abbé's eyes, he demanded:
"Do you know him?"

The priest took a step forward to look and grew pale, for it was his own likeness that he had given Her years ago.

Failing to grasp the meaning of the situation he remained silent.

The tramp repeated:

"Do you recognize him?"

And the priest stammered: "Yes."

"Who is it?"

"It is I."

"It is you?"

"Yes."

"Well, then, look at us both, — at me and at your picture!"

Already the unhappy man had seen that these two beings, the one in the picture and the one by his side, resembled each other like brothers; yet he did not understand, and muttered: "Well, what is it you wish?"

Then in an ugly voice, the tramp replied: "What do I wish? Why, first I wish you to recognize me."

"Who are you?"

"Who am I? Ask anybody by the roadside, ask your servant, let's go and ask the mayor and show him this; and he will laugh, I tell you that! Ah! you will not recognize me as your son, papa curé?"

The old man raised his arms above his head, with a patriarchal gesture, and muttered despairingly: "It cannot be true!"

The young fellow drew quite close to him.

"Ah! It cannot be true, you say! You must stop lying, do you hear?" His clenched fists and threatening face, and the violence with which he spoke, made the priest retreat a few steps, while he asked himself anxiously which one of them was laboring under a mistake.

Again he asserted: "I never had a child."

The other man replied: "And no mistress, either?"

The aged priest resolutely uttered one word, a proud admission:

"Yes."

"And was not this mistress about to give birth to a child when you left her?"

Suddenly the anger which had been quelled twenty-five years ago, not quelled, but buried in the heart of the lover, burst through the wall of faith, resignation, and renunciation he had built around it. Almost beside himself, he shouted:

"I left her because she was unfaithful to me and was carrying the child of another man; had it not been for this, I should have killed both you and her, sir!"

The young man hesitated, taken aback at the sincerity of this outburst. Then he replied in a gentler voice:

"Who told you that it was another man's child?"

"She told me herself and braved me."

Without contesting this assertion the vagabond assumed the indifferent tone of a loafer judging a case:

"Well, then, mother made a mistake, that's all!"

After his outburst of rage, the priest had succeeded in mastering himself sufficiently to be able to inquire:

"And who told you that you were my son?"

"My mother, on her deathbed, M'sieur le Curé. And then — this!" And he held the picture under the eyes of the priest.

The old man took it from him; and slowly, with a heart bursting with anguish, he compared this stranger with his faded likeness and doubted no longer — it was his son.

An awful distress wrung his very soul, a terrible, inexpressible emotion invaded him; it was like the remorse of some ancient crime. He began to understand a little, he guessed the rest. He lived over the brutal scene of the parting. It was to save her life, then, that the wretched and deceitful woman had lied to him, her outraged lover. And he had believed her. And a son of his had been brought into the world and had grown up to be this sordid tramp, who exhaled the very odor of vice as a goat exhales its animal smell.

He whispered: "Will you take a little walk with me, so that we can discuss these matters?"

The young man sneered: "Why, certainly! Isn't that what I came for?"

They walked side by side through the olive grove. The sun had gone down and the coolness of southern twilights spread an invisible cloak over the country. The priest shivered, and raising his eyes with a familiar motion, perceived the trembling gray foliage of the holy tree which had spread its frail shadow over the Son of Man in His great trouble and despondency.

A short, despairing prayer rose within him, uttered by his soul's voice, a prayer by which Christians implore the Savior's aid: "O Lord! have mercy on me."

Turning to his son he said: "So your mother is dead?"

These words, "Your mother is dead," awakened a new sorrow; it was the torment of the flesh which cannot forget, the cruel echo of past sufferings; but mostly the thrill of the fleeting, delirious bliss of his youthful passion.

The young man replied: "Yes, Monsieur le Curé, my mother is dead."

"Has she been dead a long while?"

"Yes, three years."

A new doubt entered the priest's mind. "And why did you not find me out before?"

The other man hesitated.

"I was unable to, I was prevented. But excuse me for interrupting these recollections—I will enter into more details later—for I have not had anything to eat since yesterday morning."

A tremor of pity shook the old man and holding forth both hands: "Oh! my poor child!" he said.

The young fellow took those big, powerful hands in his own slender and feverish palms.

Then he replied, with that air of sarcasm which hardly ever left his lips: "Ah! I'm beginning to think that we shall get along very well together, after all!"

The curé started toward the lodge.

"Let us go to dinner," he said.

He suddenly remembered, with a vague and instinctive pleasure, the fine fish he had caught, which, with the chicken, would make a good meal for the poor fellow.

The servant was in front of the door, watching their approach with an anxious and forbidding face.

"Marguerite," shouted the abbé, "take the table and put it into the dining-room, right away; and set two places, as quick as you can."

The woman seemed stunned at the idea that her master was going to dine with this tramp.

But the abbé, without waiting for her, removed the plate and napkin and carried the little table into the dining-room.

A few minutes later he was sitting opposite the beggar, in front of a soup-tureen filled with savory cabbage soup, which sent up a cloud of fragrant steam.

III.

When the plates were filled, the tramp fell to with ravenous avidity. The abbé had lost his appetite and ate slowly, leaving the bread in the bottom of his plate. Suddenly he inquired:

"What is your name?"

The man smiled; he was delighted to satisfy his hunger.

"Father unknown," he said, "and no other name but my mother's, which you probably remember. But I possess two Christian names, which, by the way, are quite unsuited to me—Philippe-Auguste."

The priest whitened.

"Why were you named thus?" he asked.

The tramp shrugged his shoulders. "I fancy you ought to know. After mother left you, she wished to make your rival believe that I was his child. He did believe it until I was about fifteen. Then I began

363

to look too much like you. And he disclaimed me, the scoundrel. I had been christened Philippe-Auguste; now, if I had not resembled a soul, or if I had been the son of a third person, who had stayed in the background, to-day I should be the Vicomte Philippe-Auguste de Pravallon, son of the count and senator bearing this name. I have christened myself 'No-luck.'"

"How did you learn all this?"

"They discussed it before me, you know; pretty lively discussions they were, too. I tell you, that's what shows you the seamy side of life!"

Something more distressing than all he had suffered during the last half hour now oppressed the priest. It was a sort of suffocation which seemed as if it would grow and grow till it killed him; it was not due so much to the things he heard as to the manner in which they were uttered by this wayside tramp. Between himself and this beggar, between his son and himself, he was discovering the existence of those moral divergencies which are as fatal poisons to certain souls. Was this his son? He could not yet believe it. He wanted all the proofs, every one of them. He wanted to hear all, to listen to all. Again he thought of the olive-trees that shaded his little lodge, and for the second time he prayed: "O Lord! have mercy upon me."

Philippe-Auguste had finished his soup. He inquired: "Is there nothing else, abbé?"

The kitchen was built in an annex. Marguerite could not hear her master's voice. He always called her by striking a Chinese gong hung on the wall behind his chair. He took the brass hammer and struck

the round metal plate. It gave a feeble sound, which
grew and vibrated, becoming sharper and louder till
it finally died away on the evening breeze.

The servant appeared with a frowning face and
cast angry glances at the tramp, as if her faithful
instinct had warned her of the misfortune that
had befallen her master. She held a platter on
which was the sunfish, spreading a savory odor
of melted butter through the room. The abbé divided the fish lengthwise, helping his son to the
better half: "I caught it a little while ago," he
said, with a touch of pride in spite of his keen distress.

Marguerite had not left the room.

The priest added: "Bring us some wine, the white
wine of Cape Corse."

She almost rebelled, and the priest, assuming a
severe expression was obliged to repeat: "Now, go,
and bring two bottles, remember," for, when he
drank with anybody, a very rare pleasure, indeed, he
always opened one bottle for himself.

Beaming, Philippe-Auguste remarked: "Fine! A
splendid idea! It has been a long time since I've had
such a dinner." The servant came back after a few
minutes. The abbé thought it an eternity, for now a
thirst for information burned his blood like infernal
fire.

After the bottles had been opened, the woman
still remained, her eyes glued on the tramp.

"Leave us," said the curé.

She intentionally ignored his command.

He repeated almost roughly: "I have ordered you
to leave us."

Then she left the room.

Philippe-Auguste devoured the fish voraciously, while his father sat watching him, more and more surprised and saddened at all the baseness stamped on the face that was so like his own. The morsels the abbé raised to his lips remained in his mouth, for his throat could not swallow; so he ate slowly, trying to choose, from the host of questions which besieged his mind, the one he wished his son to answer first. At last he spoke:

"What was the cause of her death?"

"Consumption."

"Was she ill a long time?"

"About eighteen months."

"How did she contract it?"

"We could not tell."

Both men were silent. The priest was reflecting. He was oppressed by the multitude of things he wished to know and to hear, for since the rupture, since the day he had tried to kill her, he had heard nothing. Certainly, he had not cared to know, because he had buried her, along with his happiest days, in forgetfulness; but now, knowing that she was dead and gone, he felt within himself the almost jealous desire of a lover to hear all.

He continued: "She was not alone, was she?"

"No, she lived with him."

The old man started: "With him? With Pravallon?"

"Why, yes."

And the betrayed man rapidly calculated that the woman who had deceived him, had lived over thirty years with his rival.

Almost unconsciously he asked: "Were they happy?"

The young man sneered. "Why, yes, with ups and downs! It would have been better had I not been there. I always spoiled everything."

"How, and why?" inquired the priest.

"I have already told you. Because he thought I was his son up to my fifteenth year. But the old fellow wasn't a fool, and soon discovered the likeness. That created scenes. I used to listen behind the door. He accused mother of having deceived him. Mother would answer: 'Is it my fault? you knew quite well when you took ·me that I was the mistress of that other man.' You were that other man."

"Ah! They spoke of me sometimes?"

"Yes, but never mentioned your name before me, excepting toward the end, when mother knew she was lost. I think they distrusted me."

"And you — and you learned quite early the irregularity of your mother's position?"

"Why, certainly. I am not innocent and I never was. Those things are easy to guess as soon as one begins to know life."

Philippe-Auguste had been filling his glass repeatedly. His eyes now were beginning to sparkle, for his long fast was favorable to the intoxicating effects of the wine. The priest noticed it and wished to caution him. But suddenly the thought that a drunkard is imprudent and loquacious flashed through him, and lifting the bottle he again filled the young man's glass.

Meanwhile Marguerite had brought the chicken.

367

Having set it on the table, she again fastened her eyes on the tramp, saying in an indignant voice: "Can't you see that he's drunk, Monsieur le Curé?"

"Leave us," replied the priest, "and return to the kitchen."

She went out, slamming the door.

He then inquired: "What did your mother say about me?"

"Why, what a woman usually says of a man she has jilted: that you were hard to get along with, very strange, and that you would have made her life miserable with your peculiar ideas."

"Did she say that often?"

"Yes, but sometimes only in allusions, for fear I would understand; but nevertheless I guessed all."

"And how did they treat you in that house?"

"Me? They treated me very well at first and very badly afterward. When mother saw that I was interfering with her, she shook me."

"How?"

"How? very easily. When I was about sixteen years old, I got into various scrapes, and those blackguards put me into a reformatory to get rid of me." He put his elbows on the table and rested his cheeks in his palms. He was hopelessly intoxicated, and felt the unconquerable desire of all drunkards to talk and boast about themselves.

He smiled sweetly, with a feminine grace, an arch grace the priest knew and recognized as the hated charm that had won him long ago, and had also wrought his undoing. Now it was his mother whom the boy resembled, not so much because of his features, but because of his fascinating and deceptive

glance, and the seductiveness of the false smile that
played around his lips, the outlet of his inner igno-
miny.

Philippe-Auguste began to relate: "Ah! Ah! Ah!
—I've had a fine life since I left the reformatory! A
great writer would pay a large sum for it! Why,
old Père Dumas's Monte Cristo has had no stranger
adventures than mine."

He paused to reflect with the philosophical gravity
of the drunkard, then he continued slowly:

"When you wish a boy to turn out well, no
matter what he has done, never send him to a reformatory. The associations are too bad. Now, I
got into a bad scrape. One night about nine o'clock,
I, with three companions—we were all a little drunk
—was walking along the road near the ford of Folac.
All at once a wagon hove in sight, with the driver
and his family asleep in it. They were people from
Martinon on their way home from town. I caught
hold of the bridle, led the horse to the ferryboat,
made him walk into it, and pushed the boat into the
middle of the stream. This created some noise and
the driver awoke. He could not see in the dark, but
whipped up the horse, which started on a run and
landed in the water with the whole load. All were
drowned! My companions denounced me to the
authorities, though they thought it was a good joke
when they saw me do it. Really, we didn't think
that it would turn out that way. We only wanted
to give the people a ducking, just for fun. After that
I committed worse offenses to revenge myself for the
first one, which did not, on my honor, warrant the
reformatory. But what's the use of telling them? I

will speak only of the latest one, because I am sure it will please you. Papa, I avenged you!"

The abbé was watching his son with terrified eyes; he had stopped eating.

Philippe-Auguste was preparing to begin. "No, not yet," said the priest, "in a little while."

And he turned to strike the Chinese gong.

Marguerite appeared almost instantly. Her master addressed her in such a rough tone that she hung her head, thoroughly frightened and obedient: "Bring in the lamp and the dessert, and then do not appear until I summon you."

She went out and returned with a porcelain lamp covered with a green shade, and bringing also a large piece of cheese and some fruit.

After she had gone, the abbé turned resolutely to his son.

"Now I am ready to hear you."

Philippe-Auguste calmly filled his plate with dessert and poured wine into his glass. The second bottle was nearly empty, though the priest had not touched it.

His mouth and tongue, thick with food and wine, the man stuttered: "Well, now for the last job. And it's a good one. I was home again,—stayed there in spite of them, because they feared me,—yes, feared me. Ah! you can't fool with me, you know,—I'll do anything, when I'm roused. They lived together on and off. The old man had two residences. One official, for the senator, the other clandestine, for the lover. Still, he lived more in the latter than in the former, as he could not get along without mother. Mother was a sharp one—she knew how to hold a man! She had taken him body and soul, and kept him to the last! Well, I had come back and I kept them down by fright. I am resourceful at times — nobody can match me for sharpness and for strength, too — I'm afraid of no one. Well, mother got sick and the old man took her to a fine place in the country, near Meulan, situated in a park as big as a wood. She lasted about eighteen months, as I told you. Then we felt the end to be near. He came from Paris every day — he was very miserable — really.

"One morning they chatted a long time, over an hour, I think, and I could not imagine what they were talking about. Suddenly mother called me in and said:

"'I am going to die, and there is something I want to tell you beforehand, in spite of the Count's advice.' In speaking of him she always said 'the Count.' 'It is the name of your father, who is alive.' I had asked her this more than fifty times — more than fifty times — my father's name — more than fifty times — and she always refused to tell. I think I even beat her one day to make her talk, but it was of no use. Then, to get rid of me, she told me that you had died penniless, that you were worthless and that she had made a mistake in her youth, an innocent girl's mistake. She lied so well, I really believed you had died.

"Finally she said: 'It is your father's name.'

"The old man, who was sitting in an armchair, repeated three times, like this: 'You do wrong, you do wrong, you do wrong, Rosette.'

"Mother sat up in bed. I can see her now, with her flushed cheeks and shining eyes; she loved me,

371

in spite of everything; and she said: · 'Then you do something for him, Philippe!' In speaking to him she called him 'Philippe' and me 'Auguste.'

"He began to shout like a madman: 'Do something for that loafer — that blackguard, that convict? never!'

"And he continued to call me names, as if he had done nothing else all his life but collect them.

"I was angry, but mother told me to hold my tongue, and she resumed: 'Then you must want him to starve, for you know that I leave no money.'

"Without being deterred, he continued: 'Rosette, I have given you thirty-five thousand francs a year for thirty years, — that makes more than a million. I have enabled you to live like a wealthy, a beloved, and I may say, a happy woman. I owe nothing to that fellow, who has spoiled our late years, and he will not get a cent from me. It is useless to insist. Tell him the name of his father, if you wish. I am sorry, but I wash my hands of him.'

"Then mother turned toward me. I thought: 'Good! now I'm going to find my real father — if he has money, I'm saved.'

"She went on: 'Your father, the Baron de Vilbois, is to-day the Abbé Vilbois, curé of Garandou, near Toulon. He was my lover before I left him for the Count!'

"And she told me all, excepting that she had deceived you about her pregnancy. But women, you know, never tell the whole truth."

Sneeringly, unconsciously, he was revealing the depths of his foul nature. With beaming face he raised the glass to his lips and continued:

"Mother died two days — two days later. We followed her remains to the grave, he and I — say — wasn't it funny? — he and I — and three servants — that was all. He cried like a calf — we were side by side — we looked like father and son.

"Then he went back to the house alone. I was thinking to myself: 'I'll have to clear out now and without a penny, too.' I owned only fifty francs. What could I do to revenge myself?

"He touched me on the arm and said: 'I wish to speak to you.' I followed him into his office. He sat down in front of the desk and, wiping away his tears, he told me that he would not be as hard on me as he had said he would to mother. He begged me to leave you alone. That — that concerns only you and me. He offered me a thousand-franc note — a thousand — a thousand francs. What could a fellow like me do with a thousand francs? — I saw that there were very many bills in the drawer. The sight of the money made me wild. I put out my hand as if to take the note he offered me, but instead of doing so, I sprang at him, threw him to the ground and choked him till he grew purple. When I saw that he was going to give up the ghost, I gagged and bound him. Then I undressed him, laid him on his stomach and — ah! ah! ah! — I avenged you in a funny way!"

He stopped to cough, for he was choking with merriment. His ferocious, mirthful smile reminded the priest once more of the woman who had wrought his undoing.

"And then?" he inquired.

"Then, — ah! ah! ah! — There was a bright fire

in the fireplace — it was in the winter — in Decem-
ber — mother died — a bright coal fire — I took the
poker — I let it get red-hot — and I made crosses on
his back, eight or more, I cannot remember how
many — then I turned him over and repeated them on
his stomach. Say, wasn't it funny, papa? Formerly
they marked convicts in this way. He wriggled like
an eel — but I had gagged him so that he couldn't
scream. I gathered up the bills — twelve in all —
with mine it made thirteen — an unlucky number. I
left the house, after telling the servants not to bother
their master until dinner-time, because he was asleep.
I thought that he would hush the matter up because
he was a senator and would fear the scandal. I was
mistaken. Four days later I was arrested in a Paris
restaurant. I got three years for the job. That is the
reason why I did not come to you sooner." He
drank again, and stuttering so as to render his words
almost unintelligible, continued:

"Now — papa — isn't it funny to have one's papa
a curé? You must be nice to me, very nice, because,
you know, I am not commonplace, — and I did a good
job — didn't I — on the old man?"

The anger which years ago had driven the Abbé
Vilbois to desperation rose within him at the sight of
this miserable man.

He, who in the name of the Lord, had so often
pardoned the infamous secrets whispered to him under
the seal of confession, was now merciless in his own
behalf. No longer did he implore the help of a mer-
ciful God, for he realized that no power on earth or
in the sky could save those who had been visited by
such a terrible disaster.

All the ardor of his passionate heart and of his violent blood, which long years of resignation had tempered, awoke against the miserable creature who was his son. He protested against the likeness he bore to him and to his mother, the wretched mother who had formed him so like herself; and he rebelled against the destiny that had chained this criminal to him, like an iron ball to a galley-slave.

The shock roused him from the peaceful and pious slumber which had lasted twenty-five years; with a wonderful lucidity he saw all that would inevitably ensue.

Convinced that he must talk loud so as to intimidate this man from the first, he spoke with his teeth clenched with fury:

"Now that you have told all, listen to me. You will leave here to-morrow morning. You will go to a country that I shall designate, and never leave it without my permission. I will give you a small income, for I am poor. If you disobey me once, it will be withdrawn and you will learn to know me."

Though Philippe-Auguste was half dazed with wine, he understood the threat. Instantly the criminal within him rebelled. Between hiccoughs he sputtered: "Ah! papa, be careful what you say — you're a curé, remember — I hold you — and you have to walk straight, like the rest!"

The abbé started. Through his whole muscular frame crept the unconquerable desire to seize this monster, to bend him like a twig, so as to show him that he would have to yield.

Shaking the table, he shouted: "Take care, take care — I am afraid of nobody."

The drunkard lost his balance and seeing that he was going to fall and would forthwith be in the priest's power, he reached with a murderous look for one of the knives lying on the table. The abbé perceived his motion, and he gave the table a terrible shove; his son toppled over and landed on his back. The lamp fell with a crash and went out.

During a moment the clinking of broken glass was heard in the darkness, then the muffled sound of a soft body creeping on the floor, and then all was silent.

With the crashing of the lamp a complete darkness spread over them; it was so prompt and unexpected that they were stunned by it as by some terrible event. The drunkard, pressed against the wall, did not move; the priest remained on his chair in the midst of the night which had quelled his rage. The somber veil that had descended so rapidly, arresting his anger, also quieted the furious impulses of his soul; new ideas, as dark and dreary as the obscurity, beset him.

The room was perfectly silent, like a tomb where nothing draws the breath of life. Not a sound came from outside, neither the rumbling of a distant wagon, nor the bark of a dog, nor even the sigh of the wind passing through the trees.

This lasted a long time, perhaps an hour. Then suddenly the gong vibrated! It rang once, as if it had been struck a short, sharp blow, and was instantly followed by the noise of a falling body and an overturned chair.

Marguerite came running out of the kitchen, but as soon as she opened the door she fell back, frightened by the intense darkness. Trembling, her heart beating as if it would burst, she called in a low, hoarse voice: "M'sieur le Curé! M'sieur le Curé!"

Nobody answered, nothing stirred.

"*Mon Dieu, mon Dieu*," she thought, "what has happened, what have they done?"

She did not dare enter the room, yet feared to go back to fetch a light. She felt as if she would like to run away, to screech at the top of her voice, though she knew her legs would refuse to carry her. She repeated: "M'sieur le Curé! M'sieur le Curé! it is me, Marguerite."

But, notwithstanding her terror, the instinctive desire of helping her master and a woman's courage, which is sometimes heroic, filled her soul with a terrified audacity, and running back to the kitchen she fetched a lamp.

She stopped at the doorsill. First, she caught sight of the tramp lying against the wall, asleep, or simulating slumber; then she saw the broken lamp, and then, under the table, the feet and black-stockinged legs of the priest, who must have fallen backward, striking his head on the gong.

Her teeth chattering and her hands trembling with fright, she kept on repeating: "My God! My God! what is this?"

She advanced slowly, taking small steps, till she slid on something slimy and almost fell.

Stooping, she saw that the floor was red and that a red liquid was spreading around her feet toward the door. She guessed that it was blood. She threw down her light so as to hide the sight of it, and fled from the room out into the fields, run-

ning half crazed toward the village. She ran scream-
ing at the top of her voice, and bumping against the
trees she did not heed, her eyes fastened on the
gleaming lights of the distant town.

Her shrill voice rang out like the gloomy cry of
the night-owl, repeating continuously, "The maoufatan — the maoufatan — the maoufatan" —

When she reached the first house, some excited
men came out and surrounded her; but she could
not answer them and struggled to escape, for the
fright had turned her head.

After a while they guessed that something must
have happened to the curé, and a little rescuing party
started for the lodge.

The little pink house standing in the middle of
the olive grove had grown black and invisible in the
dark, silent night. Since the gleam of the solitary
window had faded, the cabin was plunged in darkness, lost in the grove, and unrecognizable for anyone
but a native of the place.

Soon lights began to gleam near the ground,
between the trees, streaking the dried grass with
long, yellow reflections. The twisted trunks of the
olive-trees assumed fantastic shapes under the moving
lights, looking like monsters or infernal serpents.
The projected reflections suddenly revealed a vague,
white mass, and soon the low, square wall of the
lodge grew pink from the light of the lanterns. Several peasants were carrying the latter, escorting two
gendarmes with revolvers, the mayor, the *garde-
champêtre*, and Marguerite, supported by the men,
for she was almost unable to walk.

The rescuing party hesitated a moment in front

of the open, grewsome door. But the brigadier, snatching a lantern from one of the men, entered, followed by the rest.

The servant had not lied, blood covered the floor like a carpet. It had spread to the place where the tramp was lying, bathing one of his hands and legs.

The father and son were asleep, the one with a severed throat, the other in a drunken stupor. The two gendarmes seized the latter and before he awoke they had him handcuffed. He rubbed his eyes, stunned, stupefied with liquor, and when he saw the body of the priest, he appeared terrified, unable to understand what had happened.

"Why did he not escape?" said the mayor.

"He was too drunk," replied the officer.

And every man agreed with him, for nobody ever thought that perhaps the Abbé Vilbois had taken his own life.

This book designed by
William B. Taylor
is a production of
Heron Books, London

© *1968, Heron Books, London*

Printed on wood free paper
and bound by Hazell Watson & Viney Ltd,
Aylesbury, Bucks

Printed and bound in England

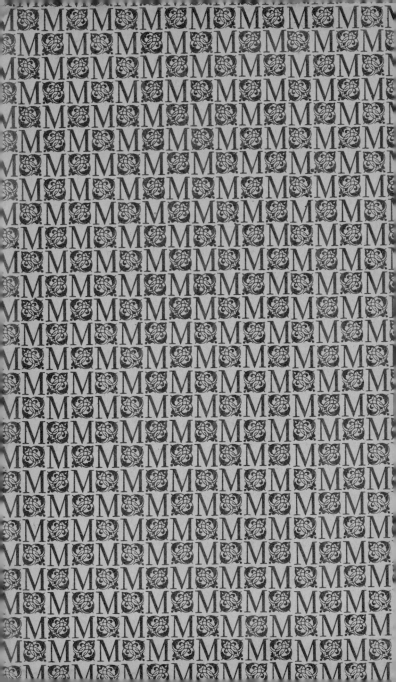